Expedition route around Africa

Contents

Introduction

Alexandria, Egypt
March 2019

B UMPING along a gravel road in Guatemala with my friend Kate I clearly remember discussing overland travel and what it might mean for my life. Two continuous years exploring foreign countries was substantially bigger than anything I had attempted before. To be perfectly honest, I still wasn't sure it was for me.

"There are really only two options," I said.
"Either this Alaska to Argentina drive satisfies my urge and I'll never do this kind of thing again, or I'll be addicted for life."

The fact this book exists tells you which way that went.

When I set out to drive from Alaska to Argentina I didn't know what to expect. I knew almost nothing about border crossings, bribery or if I could learn another language. My plan was to go until I didn't enjoy it any more, then do something else with my life. This meant I didn't feel any pressure. If my little Jeep got stolen or destroyed I could simply walk away. I hadn't made any promises, and virtually nobody outside my family knew of The Road Chose Me.

The Africa expedition was very different from the start. I began planning and dreaming fully aware of what I was getting into. I knew how disciplined I would have to be while saving money, and how difficult it would be to leave my comfortable life behind. I knew the depths of loneliness that were in front of me, and how hard it would be to push through my fears and doubts. To put it simply, I knew exactly what I was signing myself up for - or at least I thought I did.

I again quit my job and sold everything I wasn't taking, and I promised a lot of people I would complete the lap around Africa. Once I committed, I was all in. There would be no turning back or stopping early this time. I knew an expedition all the way around Africa would be an enormous adventure, and it turned out to be a thousand times more than even I dreamed possible.

Africa and her people taught me so much and I feel a great responsibility to do their story justice. After three months I thought I knew everything. Then after twelve months I realized that was all garbage and I had a new perspective. This learning process was continuous as I tried to keep my eyes and ears open to the world I was experiencing.

Like volume one, this book contains more than just tales of adventure, but also the lifelong lessons I will never forget. Fair warning, some lessons are controversial and will be difficult for readers in the developed world. I learned volumes about how the world views and treats Africa, making it impossible not to touch on politics. To be perfectly honest, most of what I learned makes me sick to my stomach. I hope you will keep an open mind as you make this journey of discovery with me.

Throughout the expedition the endless kindness and warmth of the African people was a constant. Without their love and encouragement my dream wouldn't have been possible.

So much is outside my control while on these expeditions I often feel as if I'm on a roller coaster, taking the unexpected twists and turns as they come. All I can do is plant a smile on my face, hold on and enjoy the ride. So strap yourself in as we embark on the adventure of a lifetime.

-Dan

Like A Donkey

Canada to Morocco
June 2015 to June 2016

EVEN before I finished the Pan-American Highway my savings ran out and I knew I'd have to return to full time work. After two years of continuous movement living in a ground tent, I was ready for a change. I was exhausted, and in need of stability. Besides going to work every day it allowed me to go to the gym, cook and eat healthy food and make solid friends who I could count on for adventurous weekends. Living in the Yukon allowed me to roam the mighty north, into the Arctic Circle and all over Alaska. I knew a savings account would be mandatory if I wanted more grand adventures, and I knew the payoff would justify the years of sitting at a desk.

For the first couple of years I wasn't necessarily saving for another huge expedition, just saving to give myself options down the road. I kept my focus on the freedom from work my savings would allow rather than any particular destination. As the years rolled by, Africa slowly became the focus. The more I learned, the more curious I became, and it climbed the long list of possible destinations to become the entire list.

I spent thousands of hours researching and planning my new dream and for inspiration I followed overlanders in Africa while researching visas, safety, immunizations and a new vehicle. The little two-door Jeep Wrangler was ideal for the Americas, though it was very small and I wanted more creature comforts. More space and a few luxuries will mean I can thoroughly enjoy years on the road rather than just tolerate them.

Φ   Φ   Φ

Watching my savings account and judging my own motivation level to begin another huge expedition, everything slowly
comes together. I watch vehicles for sale and find a 2007 Jeep
Wrangler Unlimited Rubicon in British Colombia. It's the four
door version which provides plenty of interior space, it has a
6-speed transmission and the Rubicon package comes with the
serious 4x4 equipment I've decided is necessary for the West
African mud. I fly to BC and spend a week driving it north
over Christmas and New Years. On the final ten hour driving
day the temperature hovers around -40°F/C, even in full sunshine. An hour from home I'm so distracted by a breathtaking
display of northern lights I have to pull over or risk crashing.

Looking to take on new challenges to make this expedition
different, I set a goal of getting my stories and photos published
in print magazines. I follow a few magazines on Twitter, and
one editor immediately sends me a message. Eric knew of my
Pan-Am adventure, and says right away he would love to work
together. For the first time I explain my ambitious plan to
someone outside my family, and Eric is quickly hooked. Years
ago he flew to Alaska and bought a broken Jeep sight unseen
before fixing it with his brother and driving four thousand miles
to North Carolina. Eric has been a self diagnosed Jeep fanatic
ever since, addicted to the adventures they provide. Eric
immediately commits to running my stories in his magazine,
and it feels great to know someone else believes in me, and
I'm not completely insane.

After four years of working and saving I'm finally ready to quit
my job and put my plan into action. When I give two weeks
notice colleagues try to dissuade me, certain I'm damaging my
career.
"Think of your future," they say.
"I am," is my serious reply.

I finish work, sell everything I won't be taking, and bid farewell to the Yukon. Over a few days I drive fourteen hundred miles south to Calgary where I catch up with my good friends from before the Pan-Am. I rent a room from Ian and Jamie and immediately get to work building the Jeep into a house on wheels.

I thoroughly enjoy tent camping, though as the months turned into years on the Pan-Am setting up and taking down the tent in the mud got old, and I want a better sleeping system for this expedition. After eating ramen noodles almost every day for two years I can no longer stomach them, and I want to cook and eat much better food. I'm also expecting to encounter severely deep mud and sand - especially in West Africa - so upgrades to the Jeep's off-road capabilities are in my plan.

To start I strip the interior to bare metal and remove the rear seat to see what I have to work with. I want to maximize every possible square inch so I can stand up and live inside the Jeep, which requires moving the roll bar. My friends Ian, Reg and Oscar cut and weld it for me, in part because I'm terrible at welding and also because I'm scared to cut into my Jeep.

With the rear now wide open I run wiring for a fridge, water pump, lights and charging station before building storage cabinets that my Dad and I designed to fit around a thirty-five liter fridge. I'm far from the world's best carpenter, so to compensate I work ten and twelve hour days designing and building as I go. Ian returns after a week working in the north to admire my handy work, and gives advice I will never forget. "Dan," he says, "That looks great, but at this rate it's going to take you six months to finish. You're a good friend, but you're not welcome in my house for six months. Hurry up!"
"It doesn't have to be perfect," he says, "it just has to be good enough."

With Ian's prodding and help we finish the wiring, cabinets, fridge install and add bolt down steel lock-boxes. The interior build takes six weeks of long hours, and I'm elated to move one step closer to my dreams of African adventure.

Φ   Φ   Φ

Somewhere during all the planning I became obsessed with putting a diesel engine in the Jeep. On paper there are numerous advantages for an expedition burning diesel. Diesels get better mileage and in Latin America it was sometimes half the price of gas. Typically diesel engines are simpler, more reliable and require less maintenance because they are more industrial in nature. They also generate less heat, and an older engine doesn't have electronics to cause problems in remote Africa, even with terrible quality fuel. On paper these advantage are huge, and I couldn't leave it alone. Many knowledgeable people tried to talk me out of it, but I only became determined.

After hundreds of hours of research I located a mechanic in the US with the skills and experience to do the job, and I pulled the trigger. Don quotes eight weeks to complete the engine swap, and I immediately dreamed of a powerful, reliable and efficient conversion.

Fully committed to the engine swap I drive to the US and pitch my old three man tent in a beautiful lakeside town. Finally meeting Don the mechanic face to face, I soon get a bad feeling. I see at least five or six half-finished vehicles lying around, and I'm dismayed to see Don has not made any inroads into the diesel engine I purchased months ago. In my mind he had been preparing to make the conversion go as quickly as possible, though that was clearly not the case. With little choice I leave the Jeep with Don, keeping all my fingers crossed.

Having recently worked long days building the interior, I suddenly feel at a complete loss doing nothing. I've always been in charge of making my dreams come true, and now I'm utterly dependant on Don to keep moving forward. I don't have a drop-dead date I must arrive in Africa, though every day I wait costs money, so I'd rather get moving. I soon realize I'm terrible at doing nothing, and even worse at leaving my dreams at the mercy of someone else.

As the weeks go by I adjust to life by the lake. I borrow an old mountain bike and play a lot of frisbee golf. I swim in the lake and explore the immediate area on foot all while living full-time in my tent and cooking meals on my tiny camp stove. While most of my gear has long-since fallen apart, I still use the same sleeping bag and hiking stove I took to Argentina.

There are numerous other upgrades I need to make to the Jeep, and Don is happy for me to work one day a week in his garage. I spend a day installing a new rear bumper and tire carrier setup, and another day installing heavy-duty suspension. Each time I see the Jeep I'm dismayed by the lack of progress on the new engine. The old engine came out relatively quickly, but week after week I see no noticeable progress. Don has other projects on the go and evidently works at his own pace.

The quoted two month timeline comes and goes while the Jeep is still very far from complete - in fact the replacement engine is not even bolted in. Now at Don's mercy all I can do is ask him to keep at it and hope for the best. Slowly I become more and more stressed about the situation because my dream is completely out of my control. I'm given the opportunity to display the Jeep at SEMA in Las Vegas, the world's biggest automotive show. This is a huge opportunity for more media coverage and to prove my professionalism, so I desperately want the Jeep to be finished. I try to impart on Don just how important this opportunity and deadline is, and he assures me the Jeep will be finished, still a month away.

One morning at a coffee shop I meet Richard, a friendly local who drives a Jeep just like mine. He offers a ride to the supermarket, and we become fast friends. Richard is thoughtful and kind, and full of outrageous stories from his thirty-five year career as an LAPD detective. He's shocked to learn of my situation and my complete dependence on Don.

Living fill-time in my tent becomes a problem when the leaves begin to fall. Snow will be flying soon, and I can only hope the Jeep will be finished before it does.

The deadline for displaying the Jeep at SEMA comes and goes, and it's still far from complete. I feel terrible breaking commitments, though there is nothing I can do. My personal reputation is now at stake, and I realize it's just taken a huge blow.

Not only is the engine conversion taking much longer than quoted, every step is costing more than estimated. It's become a money pit, and to top it off the extra months mean I'm spending more on camping and food than planned.

When the campground finally closes for the winter I take Richard up on his generous offer to stay in his spare room. He's a massive car guy and has a lot of expertise restoring classics in his well-equipped home garage. We talk endlessly about my plans, the lack of progress and how I can get back on track.

The stress mounts, and I begin to seriously worry if I'm ever going to make this trip come true.

Φ   Φ   Φ

Don finally installs the engine and fires it up, and it appears to run well. The main Jeep computer is extremely unhappy, and after long nights of troubleshooting we discover an important sensor ring on the front of the engine has been installed backwards. Don says it's a major operation to correct this, and though he doesn't say it, in my mind that means many more weeks. My patience has long since run out, and I've been losing sleep for weeks about what to do.

I'm fed up with Don and being locked into his glacial pace, and I want to take matters into my own hands. Richard and I decide the best path forward is to finish the incomplete Jeep ourselves. Fifteen weeks after starting an eight week conversion, I gingerly drive my Jeep the few miles to Richard's house. With all the quirks and small issues it becomes clearer than ever just how far from complete it actually is.

Over the next two weeks Richard and I put in ten hour days ticking off all the remaining tasks. Progress is slow, and eventually I drive to a Jeep dealer hoping their diagnostic computer can give insight into the computer problems. We need to trick the Jeep computer into thinking it has a regular engine so systems like ABS and airbags will function normally. I drive the twenty miles to the dealer without gauges or lights on the dash, and I'm pleased it does actually drive fairly well. With the diagnostic computer we pinpoint the problem in five minutes, and I feel better with a clear game plan.

For the first time I think maybe the end is in sight.

On the drive back I change down to first gear to climb a steep hill and without warning the engine begins to spin extraordinarily fast. I turn off the key though it keeps spinning faster and faster as if the throttle pedal is stuck to the floor. The engine screams unimaginably loud, and I'm sure people will flood from their houses. A tremendous cloud of white smoke pours from the back of the Jeep while the engine continues to scream, completely out of control. I'm utterly terrified, and have no idea how to make it stop, or what damage is being done. If this continues I fear it will actually blow up, and I wonder briefly if I should run for cover.

In my mind this unimaginable screaming continues for thirty seconds, though it's probably only ten. Finally the engine coughs to a halt, never to start again. The silence is deafening.

Over the coming days Richard and I discover a huge diesel leak inside the valve cover that had gone unseen. On the steep hill that diesel sloshed and was sucked through the breather hose, through the air intake, and then freely into the engine. With access to unlimited diesel the engine spins faster and faster until it destroys itself, and there is almost nothing that can stop it. Known as 'diesel runaway', this type of accident is notorious for destroying diesel engines.

Five months and almost twenty thousand dollars after attempting to replace the heart of my Jeep, the new engine has been completely destroyed. While trying to wrap my head around this disaster, I can't stop thinking I might have just lost my Africa dream.

Φ   Φ   Φ

Not only has it taken five months and been a complete failure, this engine conversion has cost significantly more than planned and I've been slowly eating up my travel budget causing me to seriously worry I don't have enough money to get back on track and salvage the dream. In the coming weeks I hit a point in my life lower than ever before. Completely out of character I don't even want to get out of bed to face the day because I know nothing good will come. I become increasingly stressed about how I will live up to all the commitments I've made, and if I will ever make it to Africa at all.

I look for a cheap car to buy, and wonder if I can go back to my old job, tail between my legs.

Φ   Φ   Φ

Richard and I spend hours talking around my options and I speak with friends and family repeatedly. I'm sure they can sense my fear and desperation and I'm given words of encouragement I will remember as long as I live.

On the phone my brother Mike tries his best to cheer me up with some motivation:
"You're always trying ambitious things Dan, sooner or later one of them wasn't going to work out. That's OK, it's better to aim high and not reach your goal than to just aim low all the time. Keep going Dan, I know you'll get there."

While at the local coffee shop a friend issues a challenge:
"These things happen in life Dan, it's how we react to them that makes us who we are."

My Mum always tells me straight, and says:

"Dan, this is your life. Right now. Today. You have to find a way to enjoy it, even when things don't go your way. Be happy anyway, and get on with finding another way. You'll get there, I know it."

And finally, my friend Etienne in Whitehorse says:
"Sometimes to make big dreams come true you have to be stubborn like a donkey. Just keep pushing forward Dan. Whatever it takes, it'll be worth it."

At the time I was so emotionally invested I couldn't see it, but in hindsight I realize that trying to reach a goal and not getting there is not failure at all.
Failure would be never trying in the first place.
I'm a firm believer that I will only regret the things I didn't do in life, so I'm happy I attempted the diesel conversion, even after all the time, money and heartache.

Φ   Φ   Φ

When I stop moping around Richard and I discuss what I actually need to get this dream back on track. Without a doubt the best course of action is to sell the broken diesel Jeep for peanuts and buy a replacement. The little Jeep I drove to Argentina never had a single mechanical issue, so there's no reason to think another Jeep with a completely stock gas engine won't handle the challenge. Messing with factory reliability got me into a world of trouble, and I'm determined not to make the same mistake. I won't be upgrading anything on the drivetrain, and I ignore friends that say I should install a V8 engine, a supercharger or monster axles. This is a huge blow to my overall budget, though if I'm extremely careful - and manage to earn some money on the road - I should just be able to manage.

Now with a clear plan I feel much better. Evidently I do well when my back is to the wall, I just have to know which direction is forward.

I buy a replacement Jeep identical to the original, this time in my favourite color, called 'Sahara Tan', perfect for an African expedition. In just two weeks Richard and I transfer all the modifications across, and I couldn't be happier with how it comes together. Now with a gas engine I add a thirteen gallon auxiliary tank, and can only hope six hundred miles of range will be enough. As a finishing touch we design and build a drinking water tank, pump, filtration and UV treatment system which provides running drinking water inside the Jeep.

Without Richard the expedition would have failed before it even began, and I get choked up saying goodbye. Phase two of my Jeep is finally complete, six months and tens of thousands of dollars behind schedule.

Φ   Φ   Φ

In San Diego I buy a pop-up camper roof for the Jeep, which has been the plan from day one. Combined with the roll bar modifications I can now stand up and walk around inside meaning that when it's pouring rain or the mosquitoes are horrendous I have a small retreat where I can read a book or eat a sandwich. When I make the removable sleeping platform the entire roof of the Jeep becomes a large and comfortable bed, six feet off the ground away from hungry animals. Solar panels are mounted to the roof and I get new wheels and tires, finally finishing my house on wheels.

My vastly altered timeline means I can attend Easter Jeep Safari in Moab, the biggest Jeep event in the world. I finally meet Eric the magazine editor face to face, and we get along like old friends. He's been behind the scenes through all of this, and we thoroughly enjoy all things Jeep for the week.

I ride shotgun for a huge day of serious 4x4ing with Eric's buddies, and I watch them go places in their Jeeps I had no idea was even possible. Driving back into Moab we spot a couple of Jeep's concept vehicles that have yet to be shown to the world. Eager to learn more we follow them into town, and we're shocked when they pull over. These are multi-million dollar concept vehicles and now they're just parked in broad daylight for us to stare at.

One driver is looking a little sheepish, so we offer to help. He explains the engine just died, and he has no idea why. Of course we're eager to help, and with everyone being a Jeep fanatic soon we're actually climbing on and under the one of a kind vehicle, grinning like mad. It's not hard to determine it's out of gas, so we block the main highway and tow it to a station. Through all of this we chat to the drivers, and it's a whole ten minutes before the penny drops. This entire time I've been talking to Mark, the head of Jeep design.

I've always wondered if Jeep know who I am or are curious about my expeditions, and now here I am talking to the very well known head of design, who is a self-confessed Jeep fanatic. I give the cliff notes of my Pan-Am expedition, my new Jeep and my imminent expedition around Africa. We swap details, and a week later at Jeep HQ outside Detroit we film a short YouTube video about my Jeep expeditions. I'm immensely proud Jeep have taken even a small interest in what I'm doing, and I have a great morning pretending I'm famous after one of the camera guys calls me 'The Talent'.

Φ Φ Φ

I continue across the continent to Halifax in Nova Scotia, one of the biggest shipping ports on the East Coast. On a rainy afternoon I drive to a nondescript warehouse on the edge of the city before driving the Jeep into a twenty foot shipping container. After strapping it down the door is closed and a truck immediately whisks it out of sight. After so many months of pouring my blood, sweat and tears into the Jeep, I can't believe it's gone. Walking back to a hostel in the rain I realize I didn't even get a receipt.

Φ   Φ   Φ

I fly to England and spend two weeks with my sister Liz and her fiancé Simon while the Jeep crosses the Atlantic. I've never been to Europe, and have a great time slowly coming around to the idea the expedition is finally underway and I have years of adventure in front of me.

The Jeep ships into Antwerp in Belgium, and on another rainy day I walk from downtown to the enormous shipping port where I'm happy to find the Jeep is unmarked from it's journey across the sea. After re-connecting the battery it fires right up, and I drive onto the streets of Belgium, finally underway.

Trying to gain more media attention and followers, I post my Jeep build and expedition plans to the social sharing website Reddit. In just a few hours the post gets thousands of comments, virtually all saying I'm going to be murdered in horrible ways in Africa. At first I brush them off, though as they continue for hour after hour I become rattled. I stay up until 2am trying to reply and make sense of the ongoing flood of comments. Many people are adamant I'll be beheaded and my Jeep will be stolen in just the first country, and that I'm a moron for even thinking about setting foot on Africa.

The sheer number of such comments is overwhelming, and I begin to have second thoughts. Even my Mum reads the discussion, and soon my family are concerned. I reach out to a few overlanders I follow online who've been exploring Africa for years. Without fail they all offer the same advice: "You would be crazy **not** to go."

Φ   Φ   Φ

I drive non-stop through Belgium, France and Spain only stopping for gas and to camp at night. I would love to explore Europe, but it's just not the time, and I feel desperate to get this Africa expedition underway. In the far south of Spain I'm shocked I can actually see Morocco, only twenty miles away across the Strait of Gibraltar.

It's been more than five years of planning, dreaming and working towards this day, and it hardly feels real.

A year after I quit my job I drive onto the ferry to Tangier, shaking with excitement.

My dream of African adventure starts now.

Into Africa

Morocco
June 2016

M Y passport is stamped on the ferry, and after what feels
like no time at all I drive into the secure Customs area,
ready to enter Morocco. Along with about a dozen other
vehicles we're held behind a large gate until the required
paperwork is complete. I can't help but smile at the shiny new
Porsche beside the Jeep, and the many new Land Cruisers
and Land Rovers also entering Morocco. The comments on
Reddit said my Jeep was too expensive and it would make me
a target, but in reality it's not nearly as expensive as these
other vehicles.

A Police officer has me write the pertinent details on a card
before sending me upstairs to get my passport registered as a
driver. The same Policeman then conducts an extremely quick
search of the Jeep and our conversation in Spanish is brief and
to the point:

"Any guns?"
"No."

"Any drugs?"
"No."

"OK, you can go."

I'm handed a small piece of paper that is the ninety day
Temporary Import Permit for the Jeep in Morocco, and I'm
free to drive forward. I stop to buy insurance from a friendly

lady in a small office and ten minutes later I drive onto the bustling streets of Tangier, unable to wipe the grin off my face.

I haven't driven in a chaotic country since Argentina, and it's a shock to be thrown back so deeply into 'Make It Up Driving' as I like to call it. Turn signals, stop signs, red lights and lane markings mean absolutely nothing. The rules are much simpler than all of that - the biggest vehicle has the right of way. Go when there is space. Jam in when there is not. After a few hectic intersections where I cause mayhem the memories come flooding back and soon I effortlessly flow with traffic.

I decide an easy introduction is best, so I make my way to the stunning city of Chefchaouen in the Rif Mountains. The entire city is painted a rich blue which makes for a stunning backdrop to the bustling market. Different people tell different stories about why it's all painted blue – some say it's to reduce mosquitoes, some say it keeps the concrete city cooler and some say scorpions don't like the blue. Whatever the reason, it's certainly beautiful.

I walk from the campground above town and am soon inundated with the sights, sounds and smells of the lively market. From fresh fish, spices and vegetables to clothes, rugs and leather goods, the market is packed full of goods for sale. The new languages, bright stalls and striking blue city combine to make it abundantly clear I've driven my Jeep into a different world. There is no mistaking it, this is like no place I've been before.

When I buy fruit and vegetables from stalls and local dishes from small restaurants it quickly becomes clear I need to learn French, and I need to learn it now. I took beginner lessons in Canada, which were a disaster. They tried to teach useless words like 'Grandmother' and 'window' while I wanted to learn the words I found most useful in Latin America. Learning in the classroom environment brought back strong memories of learning a language in high school which was a complete waste of time. I do much better in the deep end, and soon my small notebook is scrawled with the twenty most useful words I need to memorize for today.

Though everything is unfamiliar on the surface, deep down I feel a familiarity I've longed for. Over the next couple of weeks I feel myself sinking back into my previous expedition self. I'm comfortable haggling over prices in street markets, chatting at gas stations about the Jeep, driving free-form, camping and living out of my vehicle, learning a new language and simply smiling and using hand gestures when my French is woefully inadequate. It all comes flooding back, and I enjoy every second.

Φ   Φ   Φ

In Fez I leave the Jeep in a campground outside the city and catch a taxi into town. This is the oldest city of the entire Arab world, and I feel like I've stepped back in time as I wander the labyrinth of narrow alleys and side streets. Founded in 789 everything is clearly ancient - the buildings, the stones, even the donkeys pulling carts look exceptionally old. In many places the cobble stone streets actually have grooves worn into them from centuries of cart traffic. Vendors are crammed into every possible square inch, selling products as diverse as local arts and crafts to Chinese-made plastic tubs and flip flops.

I stand to the side and practice the words in French before approaching a stall selling an array of olives. I plan to buy fifty cents worth of multiple different kinds, though after the first bag is filled so full I can hardly hold it with one hand I realize fifty cents worth of the world's freshest olives will last me a week.

The market, or *medina*, is packed with restaurants selling foods I've never seen before including the famous *Tagine* - a kind of crock-pot made with forty-two spices. I can't resist trying *pastilla* - pigeon pie. The pastry and sugar on top make it dessert-like, and the pigeon filled center tastes somewhat like the dark meat of a turkey, with a delicate mix of spices making a very rich flavor. Later I have a camel burger for dinner, which has a delicious wild flavor. It's amusing to place a food order then watch the restaurateur walk around the market buying the ingredients – flour, eggs, vegetables and a little meat, which they quickly whip into a delicious meal.

I'm so enthralled I stay in the Medina until dusk, before realizing I probably should have found a way home before dark. I struggle to explain where I'm going, and a friendly stall owner is happy to translate, assuring me the driver knows the way. Driving through the bustling and now dark city I become disoriented, and I'm not certain the driver is going the right way. I can hardly communicate with him, and what I'm expecting to be a twenty minute drive drags on for forty-five. My mind starts to run away, and I wonder if he is intentionally taking me to the wrong place. Maybe I'm trusting this guy when I shouldn't be. He has seen my big camera, and surely knows I have cash. I worry I might really be in trouble.

I'm relieved when we reach the campground where the driver comes inside and asks the security guard to translate. He invites me to visit his family if I'm ever back in Fez. He has a wife and two young children, and would like to share a meal in his house some day. He goes to great lengths to write down his name, address and phone number making me feel embarrassed for thinking ill of him earlier.

Φ   Φ   Φ

In the world-famous Marrakesh market I can hardly believe my eyes as I watch a snake charmer coax a cobra to sway and stare hypnotically, something I never dreamed I would see in real life.

A few days later in the Atlas Mountains I'm woken at sunrise by a troop of monkeys climbing on the roof of the Jeep. Once they realize I'm not trying to scare them away they're happy to pose for photos, enjoying the morning sun.

On the edge of the Sahara Desert in Merzouga I trade the Jeep for local transportation and ride a camel into the desert before spending the night in a traditional berber tent. At sunrise I climb the enormous dunes and am staggered by the enormous desert that surrounds me. Huge dunes stretch to the horizon in every direction, and it's simply breathtaking.

During each of these experiences I pinch myself, making sure it's all real and my dreams are actually coming true.

In Southern Morocco the landscape quickly changes to an extremely dry and rocky desert, completely void of features. Away from the coast the temperatures are scorching, often over 110°F before 10am.

Much to my surprise I learn Western Sahara is not currently considered a separate country from Morocco. Technically it's labeled a 'Disputed Territory', with the UN saying it's not self-governing. This is the politically correct way to say Morocco invaded their neighbor to extract the rich natural resources, and it's been that way ever since. The international community don't do anything because they simply don't care. For me this means there is no border into Western Sahara, because I'm still driving through Moroccan controlled territory.

The region is heavily patrolled by the Moroccan Military and I pass through endless checkpoints as I continue south. The checkpoints are always polite and friendly, and it's nice to know the Military are patrolling the highway and keeping me safe. Distances are vast as I follow the coast, skirting the edge of the mighty Sahara desert. I drive hundreds of miles between towns, often little more than a Military checkpoint, a few concrete buildings or a gas station if I'm lucky. In these towns I see many vehicles with 'UN' painted on the side, a first for me.

In many places sand dunes have drifted over the highway, and I'm constantly on the lookout for wild camels wandering on the road. The relentless sun is scorching hot during the day and the temperature quickly plummets at night in the barren and windswept desert.

Φ   Φ   Φ

There's only one border crossing from Western Sahara into Mauritania, and the sandy track passes directly through an active minefield. An estimated seven million landmines litter this highly disputed territory, and while I would obviously prefer an alternative route, I have no choice.

Gas is in short supply in Mauritania, so twenty miles before the border I fill the Jeep and auxiliary tank at the last Moroccan station. I arrive at the dusty and isolated border mid-morning, and it's already above 110°F in the shade. Wind howls relentlessly, whipping sand into faces while threatening to rip paperwork from clutching hands. I drive slowly along the crumbling paved road, moving past hundreds of heavily-loaded trucks waiting to exit. They're all stacked dangerously high, and I shudder to think how much each one weighs.

A uniformed officer waves me forward through a huge steel gate before another throws up his arms and yells at me for moving forward without his permission. All I can do is plead ignorance. Now inside the huge gated compound I see crumbling buildings dotted around an area enclosed by an impressive fence with large steel gates at each end. The gates apparently keep out the riff-raff, so inside it's relatively calm as far as borders go. Nobody hassles me or offers to help with paperwork and I see scores of uniformed officers sitting around, apparently doing nothing.

I park behind a few other vehicles and wait in line for an exit stamp in my passport before a random officer sitting in the shade scribbles on my Temporary Import Permit and points across the road. In a tiny brick building a copy of the permit is taken before I collect another scribble. My details are hand-written into an enormous ledger, and finally I'm free to drive through the far steel gate out of Morocco.

The instant I drive into 'No Man's Land' the Jeep is surrounded by young men yelling and banging on the windows. Some of them even grab the mirrors, door handles or bumpers as I continue to crawl forward on the remains of a rough and badly broken road. These men want to exchange money, sell me something, or guide me across the minefield to the Mauritanian border post.

I'm now between the two countries in a region that has no law, no roads and no signs. I must drive a few miles across desert sand through the active minefield to reach the Mauritanian border post. I've been warned against paying for a guide because they're known to lead people directly into the mines then demand $100 while threatening to leave. I'd much rather rely on my own instincts than deal with that. In theory I should be able to follow another vehicle or stay in tire tracks to avoid the mines. Their tire didn't set off any mines, so my tires shouldn't either.

That being said, things can and do go wrong here. In 2007 a French overlander was tragically killed and another seriously injured after they strayed off course in their Land Rover and hit an anti-tank mine. The danger is very real and I'm anxious about driving across.

A few pickups and 18-wheelers are making the crossing, so I ignore the extremely persistent guides and crawl forward, trying to keep my tires on existing tracks. I pass close to dozens of burnt-out vehicles, a clear sign this is no joke. I take the most direct route on a badly crumbling paved road built by the Spanish decades ago. When the road completely disappears I drive through sections of deep sand where four wheel drive is needed to keep the Jeep moving.

Arriving at the Mauritania border post I'm surrounded by men I recognize as border helpers, or 'fixers'. They want to help me with the paperwork for a fee, and they try to snatch my passport or paperwork from my hands. Of course they say the border will take many hours without their help, and I really need them. It's clear the Military and Police will get a cut of any money I pay the guides, so they do nothing to stop the constant harassment. No matter how many times I say "No thanks," each one comes back for more, tagging along every step of the way. I only speak to men in uniform, and never hand my passport or documents to anyone who demands it. To enter Mauritania I bounce between multiple unsigned buildings to find uniformed officers who are taking an afternoon nap or otherwise doing nothing. I buy a one month visa at Immigration and am soon stamped into the country.

I watch the grumpy Immigration officer tell a car load of Senegalese they must pay for their stamp. Exactly how much they must pay is unclear, though he makes it abundantly clear they won't get the stamp they need unless money changes hands. Each takes their turn passing across a wad of bills and the officer either grunts and waves them away or stuffs the bills into the top drawer of his battered desk. I can't help noticing it's literally overflowing with grubby bills.

My experience in Latin America has prepared me for all the waiting and I know to avoid the guides and fixers, though this blatant extortion is a first for me. I've been told repeatedly Africa runs on bribes, and here it is directly in front of my face.

After getting an import permit from Customs I drive to a chain blocking the road, but it soon becomes clear I've missed a step. I know this because the old man standing beside the chain waves wildly while pointing at yet another crumbling building across the road. After my details are hand-written into yet another giant ledger the old man outside smiles widely and asks for *Un petit cadeau* - A small gift - to which I play dumb until he lowers the chain blocking my progress.

Four hours after arriving at the Moroccan border I drive into Mauritania, African country number two.

Φ   Φ   Φ

After many hours of research, I decide not to explore Mauritania. The distances are vast, and I'm not certain I will find gas in the remote parts of the desert I'm interested in exploring. I've enjoyed my time in the desert, but I'm also excited to get into 'real' Africa, so I decide to quickly cross the country.

In the capital of Nouakchott I'm granted visas for onward travel before moving south, aiming for what is commonly called 'The Worst Border in Africa'. Horror stories abound of days spent paying hundreds of Euros in bribes at this border, only to move onto the next officer to start the whole process over. Many seasoned West African overlanders swear they'll never cross this border again and some have even sworn off the entire continent because of their experiences here.

On the main highway I'm stopped at multiple checkpoints, which is nothing new for Mauritania. What is new, however, is the insistence that I buy vehicle insurance for Senegal. They even say I can't continue without it, which is a blatant lie given I'm still sixty miles from Senegal. It's clear they want to trick foreigners like me into buying insurance at highly inflated prices and the disappointment on their faces is clear when they learn I have insurance that covers the Jeep for all of West Africa.

The small dirt track to the border at Diama parallels the Senegal River, and I'm elated to see a family of warthogs dart across the road. These are the first genuine 'African' animals I've seen, and I can't wipe the smile off my face thinking about the larger ones I will undoubtedly see in the coming years.

The border itself is a collection of small shabby buildings

situated on either side of a concrete dam, with the road running two hundred yards down the wall. A few vehicles are crossing, and only a couple of people mill about, none of which even glance in my direction. The midday sun beats down relentlessly, and I feel sunburnt even under a thick layer of sunscreen. I'm already relying heavily on my water setup and fridge, drinking more than a gallon of water each day.

Inside the crumbling Customs building I find five Military men sprawled across a grubby mattress on the floor snoring loudly. An old TV is blaring, but they're dead to the world. Most have taken off their uniform, and only wear undershirts that stopped being white years ago. A very young man appears from a side room and ushers me into an adjacent office. It consists of a large wooden desk with two desperately broken and sweat-stained office chairs in front. A computer from about 1995 has been shoved to the side and is covered in a thick layer of dust. The young man motions for me to sit before he writes my details in a massive paper ledger, and cancels the stamp in my passport. When everything is finished he glances up and mumbles for ten Euros, clearly lacking confidence. I smile broadly as I say:
"My friend said you would say that! Haha!"
I pickup my passport and stride out confidently, hoping to call the young man's bluff. He doesn't say or do anything to stop me.

I walk next door to the decrepit Immigration building, where the story is replayed. The slightly older and more serious looking officer stamps me out, writes my details into yet another enormous ledger, then asks for ten Euros. He's still holding my passport, and doesn't smile when I use the same line as before. In fact, he scowls down his nose at me, looking very unhappy.

After a few minutes of back and forth in my very poor French, multiple other officers enter the room and insist I must pay ten Euros. They're close to yelling, which leaves no room to discuss, so I just keep my cool while smiling and being very polite. The most senior man easily identified by a dazzling collection of silver on his uniform makes it clear he wants my money.

Practicing skills learned years ago I remain completely unfazed before smiling, shrugging my shoulders and wandering outside to get a cold water bottle from the fridge. I sit in the shade, and do my best to look relaxed, making it abundantly clear I can spend hours waiting. Less than five minutes later one of them wordlessly hands back my passport before stomping away.

I drive two hundred yards across the dam wall to find Senegal Immigration in a large olive green tent, Inside I see a senior and very dignified man in a crisp uniform. The tent has been transformed into the Taj Mahal, clearly serving double duty as border post and living quarters and everything is neat and orderly. The man is clearly proud of the fan blowing on him from less than a foot away. In this heat, I'm sure a fan is worth it's weight in gold. Taking a good look around I'm impressed to see a beaming color photo of the Senegalese President hanging proudly on the canvas wall. The entrance of the tent is extremely low and the large desk completely blocks the entrance. I'm forced to half squat and half kneel simply to talk to him and his look of satisfaction tells me how much he enjoys having me kneel.

After my details are again written into an enormous ledger I'm stamped into Senegal and walk across the dirt track to a tiny shack that is apparently Customs. A young man there talks on his cell phone, and barely glances at me or my paperwork as he begins filling out a Temporary Import Permit for the Jeep. He doesn't ask me a single question, or ask for any complicated paperwork I don't have, so I'm perfectly happy to say nothing.

Less than an hour after arriving on the Mauritanian side I quickly drive through the lifted boom gate before the man holding it open can demand money. I'm happy for the easy border crossing, and that I didn't pay a cent.

In the next few miles everything changes dramatically. The barren desert drops away and lush green fields and enormous trees stretch to the horizon. For years I've dreamed of mighty baobab trees, and now the road is lined with dozens on the ancient wonders. Within another mile the road is bustling with vibrant people walking and on bicycles and motorbikes. In stark contrast to Mauritania I see groups of people chatting and laughing and ladies wear extremely colorful clothing while balancing baskets, clothes and plastic tubs on their heads. Amazingly they also carry bags or children in their hands, and some manage all of this sitting on the back of motorbikes.

I'm inundated with the new sights, sounds and smells of Senegal, and I love it.

The Guinea Gamble

Guinea
August 2016

T URNING back would mean hours on muddy and potholed
jungle tracks.

"Road closed," the immaculately uniformed officer leaning on a
battered old AK-47 says offhand.
"The ferry washed downstream last week," he adds, giving all
the explanation I need.

So much for best laid plans.

As is customary in these situations, I lay maps on the hood
while a small crowd of Military and regular spectators gathers,
everyone pointing to a different place on the map, trying to
determine our location. I planned to cross from Guinea-Bissau
at an isolated border post with a river crossing and a tiny
track not shown on many maps. Without a ferry to cross the
swollen river, this route is off the table. For the first, though
certainly not the last time in Africa, I must make a new plan
on the side of the muddy track.

It's mostly agreed I can continue a few miles before branching
onto a smaller track that winds to the bigger road, and eventually another border post at Kandika. I will find Immigration
and Customs there, I'm told.
Well, probably.

Φ   Φ   Φ

Overlooked by most overlanders in the mad scramble to traverse the West Coast of Africa, Guinea sits to the south of Senegal and Mali, hugging Sierra Leon and Liberia. The capital of Conakry sees more rainfall in a month than the famously wet Pacific Northwest of the USA sees in an entire year. I pay particular attention to this point given I'm arriving in early August, the wettest month. Guinea was declared free of the massive Ebola epidemic by the World Health Organization only a few months earlier, and has seen essentially no tourists since. Major guide books have no information about Guinea, citing a general lack of interest. This is exactly the kind of place I dreamed of when I wanted to explore 'off the map', and I'm giddy thinking about how remote it might be.

I have a paper copy of the Michelin map of West Africa, commonly regarded as the best in print. It shows the first major road I will reach as 'impassable in the wet season' and the majority of roads I plan to drive are variously marked as 'less improved', 'unimproved' and 'track'.

Given the season and lack of information available I wonder what I'm going to find. I can't help wondering if I'll be hopelessly stuck in the mud and perpetually soaked to the bone from endless rain.

These thoughts bounce around my head as I take a deep breath, roll the dice, and plunge into Guinea, African country number six.

Φ   Φ   Φ

After the unplanned detour I wind along small tracks, mostly following my nose before arriving at the sleepy border post marked by two crumbling buildings and a log blocking the road. I notice there are no tracks in the mud, indicating no vehicles have passed this way in at least a couple of days. The lone dog lazing in the shade follows me with his eyes but doesn't bother to lift his head as I walk to the old Immigration building. Inside a grubby but cheery man enters my details in yet another ancient hand-written ledger.

Immigration and Customs duplicate my details into similar ledgers before I'm free to exit Guinea-Bissau and continue forward to the Guinea side, a handful of miles further. In the first few hundred yards the road deteriorates badly and I'm forced to use low-range first gear to cross ruts and deep mud pits in the middle of the road. If this is a taste of things to come Guinea might get *really* interesting.

For the first time in Africa, Guinean Customs ask to see my *Carnet de Passage* - a kind of passport for vehicles. My reply of 'No Carnet' causes a lot of confusion and I'm asked a few more times before the chief is summoned from his midday slumber. After a lot of head scratching he gives assurances I can figure it out at the regional Customs headquarters in the larger town of Koundara, sixty miles away.

I walk across the road to Immigration where I'm shocked to find four well-dressed officers sitting behind huge wooden desks, apparently awaiting my arrival. It's easy to infer rank and status from the number of medals on each chest and the girth of each man, and I slowly move up the chain, shaking hands with warm greetings, handing over my passport and having my details dutifully recorded. I'm amused to watch one man painfully rule lines and use multiple coloured pens in his huge paper ledger containing years of entries while he continually plays with and changes the music on his touch-screen phone. If only there was a better way to record all this Immigration information. On the way out I'm warmly bid farewell and '*Bonne Route!*' all round.

Φ   Φ   Φ

"Oh, that road is terrible," becomes the story in the morning. After sorting out the Jeep paperwork and buying gas and food, everyone warns me the road to Maliville is a disaster, even by local standards. A few miles after departing the regional capital of Labè, I understand why. The road had deteriorated severely, to little more than a mild rock scramble interspersed with muddy potholes. In places the road narrows to one lane, in others it fans out into a maze of impassable tracks in the mud. After lowering tire pressures to 20 psi I continue creeping forward, exclusively in first and second gear. My goal of Maliville lies at an elevation of 4,800 feet, making for a continuous climb of 1,500 feet in the next seventy miles.

The enormous rainfall and impressive mountains in Guinea mean virtually all of the largest rivers in West Africa make their start here. The Niger, The Gambia, The Senegal and many more all start high in these mountains, and I'm grinning broadly as I cross the source of The Gambia. Here it's little more than a tiny stream which is in stark contrast to the massive flow I crossed a month ago.

Around the next bend a lanky uniformed man blows his whistle loudly while furiously waving his arms for me to pull over and the chain stretched across the road leaves me with little choice. Before I can even speak I overhear a junior officer whisper in French
"He speaks bad French."
These men have clearly been tipped off to my impending arrival - likely a call ahead from the gas station, or someone who spotted me leaving town to the north. After all, the road only goes one way.
I feel uneasy knowing they've been expecting me.

After each officer has carefully reviewed my paperwork, it becomes clear my insurance is not satisfactory and a tense stand-off begins. I play my old game of trying to waste as much time as possible, and these men are clearly happy to do the same in return. While waiting I watch countless cars and motorbikes slow just enough to hand-off money to the officers before they speed forward in a cloud of dust. The officers then pass the cash to the boss, a rotund gentleman with a tiny moustache, an impressive collection of medals and white shoes shined to a mirror finish. This gentleman never leaves his chair, never shows the slightest interest in what's going on around him, and barely grunts his replies. I get the feeling nobody wants to misinterpret those grunts.

After a time it becomes obvious I'm supposed to pay, though I decided long ago I will try my best not to pay bribes in Africa. Hoping friendliness will win out, I smile as I hand out cups of hot tea intentionally made with many heaping spoonfuls of sugar. My ploy works and instantly the mood changes. My insurance is deemed acceptable, I'm offered a seat and we chat about my trip and the direction I'm headed. The men insist I must stop and say hello on my return journey south.
A few days later I do just that, enjoying more sugar tea with the assembled officers who smile broadly and get a chair ready as soon as they see me approaching. They're happy to pose for photos and bid me a very warm farewell after exchanging contact details.

$$\Phi \quad \Phi \quad \Phi$$

A bone-jarring boom jolts me awake in the dead of night. I'm camping behind a stand of low trees, a hundred yards off the muddy road. The entire Jeep rattles and I hear the thunder clap echo off the near-by mountains multiple times. A flash of lightening as bright as day hits at the exact instant another boom slams into the Jeep, and I feel the rumble deep in my chest. My hair begins to rise, and I can feel and see sparks of static electricity coming off my sleeping bag. Now wide awake, I realize the open roof of the Jeep is higher that the surrounding trees, and my brain moves at a hundred miles an hour. I wonder if the solar panels attract lightning, I wonder if rubber tires are enough insulation, and I wonder about damage to the Jeep in the event of a direct strike. My heart races, and soon I'm sweating profusely.

A few minutes later the rain comes - sheet after sheet of

torrential downpour, loud enough to drown out every other sound. I listen to the water pouring off the roof, and judge by the sound alone it must be a literal river. I lie awake for hour after hour worrying about the state of the already muddy roads, my stomach churning at the thought of tomorrow. For hour after hour the sound of the rain is deafening, easily the heaviest I have ever experienced.

This close to the equator sunrise is almost instant, and at almost exactly 6am. Early mornings are simply a way of life whether you're a morning person or not. I'm relieved to find the road north in much the same condition as the day before. At this elevation, the road is mostly solid rock and only rarely completely dirt. Most rivers have concrete bridges in good enough condition to cross which means monster mud pits are the exception rather than the rule.

That being said they do come up every hour or so, and without fail they're always a source of entertainment and hard work. Locals packed into rusted old Mercedes vans accept the mud with little fuss or fanfare, somewhat like paying a toll to pass. All passengers cross on foot, walking on whatever they can find in an attempt to stay as mud-free as possible. I admire their tenacity, though I don't see many clean shoes on the far side.

The driver of the now empty van slams into the pit at full speed, bald street tires spinning furiously in the thick, sticky mud. Mechanical sympathy is apparently unheard of in this part of the world, and drivers repeatedly bounce their engines off the rev limiter until one of three things happens. One - the vehicle breaks and is stuck in the middle of the mud pit. Two - the vehicle spins it's tires while sinking helplessly deeper, or three - the vehicle miraculously makes it across. With each successful crossing the crowd cheers before climbing aboard to continue their slow forward progress. To rescue vehicles stuck in the thick mud a few brave men dive in and push, pull, dig and throw rocks and logs for traction until forward progress is made. The instant a vehicle is clear, another dives in at full speed. I've never before seen such an amazing display of reckless determination, and it's on an endless loop.

Transport trucks are dangerously overloaded well beyond capacity and never get off so lightly. Their monumental weight causes them to sink deep in the mud, often well past the axles. Though they try valiantly, no amount of man power can budge their immense bulk. Workers toil for days in the mud to unload cargo while hoping for something big enough to pull them out. One crew I spoke to had been waiting a week in the blistering sun, blocking the centre of a massive pit. Every thirty minutes the driver fires up, and belches thick black smoke while spinning the tires hopelessly, before shutting down to again wait in silence. With low range 4x4, differential locks and good tires the mud pits don't present a huge problem for me, and I'm able to continue the slow and steady climb north, higher into the mountains.

Φ   Φ   Φ

After just ten minutes in the small mountain town of Maliville I meet Mohamed, a retired schoolteacher and the self-appointed head of tourism. With a warm smile, kind eyes, and an infectious laugh there is nothing not to like about him. Mohamed proudly displays his precious tourist log indicating a grand total of twelve tourists have visited Maliville in all of 2016. It's heartbreaking to see a steady increase in the number of visitors - up to 1,300 in 2008 - before a massive decline to present numbers. The Ebola epidemic has decimated the tourist industry in this part of the world.

Mohamed insists I stay in his rustic hut outside town, situated directly below the famous 'Dame of Mali' rock formation. He positively beams while showing me around the area, introducing me to friends and family and hosting me for dinner. I plan to stay one night, which turns into two, and then three. The warm company and refuge from the rain are impossible to turn down. During the day I wander through town chatting to locals, re-supplying and hiking up nearby mountains. Everyone smiles proudly and laughs when I express my shock at the never ending rain. "Of course," they say warmly, "This is Guinea."

Men on the street wave enormous wads of cash, hoping to exchange money using the black market rate, about 30% better than the official rate I would get from an ATM. I exchange just over one million Guinean Francs, an impressive pile of money when the largest single bill is twenty thousand. Notes come in bundles of one hundred or two hundred thousand, and I can't help noticing nobody ever counts individual bills, they simply trust each other to do the right thing. It feels great to be a millionaire, though it's short lived when I later spend a third of that on a single tank of gas.

Φ   Φ   Φ

I leave Maliville and venture into the heart of Guinea, where I find my way to the Fouta Djallon mountainous region. Perched on the edge of a spectacular gorge, the tiny town of Doucki boasts some of the best hiking in West Africa. Hassan and his family have been leading visitors on signature hikes for over a decade, and they're extremely happy to welcome me into their home and guide me on hikes. During the day we hike far into the mountains - regardless of the rain - swimming in cliff top pools and waterfalls, canyoneering and drinking tea with friendly locals in tiny huts. In the evening we relax in mud and straw huts, chatting about tourism in Guinea and what the future might bring.

Again I'm treated like family, and soon even the small children come running to greet me after a hike. These people have little more than mud huts and rice they've grown with their own labor, yet they insist on sharing it with me. Something about their relaxed attitude and huge smiles is contagious, and soon I feel more at home than the one I left behind.

Record rainfall, monster rivers and rocky mountains make Guinea the ideal place for breathtaking waterfalls. Many are deep in the jungle, requiring exploratory side trips down narrow tracks. Time and again my jaw drops as I approach enormous waterfalls carved into the stunning landscape. Elsewhere in the world they would be huge tourist destinations while here in Guinea there is rarely a sign, and absolutely no fences or guard rails to stop me venturing much too close to the edge where I repeatedly scare myself. I also never pay a cent to visit a single waterfall.

Φ   Φ   Φ

One track is much longer and slower than planned, and I'm not back on the main road until sunset. With no choice I break my only golden rule and continue driving after dark. The dangers of driving in the dark are very real - animals, people, broken down vehicles and other obstacles lay around every bend. The road itself is extremely broken and seemingly more pot hole than road, all of which hides perfectly in the dark. I don't enjoy driving in the dark one bit, though finding a suitable place to wild camp now is essentially impossible. To add to the danger a thick fog rolls in, making the hazards even harder to spot.

With a huge transport truck barreling along behind I'm pushing too hard in the darkness when I hit a massive pot hole, completely unseen. All four corners of the Jeep smash into the bump stops, causing the rear end to bounce off the pavement and I actually hear the tires chirp as they land, a first for me. After letting the truck pass I continue a hundred yards before I hear a worrying clunk as I crawl into and out of the next series of potholes.

It's now pitch black, cold and drizzling rain. With only a headlamp I lie in the mud and make a careful check of the suspension. On my second time around I see the damage - a sway bar end link on the front has been torn off it's rubber mount, and now hangs uselessly from the sway bar, hitting the mount on the axle each time the suspension cycles. A few locals materialize out of the foggy darkness and offer help. Given the engine is still running and the wheels are able to turn, they don't see a problem.

Weighing my options, I come around to their point of view. That, and I really have no choice. The nearest Jeep parts are thousands of miles and multiple border crossings away and the sway bar isn't essential. Hoping to avoid further damage I cable tie the useless end link out of the way and continue through the thick fog, much slower than before.

Φ   Φ   Φ

A month of relentless rain and intense humidity has left everything inside the Jeep damp and muddy. With no way to completely dry out, I inevitably find mould growing inside and on my clothes. My shoes and feet have not once been dry, and are much the worse for it. The warm people, beautiful sights and adventure have been exactly what I dreamed of, though I'm ready to dry out. The relentless rain means I'm not enjoying myself as much as I should be, so I look to move on.

A few borders are still closed from the massive Ebola outbreak, so I can't continue around the coast through Sierra Leon and Liberia as I originally planned. With my visa running out I set my sights to the north, hoping the rainy season is finished in neighbouring Mali.

On my final day in Guinea I wind north along the banks of the enormous Niger River and replay the previous month in my mind, thinking about the challenges faced and the many smiling faces that always accompanied every experience.

I squat on the side of the road, scooping handfuls of burning-hot rice and fried onion from a communal bowl. I've been warmly invited by a group of Police to share their meagre meal, their pride clearly evident. They were trying to get a bribe from me only ten minutes prior, though after a cup of tea and warm smiles, that's all water under the bridge. From my shady spot I watch fishermen cast nets and women wash clothes on the shores of the massive Niger, a swirling, muddy torrent of water. The scene is so peaceful and everyone is so happy I have to pinch myself to make sure I'm not still dreaming about adventures in Africa. The more I travel, the more I realize a country is made up of people, and it's the people that make a country unforgettable.

I decided to play the odds, and I'm extremely happy I made the detour into Guinea for a month of adventure in the mountains and jungle of this little-known West African gem. My French has progressed enough I can easily get around, chat to locals, buy street food and deflect bribery attempts.

I'm sinking into Africa and this expedition, and I can't stop grinning about Guinea being only country number six. I have years of adventure like this in front of me.

West African Visas

Bamako, Mali
September 2016

M ALI'S capital of Bamako lies on the mighty Niger River and just a stone's throw from the heart of the city lies the famous 'Sleeping Camel' hostel/hotel/campground. In years past The Camel was *the* overlander and backpacker hangout in this part of West Africa, though the ongoing conflict in Northern Mali and Ebola in nearby countries means overlanding and tourism in general on the West Coast are much less common.

I'm excited to see an old Land Rover with a roof top tent setup in The Camel, the first overlanders I've seen in two months. I quickly strike up a friendship with laid back and friendly Danny and Alice, as always happy to speak to people I have so much in common with. After living and working in Tanzania for five years they set out to drive to Alice's home in England. They've been on the road a year and I quickly see they're exhausted and ready to be finished. Over a cold drink Danny explains they were unable to get a Nigerian visa, and with no other choice were forced to ship their Landy from Gabon to Togo on a vehicle and passenger ferry. Just a day into the voyage the ferry grounded on a sand bar, and they were stuck on the ferry for an entire month.

Conditions quickly deteriorated into a *Lord of the flies* style scenario, with overflowing toilets full of maggots, a severe lack of drinking water and very little food. Without multiple entry visas for Gabon they couldn't leave the ferry, though thankfully they were able to buy fruits, fish and water from the fishermen who were kind enough to row to the stricken ferry.

A month later when they finally arrived in Togo the nightmare continued with Customs making life extremely painful and not accepting their vehicle paperwork. During the negotiations Alice wasn't permitted to leave the ferry, and started to feel a lot like a prisoner. After many days negotiating in the hot sun Danny also hit his limit and paid thousands of dollars to get the Landy into Togo for just a week. Combined with a round of Malaria each they're understandably ready to finish their West African adventure. Even still they fill my head with advice and recommendations for out of the way places to explore.

The owners of The Camel are also interesting guys who've lived in Mali for ten years each. Both have permanent smiles, speak fluent French and love the Malian way of life. Matt is originally Australian, is six foot five and smiles with his entire face while enjoying his bottomless cool beer. Originally American, Phil is expecting a baby with his Malian wife and clearly couldn't be happier or prouder. They both have endless crazy stories about life here, like when Phil arrived in 2012 on the last flight before the massive Military *Coup d'état* that ousted the President. Always curious I drill him for details, though he just says everyone laid low until the dust settled, and it really wasn't a big deal.

The Camel is such an inviting and friendly place I stay longer and longer, and I relax for two weeks before someone mentions the hot shower.
"Which shower is hot?" I ask.

There are hot and cold taps, though I didn't even bother trying the hot one, simply assuming it didn't work like every other shower I've seen in Africa so far.

In the evening I take my first hot shower since Morocco, many months ago.

Φ Φ Φ

It's common to assume West African countries would be happy to issue travel visas to foreigners like Danny, Alice and myself. While that would make life easier, it's unfortunately not the case. Tourism is very uncommon in this part of the world and dealing with the governments is never straightforward. The Embassies of many West African countries won't issue travel visas to foreigners and insist a person must obtain visas from Embassies in their home country. While this is extremely frustrating, I understand why it's done this way. Embassies in Africa are staffed by people who speak the language and understand the needs of locals here. They know what paperwork these people will have, and can get if required. They don't know anything about foreigners like me, and they have no reason to. After all there is a perfectly good Embassy in my home country staffed by people who can issue me a visa, so I should just go there.

I need to secure a tourist visa in my passport before I arrive at the border of virtually every country in West Africa, and I've already been denied at two separate Embassies. Because I'm a foreigner, they wouldn't even talk to me.
"We can not help you."
"Please go to your home country."
Ouch.

This presents a huge problem given I need roughly thirteen visas to successfully traverse the west coast and reach South Africa. In theory I could go to Australia and obtain all the visas I need in one fell swoop, though unfortunately there are two reasons that won't work. Many of the visas have strict time limits and expiry dates, often a maximum of thirty days after they are issued. Some even begin the day they are issued and only last thirty days. Even if I somehow managed to obtain them all, I simply wouldn't have enough time to drive the length of the massive continent. Furthermore many West African countries don't actually have Embassies in Australia, instead they nominate the closest one to serve Australians. After extensive research I learn I will have to visit the Angolan Embassy in Singapore in order to secure that all important visa. Not only is this prohibitively expensive, but I might need a visa for Singapore. This rabbit hole quickly gets *very* deep.

Φ   Φ   Φ

To solve this problem, I will rely on Africa being Africa. Virtually everything here is negotiable with the right smiles and handshakes. Talking with overlanders like Danny and Alice I've learned some Embassies are not so strict about enforcing these rules. So even if the Nigerian Embassy in virtually every country tells me to take a hike, it's well known among travelers the Nigerian Embassy in Bamako will probably issue me a visa. Why they do this is hard to say. Maybe the Ambassador is just a nice guy who is happy to help. Maybe they didn't get the memo from headquarters - after all they're thousands of miles away in a country that speaks a different language and has unreliable communication networks. Most likely they're just going rogue and pocketing the visa application fee.

I don't care why it works, I just need it to work.

With all of this in mind I begin the game of applying for each visa as I move south. I don't want to get any visa too early because I won't have enough time to reach that country. I also don't want to leave it too late, and risk being denied. Most worryingly, I've learned it's entirely possible to become stuck with no legal path forward or back. For example if I manage to get through Nigeria into Cameroon without first obtaining a visa for Gabon I will be stuck. The Gabon Embassy in Cameroon won't issue me a visa to continue forward, and the Nigerian Embassy there also won't issue me a visa to go back. If that happens I may be forced to ship the Jeep around a few countries, if that's even possible.

All of this visa bureaucracy, a severe lack of information,

terrible roads and infrastructure and safety concerns combine to make West Africa one of the hardest places to travel on the planet, which also means it contains some of the least explored regions on the planet.

On top of that, these tourist visas are not cheap. When I do manage to obtain one I'm paying anywhere from $50USD to $150USD for a one month visa to each of the roughly thirteen countries in West Africa alone.

Ф   Ф   Ф

Hoping for the best I put on my cleanest collared shirt and nice pants before walking across Bamako in the scorching sun to the Nigerian Embassy. I'm on my best polite behaviour as I explain myself to the security guard, while showing him a map of Africa explaining my route with a photo of the Jeep to emphasise my point. I'm directed to wait with a few other people, and I'm more than happy to sit under the air conditioner on a comfortable couch. On the far wall is a large flat screen - the first TV I've seen in many months.

English is the official language of Nigeria, so the TV is easy to understand. It's an American show depicting soldiers in a far away land literally fighting for their lives. They're in some horrible place, constantly being shot at and are very clearly hated by everyone. I see images of roadblocks where women and children are violently pulled from cars and men are smashed in the face with the butts of rifles before being shot in the head. It's extremely violent and gripping, and looks like a war documentary. I become completely sucked into the bright images and fast-paced action, never mind the gripping action and desperation.

Without TV or movies in my life I haven't seen violence, anger or desperation like this in months and it quickly captivates me. I realize I only ever see this kind of anger and hatred in movies and TV, and living without them for a few months highlights just how unlike real life they are.

Everyone else waiting is Nigerian, so they clearly speak English and perfectly understand the show too. I'm jarred back to reality after forty minutes when one of the characters desperately fleeing for their life says they must get to Bamako.

Wait a minute, I think.
I'm in Bamako!

The show depicts a horrendous war zone, and the style and tone makes it feel like a documentary rather than a fictional drama. My brain reels as the implications sink in. Anyone back in the developed world would assume these images on TV are an accurate picture of Mali, while I've been exploring the capital of Bamako and all over southern Mali having a great time. For five weeks I've been walking the streets, eating street food and enjoying live music and drinks in the evenings. Never once have I felt remotely unsafe. In fact I've been invited into more homes to share food and tea than I can count. The images on TV are the polar opposite of what I've been experiencing, but nobody in the developed world has any way of knowing that.

Hollywood has become so good at making fiction look real, it's extremely easy for them to depict far away lands in a way that is nothing like reality. In the quest for higher ratings these shows distort reality with complete disregard for their portrayal of the millions of friendly people who actually live there. I feel horrible knowing anyone watching the show will think Mali is one huge war zone and the people are all either causing great harm or fleeing for their lives. The reality couldn't be any more different - in five weeks I've experienced the friendliest and warmest people of my entire life.

Feeling embarrassed and awkward I move my passport on the table so the world 'Australia' is clearly visible.

Φ   Φ   Φ

After waiting a few hours the Ambassador speaks with me very briefly. He wants to know why I want to visit Nigeria, where I will stay and for how long. He seems satisfied with my rambling tale, and asks me to return at the end of the week. I leave my passport hoping for the best.

I'm overcome with emotion as I step outside onto the streets of Bamako to walk back to The Camel. Even though my personal experience tells me everything is fine, the lasting impact from the Hollywood scenes is intense. The vivid images of the brutal war zone linger in my mind, and it's difficult to convince myself I'm not about to be violently attacked. Even after five weeks on the ground I struggle to believe my own experiences, and I realize anyone who has never visited Mali has no chance of understanding the reality if they've seen a show like the one I did.

Φ   Φ   Φ

I return on Friday afternoon just as the Embassy staffer is locking the front gates. He seems flustered but does remember me. He grabs my passport from a top drawer, replacing it with the wad of cash I hand over - the official visa application fee. He immediately jumps on his scooter and zooms off in a cloud of dust, leaving me alone to celebrate the shiny Nigerian visa glued into my passport.

On The Media

V IRTUALLY everything we in the developed world know about Africa comes from the mainstream media. The TV, radio and newspapers have inundated us with images of civil war, famine and disease on an endless loop. So shocking are these images and stories of horror it appears as if Africa is horrible, and it's horrible everywhere.

So pervasive is this narrative people are often dumbfounded I would willingly travel around Africa. They assume I have an armed escort and I'm rushing through endless war zones, famine and disease. Clearly, I'll be lucky to escape with my life.

It was always shocking to be on the inside of news headlines, and to experience the reality compared to the news reports. I repeatedly felt as if a mistake had been made, and the report was actually about somewhere else. Even worse, I wondered if the cameras had intentionally been pointed in the worst direction they could find while ignoring all the good.

I don't want you to read another page if you think Africa is a disgusting hellhole, because you won't be able to understand Africa the same way I do. The images the media has put in your head of dodging bullets, famine and disease are so unrepresentative of what I saw and experienced I feel compelled to set the record straight before you read any further.

Chronologically this chapter should be at the end of this book, because I didn't come to this understanding until I'd been on the ground in Africa for years. It's important for you to read this now so you have the same perspective on Africa and the media that I do.

Φ   Φ   Φ

It's extremely easy for a report to simply leave out a great deal of information about a topic, often called lies of omission. A report can be entirely factual about the things it does cover, but by omitting certain details it can leave a lasting impression that doesn't give an accurate picture of the entire scene.

One sided reports from Africa are the only kind of report from Africa, and they're always reports about bad occurrences. These attention grabbing headlines only show the very worst happenings gathered from around the continent because they're so gripping. Africa is enormous and diverse, and while bad things do occur, the overwhelming majority of daily occurrences are good. Every day there are tens of thousands of weddings filled with endless joy and happiness. Babies are born to proud parents, kids graduate school, hospitals are built and people celebrate at every opportunity - in fact much more than in the developed world. Because the mainstream media only reports on the very worst occurrences, people following the news in developed countries don't hear about any of that. In fact, they never hear about anything good from Africa.

I want you to imagine you live in a far away country, on a tiny island isolated from the world. You don't hear a lot about other countries, but when you do it's always from the TV, radio or the newspaper. There is one very large and prominent place in particular you only hear bad things about - mass shootings, natural disasters, violence when the new President is inaugurated, race riots and even scores of children being killed by gunfire at school. Given all of that, it's clearly a terrible place and you certainly wouldn't choose to visit. As long as the media only covers the bad stuff, it's easy to paint this far away place in a bad light. As the years roll into decades and these kinds of stories keep coming up, it simply becomes common knowledge this far away land is a hellhole. The media doesn't tell you about anything else going on in this place, because there is an endless stream of bad to keep you hooked. While it sounds horrible, in fact all of those bad occurrences are from the USA in just the last few years.

By reporting on only the worst occurrences it's simple for the media on your little island to make you think the USA is a horrible place, and it's extremely important to see this is *exactly* what the mainstream media has been doing for decades reporting on Africa. News headlines from Africa are factual, but because they only talk about the bad occurrences they don't give a complete or accurate representation of day to day life, in the same way the events above don't give a good feel for the everyday lives of three hundred and thirty million Americans.

After meeting thousands of friendly people living happy lives all across Africa, this realization made me extremely angry. The media is doing an immense injustice to the more than one billion friendly and happy people who live across Africa. I didn't understand why they would do this to people who are kinder, warmer and more generous than anyone I had met before. More than angry, I was furious and upset that the world thinks Africa and her people are horrible when the reality I was experiencing was the polar opposite. Once I got past my anger I was able to move onto understanding and eventually acceptance.

I realized the mainstream media is a business just like any other. They have profits to make and targets to reach. It's literally someone's job to increase viewership. That person likely has a family to feed and bills to pay, and they'll lose their job if they don't succeed. They aren't measured on how accurately they portray everyday life in foreign lands, or how balanced the reporting is each day, they're measured on how much they increase readership. Naturally they will choose to run the most shocking, awful and attention-grabbing stories available from all around the globe. These stories are intentionally chosen to tug at our heartstrings and trigger overwhelming emotions in the hope we will be forever hooked on the seemingly endless stream of stories too shocking to ignore. Teams of people work tirelessly every single day to dig up the most sensational and shocking stories from the entire planet, so it shouldn't be a surprise they manage to find some.

There's no conspiracy here, and the media aren't going out of their way to intentionally lie about Africa and other far away lands, they just don't have the time or motivation to tell the entire story. They have to pack as much as possible into their thirty minute segment, so after reporting on a few horrible occurrences from around the globe they switch back to more local matters. If there is a good news story for the day, they would much rather make it about something nearby, likely in their own country or region.

It's an unfortunate fact the mainstream media long ago stopped focusing on actual news, and simply became about entertainment and shock value. Especially when it comes to reporting on far away lands, there's zero incentive for balanced reporting. We will never see a report on a mundane plane landing, but accidents and crashes will always make headlines because they're attention grabbing. This leads many to think plane crashes are relatively common, and that air travel is dangerous. In fact, plane crashes are exceptionally rare. Every day of the year around the world there are more than one hundred thousand flights, and 99.999975% of them land safely[1].

Not only does the mainstream media leave out almost all the good events around the world, they also fail to give us any sense of scale or perspective. When we're told about a shocking

---

[1]See the next footnote

event we're given no context to know how often this kind of thing happens, what percentage of people are impacted by the event or if it's likely to happen again. This is done intentionally to make minor events seem much more dramatic than reality so you become hooked to the news as the story develops. I will never forget when I was working at Kirkwood in California and my roommate insisted I watch the TV coverage of some huge disaster in Australia. Over the next four hours I was glued to the TV trying to decipher the story, and although there was a lot of American coverage, none gave simple facts, instead they chose to focus on the deadly situation and how distraught people should be about what had happened. Eventually I learned it was about a shark attack, and I assumed one or more people had died from all the fanfare and hype the media was giving the story. In actuality one surfer had been bitten on the foot and needed just five stitches. The media hyped the story beyond belief, and they succeeded in sucking me into their coverage.

This lack of scale and perspective is complicated by the fact Africa is simply enormous. It's so large we can't easily comprehend it, and our intuition fails us because we have nothing to compare it to. Unfortunately maps don't help because the way the round globe is printed distorts landmasses making Africa appear much smaller than it really is. In reality Africa has more than three times the landmass of the USA and has four times as many people. Africa comprises 20% of all land on earth, and contains 15% of all human beings on the planet. At that scale, it's not surprising Africa is often in the headlines for bad occurrences - it's so enormous there is simply a lot happening each day.

I also need to emphasise how utterly useless it is for the media to report on a disaster or horrible event in 'Africa' in a way that implies it's just one place, or that the event impacts all of 'Africa'. Not only is the continent of fifty-four countries simply massive, but African countries are vastly different and diverse from each other and they're separated by strictly controlled international borders. Even when bad things happen in one country, life in the immediate neighbours continues as normal. For example I doubt anyone living in Oregon was concerned for their safety during the recent civil unrest in Nicaragua. That trouble was many thousands of miles and multiple international borders away, making it virtually impossible for it to spill over into Oregon. This is exactly the case with Africa, only the distances and therefore separation are much bigger.

Φ   Φ   Φ

If we're to form an accurate understanding of the world we must change the way we process the sensationalist headlines pumped out by the media. In his phenomenal book *Factfullness*[2], Hans Rosling teaches us how to do exactly that. He recommends slowing down and thinking about the story carefully, rather than getting caught up in the hype and letting our emotions overwhelm our thinking brains. It's easy enough to become outraged over a headline about some horrible event on the other side of the world, but it takes time and effort to dig deeper into the details.

For example, an American tourist was recently kidnapped in Uganda, and this terrible event made headlines around the world. There was so much coverage that many people contacted me and expressed their concerns that I might suffer the same fate if I were to visit Uganda. This kind of event and the coverage it generates leads millions of people to jump to the conclusion that Uganda is unsafe for tourists. If I just saw the headline and didn't dig deeper, it would be easy to assume I should avoid Uganda altogether. Rather than jumping to conclusions like this from sensationalist headlines, I prefer to dig into the details before I draw any conclusions and make decisions about my route.

A quick Google tells me approximately 1.4 million tourists visit

---

[2] *Factfullness* - Hans Rosling, 2018

Uganda each year, and kidnappings are extremely rare, this being the only one in many years. If we horribly exaggerate and say one tourist is kidnapped each year, then the likelihood of any tourist being kidnapped in a year is half that of a person living the USA being struck by lightening in any given year[3]. Virtually nobody living in the USA worries about being struck by lighting in their regular life, even though it's twice as likely as getting kidnapped if they visit Uganda. Keep in mind we vastly exaggerated the number of yearly kidnappings in Uganda, so probably a person is three or five times more likely to be hit by lightening than kidnapped in Uganda. By digging into the story I see the headline isn't so scary[4], and I conclude Uganda is plenty safe enough for me to visit.

Decades of one sided reports from the media have permanently burned images of war, disease and famine into our brains. Because of this it's perfectly normal to assume Africa is horrible and extremely dangerous. Certainly there are dangerous places, and bad things do happen. I'm not sugar-coating it and saying everything is fine, that is simply not true. After years on the ground I've come to learn it's extremely difficult to get an accurate and complete picture when information only comes from the mainstream media. To gain a more complete understanding of the realities in Africa we must slow down and use our brains to dig into these headlines. We must seek out and talk to people that have visited and lived there, and we must be willing to update our outdated understanding formed from outdated information.

The fact is that all African countries are developing extremely quickly, and conditions for the vast majority of people are enormously better than they've ever been at any point in history. That is not just my opinion, these facts are confirmed by UN data on global development.

---

[3] 1 in 1.4 million vs 1 in 700,000

[4] The kidnapping victim was released unharmed for a $500,000 ransom after five days.

Next time a headline screams for your attention about a bad event in a far way land - as it undoubtedly will - ask yourself how many good things also happen there on a daily basis. How many people got married, how many people cried with joy at the birth of their first child, and how many people partied at a birthday celebration or festival. Remember there is *a lot* more happening in that country than just the news headline you're shown.

Φ Φ Φ

What does all of that mean for my experiences on the ground every single day in Africa? After all the media hype, the reality on the ground turned out to be vastly different than the commonly assumed situation in Africa.

During the entire expedition I never once saw or experienced any violence. I never had a gun pulled on me, no knives were pulled and no punches were thrown. Not a single thing was ever stolen from myself or the Jeep. In all the border crossings, roadblocks and street markets not a single person uttered a threatening word. Nobody even once said anything remotely like "or else."

In Southern and Eastern Africa I bumped into many hundreds of European overlanders driving all over the place, having the time of their lives. Many retirees have been doing so for years on end, and have never had a single problem. Right now there are literally thousands of foreigners driving all over Africa, simply loving it.

The reality was so different to the media narrative, in fact, I never heard a single gunshot in all of Africa.

Malaria Round One

Bamako, Mali
September 2016

M ALARIA presents a very large problem on a multi-year expedition around Africa. There's no vaccine, so conventional wisdom says to regularly take an anti-malarial pill in the hopes of preventing infection. Unfortunately, these anti-malarials are not 100% effective, and I met plenty of people throughout Africa who were taking the daily pill and still contracted malaria anyway. Furthermore, all anti-malarial pills come with a slew of side effects, some of which are very nasty.

Virtually all the different pills bring increased sensitivity to the sun, and I learned quickly it's virtually impossible to avoid the sun in Africa. A couple of the pills are notorious for causing demented dreams and more than a few people swear they'd rather have malaria than experience those dreams again. The US Military issued one popular pill to their personnel for many years, and only stopped when it was discovered 10% of all people taking it developed *permanent* psychosis.
While malaria sounds bad, I'm sure that's worse.

All the different prevention pills are also very hard on the liver when taken long term, and doctors recommend taking them for a maximum of about six months. Besides the nasty side effects, the logistics are also prohibitive. Most have to be taken daily, and I can't imagine trying to cross borders with a stash of over a thousand pills - the first border guard to find them would undoubtedly confiscate them.

The most effective way for me to avoid malaria is actually very simple. The particular mosquito that carries malaria is only active at dawn and dusk, so at those times I need to use strong repellent, wear long pants and sleeves and do whatever it takes not to get bitten. I do my best, though when it's 95°F and 95% humidity at 5pm I find it extremely difficult to put on a long sleeve shirt, long pants, socks and shoes.

Φ   Φ   Φ

On my first afternoon in Bamako I venture into the city with a new local friend, and I don't plan ahead. I'm wearing shorts and a t-shirt, and I don't bring any bug spray with me. We eat dinner in a busy neighbourhood, and I get eaten alive.

About a week later at The Camel I begin to feel horrible around midday. I'm exhausted for no reason, a huge headache is building, my stomach hurts and I feel a kind of out-of-body numbness. I'm also extremely irritable, which is very out of character for me. I lay down for an hour and things only get worse. Maybe I've just eaten something bad, which is not uncommon given how much street food I eat.

As luck would have it a doctor with a lot of malaria experience is also staying at The Camel. Originally from Colombia, Sara is small in stature but takes her work very seriously and is not to be disagreed with.

Late in the afternoon Sara takes one look at me lying uselessly in the shade and says:
"Dan you've got malaria."
"Nonsense," I say, completely in denial.
I refuse to believe it might be true, though after twenty minutes of discussion, Sara is only more convinced.
"Dan, I treated twenty people with malaria *today*," she says.
"Trust me, you have malaria."

Still trying to deny reality, Sara runs through my options. We could buy a 'quick test' in a local Pharmacy to confirm the diagnosis. While they sound great, unfortunately these tests are not very accurate. If the test comes back positive I most likely do have malaria, but if it comes back negative there is about a fifty percent chance I do anyway. The only way to know with certainty is to drawn blood at a clinic and look at it under a microscope, the results of which take a day.

It's now late in the afternoon and all the clinics are closed until the following morning, so that doesn't help. Even though we're not absolutely certain I have malaria, Sara says our approach doesn't change. I should immediately start taking the 'cure' medication regardless, because if I really do have malaria the sooner I take the medication the better. If I don't have malaria, the medicine won't hurt and tomorrow I'll most likely feel fine. Sara explains the 'cure' medication is vastly more effective the sooner I start, so we have no time to waste.

Sara buys the medicine for about \$12 at a neighbourhood pharmacy, and I'm grateful. After deciphering the instructions I immediately take the first round, and pay for a room in The Camel with air conditioning. Even with the room cold enough to make Sara shiver I begin to sweat profusely. I have no appetite, and my headache threatens to crack my skull open. Before I fall asleep my fingers and toes begin to tingle and I start to get loopy, both of which are classic malaria symptoms. I tell a few morbid jokes about my own death that I know aren't funny, but somehow I can't help myself. I feel like I'm watching my actions from outside my own body, a very surreal experience.

During the night I wake multiple times bathed in sweat, even with the AC working overtime to keep the room frigid. Thankfully I sleep a lot, and the night passes without too much discomfort.

In the morning I feel a little better, and after a very lazy day and more rounds of medicine I really only feel tired and weak from not eating. Even my headache subsides, so I have no trouble taking endless naps in the amazing air conditioning.

Two days later I finish the medication and I feel ninety-five percent of my usual self. I'm extremely thankful Sara made me take the medication so early, clearly it made a huge difference. We still don't know for sure if I actually had malaria, though it is the most likely explanation.

A few days later I begin to feel sick again, so I get a blood test for both malaria and typhoid. Both are negative, and after a round of general purpose antibiotics I feel fine again a few days later and I'm happy to put the whole incident behind me.

Φ   Φ   Φ

In the coming weeks I learn much about malaria as I talk to everyone at The Camel about my experience. Here in West Africa malaria is not nearly the big deal that the western media makes it out to be and. Locals and foreigners alike contract it at least once a year, and they just deal with it. Matt and Phil at The Camel have both had it more times than they can count, and just shrug when I ask how bad it is. Sara the doctor also contracts malaria twice while living in Mali, as does virtually everyone working for the UN.

I come to learn most people that spend more than a few months in remote Africa are very likely to contract malaria at least once. It's clearly not good, and it can be really bad, but almost everyone that takes the 'cure' medication will make a full recovery. Malaria does kill a staggering number of people each year, though the vast majority are the very young or very old who don't have access to the medication.

Having learned my lesson, I put a course of the 'cure' medication in the fridge and I vow to do a better job covering up and wearing bug spray at sunrise and sunset.

Malaria was an experience I was desperately hoping to avoid. Thanks to the quick actions of Sara the doctor it wasn't nearly as bad as the hype had lead me to believe.

Healthcare In Rural Africa

Kalana, Mali
November 2016

A FTER saving me from malaria, Sara and I strike up a friendship while staying at The Camel. We wander around drinking tea with locals, buying street food Sara's favourite - delicious fresh watermelons which are in season and plentiful. Sara volunteers at a remote mission run by extremely hard working and dedicated nuns providing much needed healthcare in an isolated community. Sara recently graduated medical school in Colombia, and wants to help people who otherwise wouldn't have access to a doctor. She's flown around the world to work tirelessly in that pursuit, a genuine inspiration. It's clear Sara's been thrown in the very deep end in rural Mali, though I can see she's determined and meets every new challenge head on. Sara was given a crash course in French, and has also picked up a good many words in the local Malian language. She's always singing rather than just speaking like me, and locals love her infectious happiness and laughter. Sara has such an amazing manner with people it's easy to see why she's dedicated her life to helping others.

Always on the lookout for new adventures, I offer to drive Sara to her isolated town. For most of a day we bump along dusty and corrugated roads before finally arriving in the small town, very close to the border of Guinea. Many of Sara's patients actually come from Guinea, and just walk through the fields with no paperwork. For many locals in rural Africa, borders are virtually meaningless.

The clinic is basic, though with decades of hard work the nuns have become a very important part of the community. Not only do they offer much needed health care, they run basket making classes for women, and have just opened a school. I feel a bit useless, and when they ask me to move a few heavy boxes I think they're trying to make me feel better. Sara works tirelessly treating her patients which are mostly children suffering from malaria, malnutrition and snake bites.

Φ   Φ   Φ

I'm reading a book in the baking afternoon heat when Sara asks for my help. Of course I say yes, having no idea how I can possibly help in the clinic. Sara is treating an extremely fit and strong young man in his mid 20s, and needs my help with him. Ominously I see a bandage covering his right hand up to the elbow, and I can see right away he's in a lot of pain. His two burly brothers have come for moral support, and they all look extremely serious compared to the happiness I've come to love in Mali. They don't speak French, so Sara talks to her patient via a translator. Sara asks questions and receives answers in French, her third language. Helpfully she throws in the occasionally English word for my benefit.

A few months ago the young man got some kind of infection on his hand, and has been covering it up ever since, hoping it will go away. Evidently he's terrified and doesn't want anyone to even look at it, much less touch it. I get the feeling the big brothers have convinced him to come today, realizing there is a serious problem. After removing the bandage, Sara and I see why.

His little finger is nothing but bone, and it's jet black. I know nothing about healthcare, but I know that's not good. His ring finger is half flesh and half bone, and then his middle and pointer are covered in white fleshy lumps with patches of visible bone underneath. His hand reeks of decay and it's clear he's in a lot of pain.

Sara says this is some kind of flesh-eating bacteria - yes, that's a real thing - and his little finger is completely dead. She's worried he may soon lose more if she doesn't act, and his whole arm is at risk. Ideally she would amputate at least the little finger, but she's not equipped to do that here. He needs to go to a real hospital, but that's expensive and far away.

Sara explains her plan in English and we get to work. We pull chairs outside in the sun, and I sit facing the young man, only a foot away. I put on rubber gloves, and try my best to be calm, knowing what's coming. Sara needs to thoroughly clean the entire wound to prevent the bacteria spreading, and it's clear the pain of doing so will be excruciating. Anesthetic must first be injected into his fingers and hand in multiple places before she can scrub the wound, which is where I come in. Through the translator Sara explains what we're going to do, and the young man gingerly extends his hand, shaking like a leaf. I grasp his forearm with both hands, and do my best to stop him pulling it back. He writhes in pain as Sara jams the needle in repeatedly anywhere it will go, and it's clear he's trying with all his strength not to actually cry out in pain.

His two brothers step closer and for an instant I worry they might thrash me for holding their brother who is clearly suffering. They hover close, though they never interfere with our work. They also don't help me hold their brother, and it takes all my strength with two arms to hold his one.

Once the needlework is done we rest for a few minutes before Sara checks if the anesthetic has taken effect. When satisfied she begins scrubbing away chunks of skin while I again hold his arm steady. Sara uses scrubbing pads and scissors to rip off chunks of dead and decaying skin, and then uses cloth soaked in disinfectant to clean any salvageable skin. If she doesn't get all the decaying skin, she explains, this will all be for nothing. More than a few chunks of rotten skin and a good amount of blood drop onto the bare earth between our feet, and I struggle to keep it together. We're in the full sun, flies are buzzing around and I'm drenched in sweat from the effort and the scene only inches from my face. I've never had a close view of raw bones before, and I hope I never do again.

To finish Sara re-wraps the hand with a new bandage, and explains he must visit the real hospital. At a minimum the dead finger must be amputated, and she does her best to explain through the translator he might lose his entire arm if he continues to ignore it. I'm shocked by the display of raw medicine, and the kind of deep courage and strength the young man displayed. All the men thank Sara repeatedly, and the brothers manage to shake my hand even though they're clearly not sure if I was helping or hurting.

I never did learn that brave young man's name.

Φ Φ Φ

Later that evening Sara wants to check on a much younger patient across town, and I'm happy for the distraction. There is a Chinese scooter in the compound, and I ride a few practice laps by myself to make sure I'm not going to crash before Sara jumps on the back. My Dad, sister and brother have all had motorbikes at various times, though somehow they've never appealed to me and I'm a terrible rider. At sunset we ride into town on dusty roads, just as the streets burst to life. Now the heat has passed hundreds of people fill the streets and they hoot and holler at the sight of two white people zig-zagging unsteadily on the scooter. Many know Sara, and the greetings she sings in the local language are returned with laughter, smiles and waves.

After crossing a dry and dusty soccer field I must ride through a deep drainage ditch. I'm not sure how the scooter will handle it, so I ask Sara to jump off. A few local men stop to see how I'll make out, clearly entertained. The men speak French, so I ask if the scooter can make it through. It seems virtually everyone in West Africa is a pro at riding these little scooters, so they're clearly amused by my lack of skill.

"Of course it will." they say together.

Of course, they always say that.

As I drop into the culvert the scooter bottoms out and I get a bit stuck, spinning the back wheel. Two of the men give me a solid push and I lurch unsteadily up and over the crest of the hill, barely able to hang on. The men are all smiles and laughter, clearly happy to have helped the incompetent white guy.

I'm just happy I didn't drop the scooter.

We arrive at a local clinic on the other side of town, which is just a nondescript mud brick building with a tin roof. Sara explains she's been treating a young boy with malaria who was taken to the big hospital for a desperately needed blood transfusion. Earlier today he was brought back here in the back of a pickup, and she's eager to check on him.

I am completely unprepared for the scene in the tiny clinic.

In the only room there are six or seven extremely dirty mattresses on the bare earth, and each mattress holds a patient. Most are elderly and appear to be very close to their last breath, though it's the young boy on the far mattress that shocks me the most. He must be six or seven years old, and is having an extremely hard time breathing. His eyes are sunken into his skull, and he can't lift his head or talk. He looks extremely fragile, and barely responds when Sara tries to talk to him and take his vitals. When she draws blood it is the color and consistency of mud, and Sara says he would certainly be dead if not for the transfusion he had earlier in the day.

Gathered around his mattress is a crowd of what can only be his family who understandably look terrified and helpless at the same time. While working Sara chats quietly to each family member, offering words of encouragement and reassurance. In English she says the boy was much worse yesterday, and she was genuinely worried he would die. I can't comprehend how he could possibly look any worse than he does now, and I feel just as helpless as the family. Sara is happy with the progress of her patient, and is confident he will pull through.

Φ   Φ   Φ

A month later Sara updates me on both patients. The young man visited the hospital and the nasty bacteria was completely taken care of. His little finger was amputated, but all the others were saved. Most importantly, he kept his entire arm, and is doing well.

The small boy with malaria also made a full recovery, and Sara joined him in a soccer game with his friends, running and laughing on the dusty soccer field.

It's inspiring to see Sara and these nuns work so hard in rural Africa. It's no exaggeration to say they're saving lives on a daily basis.

Bad News

Mali & Australia
December 2016

T HE next morning I wander into the small town on foot before the heat of the day sets in. I'm hoping to buy prepaid data for my phone and I have a riot chatting to everyone who remembers our outing on the scooter last night. They're all eager to learn if I will be staying at the clinic, and want to know how I know Sara. With my steadily improving French I'm able to mostly explain myself, and the women laugh and smile when I explain repeatedly that no, Sara is not my wife. Of course they all want to know why not.

Wandering the main street I manage to buy data for about $2 per Gigabyte and back at the compound I tether off 3G Internet through the little smartphone I bought for $20 in Guinea.

It's a Saturday morning in Australia, and I haven't caught up with my family for a few weeks so I give Mum and Dad a call over Skype. Right away I know something is off. After talking about life and my recent adventures they get to the point. Over a scratchy Skype connection Mum tells me she has been diagnosed with stage four lung cancer. After a few months of neck pain Mum finally went to a doctor. They found cancer in the bones of her neck, but the really bad news is that it originated in her lungs. Now the cancer has spread it's essentially unstoppable.

Mum doesn't want to upset me, but it's important that I know the truth. Stage four lung caner is a death sentence, there are no two ways about it.

The average person with Mum's diagnosis lives only twelve months, she has been told. I think about that for the rest of the day and realize it means half of people live less than twelve months.
Sometimes being good at math sucks.

After hanging up from that call my brother Mike immediately calls and we talk for an hour, trying to come to terms with the news. To really get the tears flowing he tells me his wife is pregnant and I'm going to be an uncle for the first time.

With tears streaming down my face later in the day I explain the news to Sara, still not believing it myself. I leave first thing in the morning trying to formulate a plan. The drive is long and dusty and for the entire day I battle tears that cloud my vision. It's obvious my heart is no longer in this Africa thing.

I have a choice to make - I can spend a month exploring Ghana and spend Christmas alone on the beach as I had been planning, or I can fly to Australia to have what could be our last family Christmas. The choice is extremely easy.

Φ   Φ   Φ

In Bamako the guys at The Camel are happy to store the Jeep, and my local friend Bafou comes to negotiate the paperwork. We explain my situation to the chief of Mali Customs, and I see right away he's an intelligent man who wants to be sure I'm not doing anything shady like selling the Jeep without paying import taxes. After careful consideration he agrees I can leave the Jeep inside The Camel compound, and that I should see him when I return for new paperwork. If anyone drives it, or anything else shady happens it will be confiscated and I will never get it back, he says. I thank him profusely and assure him I won't break the rules. Back at The Camel I book plane tickets for the following morning, and I realize the price is irrelevant.

Early the following morning I'm once again on the back of Bafou's scooter as we zip through the city towards the airport. The weather has just turned, and the air is noticeably cool. This results in hilarious reactions from the locals who wear winter jackets, scarves and beanies. These items have obviously been donated from the developed world, and I even spot donation tags from the Salvation Army. Bafou himself is rugged up and freezing cold, and just shakes his head at my usual shorts and t-shirt.

As we approach the airport I see it's not like other airports I've seen around the world. The approach road is guarded by heavily armed Military personnel wearing full combat gear. Using sandbags they've built fortified .50 caliber machine gun positions, and using tanks they've blocked the road to funnel us at walking pace into the middle of it all. It's clear these men mean business, though in true Mali spirit they're all friendly. White people can often get away with almost anything in West Africa, so we're quickly waved through each checkpoint without so much as a document check.

After multiple metal detector rounds and the usual check-in procedure I'm called to board my flight along with about fifty other passengers. As we step onto the pristine tarmac I'm hit by a wall of heat, and my vision is blurred by the waves rippling off the endless black surface. There were hints before, and now it's clearer than ever - this is not a regular commercial airport in the developed world. There are numerous monster planes sitting on the runway, and only one doesn't have 'UN' painted on the side in huge letters. Instead of walking down an aisle of red carpet like a movie, I walk across the scorching tarmac to the stairs flanked on each side by fully uniformed Military men, each holding an AK 47 at the ready.
I've never seen that at an airport before.

Φ   Φ   Φ

The airline food actually tastes good and I wonder if it's because I've been eating from my tiny Jeep kitchen in Africa for six months, or because airline food has actually improved. Forty-something hours and three planes later I land in Melbourne horribly jet lagged. I can never sleep in the first thirty hours of travel then physically can't keep my eyes open for the remainder. The chip in my passport means I don't even speak to a human when entering Australia, and I'm thoroughly confused as I step through the doors onto the street. I'm disoriented by the lack of people trying to sell me stuff, trying to change money or saying I must do one more complicated step to finish the border crossing. I haven't written my details into a single paper ledger, and the whole thing is so easy and painless it doesn't feel like a border crossing at all. Not a single person pays me any attention, and actually feels a little lonely. Often in Africa I'm virtually a celebrity, now suddenly I'm nobody.

I catch a bus into the heart of Melbourne where I went to University and lived for five years long ago. I immediately feel that something is off. From my window seat I never see a single person smiling. I don't see anyone wearing brightly colored clothes, chatting excitedly or even looking the least bit happy. I certainly don't see any children laughing or running about.

The disorientation only gets worse in the heart of the city. Compared to West Africa people look downright miserable, and I'm unable to make eye contact with a single person. Nobody is smiling, laughing or singing. Nobody is washing children, and I can't find anywhere to buy street food so I can sit and eat with strangers. Everyone wears extremely well tailored clothes, fancy shoes and an intense quantity of makeup and perfume. I can't help thinking these people look fake, somewhat like an enhanced picture in a magazine.

The waves of people flowing around me look like zombies compared to the vibrant faces of West Africa and I quickly realize smiling and making eye contact is not common in Melbourne. I can't shake the feeling they're the very definition of 'live to work'. Priorities here are clearly very different.

I'm wearing my usual African uniform of shorts and flip flops, and with my scraggly hair and in need of a shave I clearly stand out.
"You look relaxed," says a guy next to me at a crosswalk.
"Do you have the day off work or something?"
"Something like that," I reply with a grin.
I'm a little surprised a stranger is talking to me, though soon it makes sense.
He's holding an iPad and is conducting market research for something or other. Clearly he thinks I'm a good victim. I explain I don't have a cell phone, I don't really have a job, and I don't even live in Australia so I'm not a good candidate for him. He obviously doesn't believe me, instead thinking I'm just brushing him off. For fun I tell him I'm driving my Jeep all the way around Africa and it's probably going to take years. Now he really thinks I'm lying. I soon learn it's often easier to shock people with the honest truth than to spend twenty minutes explaining myself. Nine times out of ten they don't believe me anyway.

I catch a train to the small beach side town where my brother is building his new house, and I soon find myself number one assistant with the construction. After years of living in Canada Mike returned to Australia, married Ashleigh and together they've bought a tiny piece of land where they're building the round house of their dreams. Mike went back to University for a year to turn his aerospace engineering degree into a teaching degree, and now he's a high school math and science teacher, just like Dad. Teaching is the family business, and the joke has always been that sooner or later I'll join the dark side.

The floor and frame of their yurt on steroids are complete,

and today the roof frames are being raised. When complete it will be a beautiful round house built from reclaimed timber and eco-friendly materials. Mike and Ash have a permit to build it themselves, and with help from a local builder they're literally creating their dream with blood, sweat and occasional tears. My eyeballs hang from my head as I help lift heavy roof trusses, and everyone laughs at my shock at the insane prices when we buy lunch at a nearby café.

Late in the day Mike, Ash and I drive a further two hours to Mum and Dad's house and I sleep from the second I climb into the backseat. I wake only once when Mike points out a Kangaroo which only adds to my disorientation.

Mum and Dad had no idea I was coming, so there are plenty of tears and long hugs when we all arrive, now home for Christmas. My sister Liz also flies in from the UK, and we've got a lot to catch up on. Mum looks great as always, and says she feels just fine.

Φ   Φ   Φ

The culture shock is extreme, and even after the jet lag and confusion wears off a week later I struggle to understand why people in this world have so much, but they're clearly not very happy. The first time I step into a supermarket is staggering, and I stumble around in a daze. I'm utterly flabbergasted by the variety and quantity of products on offer. Since leaving Morocco six months ago I haven't seen a single supermarket, only vibrant street markets and basic corner stores. Not only are fourteen different brands and types of peanut butter, but the shelf is bursting with more than a hundred jars of each type, and that's just the peanut butter. I wonder how many people could live for how many months from the food in just this one supermarket. Of course, there are six more like it in this town alone.

I also struggle with the sheer number of rules imposed on

Australians, and the number of signs required to constantly remind everyone. On the roads there are signs every ten yards warning about this or that, and then more signs explaining the penalties in detail. My brother recently paid hundreds of thousands of dollars for his land, though it's illegal for him to camp there because there was no toilet. After months of free camping I can't believe that even when you own land in parts of Australia, you're not permitted to camp there.

I also can't believe the steep fines for violating these endless rules. It seems there is a fine for literally everything, and speeding fines are issued for breaking the limit by less than two miles per hour. The more I think about it, the more my brain begins to bend. When a person breaks the law their punishment is a monetary fine. To replace that money, they must go to work more. They will either work more hours in a week, or in the case of a big enough fine push back retirement. So the punishment for breaking the law is to go to work more. Work is punishment.

It comes full circle when I learn the word for paid work in French is '*travail*', which has the same Latin base as the word 'torture'.

I can't help thinking that compared to Africa something is wrong with life in Australia. There is something missing in terms of happiness, or somehow happiness isn't the goal. It feels as if following rules, going to work, paying bills, and all of that stuff are more important and I can't help thinking Australians have been tricked into accumulating ever more money with the hope it will eventually lead to happiness. I see a lot of money and the things it buys, though I don't see the happiness and pure joy that's on display daily in Africa.

I'm clearly a fish out of water, and I wonder if I'm not really Australian anymore.

Over Christmas and New Years' my family has a fantastic time cooking food, laughing, drinking and reminiscing. Nobody knows if this is Mum's last Christmas, so family and friends from all over the country fly in for a huge Christmas lunch. Mum is director of the kitchen with many assistants as we cook a delicious meal before we finish the hot day with a walk on the beach in true Australian style.

In the new year I sit with Mum in hospital while she gets her first round of Chemotherapy. The doctors waited until after she finished multiple rounds of radiation treatment which have thankfully taken away the pain. Mum is selected to be part of a trial for a new cancer treatment drug which is very effective on certain types of cancer. Unfortunately lung cancer is not on that list, so all we can do is cross our fingers and hope for the best.

Φ   Φ   Φ

When the time comes to fly back to Africa I struggle to say goodbye. I wonder if I should spend more time with Mum instead of roaming around Africa. She encourages me immensely, and assures me I will see her again.

My flight to Mali is diverted for a stopover in Chad and we sit on the runway in the capital of N'Djamena for an hour while new passengers board. Chad is not the safest place, and I realize this is the closest I'll get to a visit. Back in Bamako I'm greeted by the familiar UN planes and armed Military on the tarmac.

The minute I step out of the airport at dusk I'm thrown back into the thick of West Africa. Men surround me negotiating in French for a taxi fare, I smell the familiar aroma of cooking fires and I see the heavily fortified Military positions. I smile at the lack of seat belts, windows and interior trim in the taxi. We stop at a gas station where the driver asks me to pay upfront so he can buy gas for the ten minute drive. When he opens the hood and fills a coke bottle that is evidently his gas tank, I can only laugh. In Australia this vehicle is so highly illegal the driver would undoubtedly go to jail, while here in Mali it's perfectly normal. Familiar sights and smells drift through the spaces where glass should be, and I thoroughly enjoy the feeling of coming home. I see ladies cooking, laughing and washing babies. I seen men crouching around coals heating tea, and I hear warm laughter and kids screeching with delight as they run in circles. Without a doubt, I see life, and it makes perfect sense.

I had much greater culture shock arriving in Australia than I have arriving back in Mali. Somehow Australia does not feel like life at all, but rather some kind of slow ticking waiting. In stark contrast Mali is bursting with vibrant life all around me.

The following morning I visit the chief of Customs to sort out the Jeep paperwork. He immediately remembers me, and begins our discussion by asking how my Mum is doing. I struggle to contain the tears as I explain our family Christmas, partly because of the cancer, and partly because I'm so touched this busy and important man remembered and took the time to ask about my Mum. He genuinely wishes my family all the best, and I can't stop a few tears sneaking out as I sincerely thank him.

It's quite a shock to realize I feel more at home in Africa than I did in Australia.

Matt from the Sleeping Camel also visited family in Australia for Christmas, and over cold beers we discuss how hard it was to drop into Australia, and how people there don't feel alive compared to Mali. We agree Australia is a facade hiding real life, whereas Africa is so real it makes us feel more human. "I'll never go back," Matt says.
"Mali is my home now."

I flew to Australia multiple times during the African expedition, spending time with Mum and Dad, soaking in every minute together and recharging my batteries. I made it home for every Christmas, and even surprised Mum on her birthday one year. I was aiming to be fashionably late to the surprise party, though I have to admit two weeks late might not count as fashionable, even for me.

The culture shock intensified with each visit.

In the mountains above Whitehorse, bursting with excitement

Reg cutting the original roll bar from the Jeep

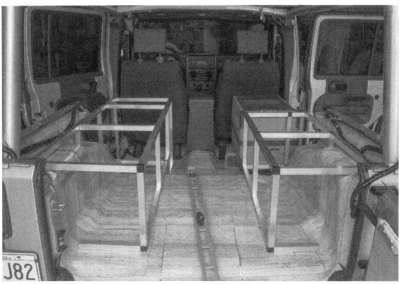
Building the rear cabinets out of lightweight aluminum tube

Transferring the cabinets into the replacement Jeep

Strapped into the container to cross the Atlantic

A friendly guy on the side of the road in Morocco

At the Mauritania border after crossing the minefield

Welcomes like this became an everyday occurrence

Hiking in the Fouta Djallon mountains of Guinea

Beautiful mud huts with thatch roofs are very common

I dreamed of mud pits like this when planning Africa

Walking Wallet

Tiébélé, Burkina Faso
January 2017

B RACING myself for what I know is coming, I drive into the village of Tiébélé, a major tourist destination in Burkina Faso. I'm not at all surprised when a man virtually throws himself under the tires trying to flag me down. He's an official guide, he says, and I must follow him. He adds that it's mandatory and I'm too tired to argue, so I follow without protest. This should be good.

At a nearby compound Bernard introduces himself, and we go over the details in French. He's a local guide, and actually lives in the ancient compound I've come to see. The local association charges $3 and his guiding fee is $8, for a total of $11. I can't be bothered haggling over the price because I spent days on nasty roads specifically to get here. Now used to this game, I confirm with Bernard three separate times I'll pay $11 and not a cent more to enter the compound and see everything.
"Rein Plus," he agrees. Nothing more.

Bernard tells me he has twenty-two children to four different wives, and I can't help but notice the two large Samsung touch-screen phones he constantly plays with. I buy the 'entry' ticket for $3, and Bernard shows me the whole compound in about twenty minutes. It's a fascinating and beautiful traditional structure, though I forget the details thanks to what happens next.

During the tour men arrive with a visitors' book for me to sign, and explain repeatedly the money is "For The Children." and "For schoolbooks and things."
Oh, how nice.
I sign the book and pay the $8 and the tour is complete.

At the Jeep I say a big thanks to Bernard and I'm just about to eat lunch when he asks for his money.
"I gave that money to the men with the visitors' book," I say.
"That was a donation For The Children," Bernard says.
Apparently it was not his guiding fee and I misunderstood.

"No problem," I say.
"We will get it back from the men, and I'll give it to you."
He quickly says that's not possible, though it's very clear he wants his guiding fee, and he wants it now.

Bernard races away and returns with the two men before explaining the situation to them. The atmosphere instantly changes and things get heated very, very quickly. Bernard first yells angrily at them, then at me. The conversation is all in French, and soon I yell right back, totally out of character. I explain it's a lot of money for me, and that Bernard assured me on three separate occasions I would pay $11 and not a cent more.

They all stare with open mouths and just repeat
"But it's for The Children."
"For schoolbooks and things."
"For The Children."

I can't help but think about how Bernard is earning $8 for about twenty minutes work, a huge amount in this part of the world. I usually keep calm and don't bite back at times like this, though I'm fed up with this crap that's happened repeatedly in West Africa.
Against my better judgement I bite back.

I tell Bernard I can't personally afford to have two children, much less twenty-two. I explain my $20 phone cost at least ten times less than either of his, and I shouldn't be pressured into giving money to support his habits. If he doesn't have enough money for twenty-two children, he should have less children, not deceive tourists into giving him more than the agreed upon price.

Bernard readily agrees he told me three times I wouldn't pay a cent more than $11. He then immediately asks for more money - 'For The Children'.
I become increasingly frustrated as we go around like this for at least ten minutes. Each time Bernard and the two men agree I'm not going to pay more before they immediately ask for more 'For The Children'.
They repeatedly agree, then ask for more. I explain I can't, and that Bernard said I wouldn't pay more and they once again agree, then ask for more.
Round and round, agree and ask, round and round.

These confrontations over money make me feel sick to the pit of my stomach, so I finally agree to donate $3 'For The Children', while still paying Bernard $8.
I just want this to be over, and I'm certain they were banking on that. I want to leave. Now. This really sucks.

I hand over the money and Bernard quickly snatches his $8 from the men with the ledger. Everyone nods and agrees I was told I would pay $11, and that I have now paid $14, and this is not a good thing. It's not right to pay more than agreed, they say.

"Give us more," they immediately say, "For The Children."

I can't take anymore. I need to leave before I really lose my cool. I'm utterly fed up and getting close to exploding, so I shake hands all round, say thanks and turn to leave.

Just then Bernard says "Give me a present," and I spin around expecting a smile, thinking he's joking because of all the tension and raised voices.
No, he's dead serious.

After all the yelling, tension and bad feelings he still has the nerve to ask for a gift.

The man has twenty-two children, two large touch screen phones, has made more money in twenty minutes than most people in this part of the world will make in a week, and looks me dead in the face asking for a gift.
"A pen or something," he adds.

Furious, I get in the Jeep and drive away without another word.

Φ   Φ   Φ

Interactions like this over money have happened on and off since my first day in Morocco, and I've had a hard time writing about them. It's difficult to explain the tension and stress greedy people put me under, constantly hounding me to give more. It hasn't been particularly bad in Burkina Faso, I've just hit my limit so I'm writing about it now.

Something is very, very broken on this continent, and it's taking me a long time to understand it. It's extremely clear generations of white people simply giving things for free has had a severely detrimental impact. I can always tell when I'm in a tourist location when the children run towards the Jeep screaming for candy, money or a cell phone while thrusting out their hands. They're utterly furious when I do not.

"White man, give me something," is unfortunately something I hear regularly from men. Even when drinking store-bought beer and food they have no shame telling me I should pay for their food and drinks.

It was kind of funny for a while, though being treated like a wallet with legs has gotten old very, very fast. The damage done by well meaning white tourists and aid workers couldn't be more obvious.

On Time

THROUGHOUT my life I've found time slides by much faster when all the days are similar. When I'm working forty hours a week the routine causes days to blend into a continuous stream of similar events. From home to the office to the grocery store and back home, days soon blend into months and years. I struggle to recall any particular day, because they're all so similar in my memory.

Time on the road passes differently than at any point in my life, and my memories are much sharper and more vivid as a result. Every day is different, and I remember them all with extreme clarity. Every day I meet people I've never seen before, I drive new roads, see new animals and try new foods. Just when I get comfortable with a country I move on and start the whole process over. Living a more dynamic and changing life makes time slow down, and I feel like I've lived more in six months on the road than in the many years of work that came before.

Φ   Φ   Φ

Lately I've been feeling like an entirely new person. I'm often in bed soon after sunset because there's nothing to do in the dark. I always sleep with the screens wide open to the breeze so I wake at the first hint of sunrise. Most mornings I try to stretch and exercise before the heat of the day, and I feel fantastic for it. Sleeping as much as my body needs completely changes how I feel.

Suddenly I have passion and energy for my long-forgotten projects. In Whitehorse it was a monumental struggle to edit photos or post a single update on my website, but now on the road I have endless energy for these passions. I delayed writing my first book for years, viewing it as a chore. Writing it while exploring West Africa has been a pleasure.

I realize I have time for all the things I've always wanted to do in life rather than only the things I have to.

I'm also in no particular hurry, so each day I can choose to move on or relax where I am. I never wake to an alarm, and I rarely have to be anywhere at a given time. This freedom from time feels incredible, like a weight off my shoulders I didn't know was there.

I learn few people in Africa really care about the time, because they live with the sun as I learned to. This means appointments don't mean much, and everything takes longer than first guessed because it's all running on 'Africa Time'.

At first I found it frustrating when trying to complete a visa application, though as the months rolled on I came to enjoy it. Because I wasn't exhausted or short on time I could just enjoy the relaxed pace of life. People are often late and things take so much time in Africa because everyone takes time for themselves. Slowing down to talk to friends and family on the street only makes sense, and trying to force things to finish faster never helps, so it's not worth the headache.

Once I fully embraced this slower pace of life I began to crave the freedom it brought, and I've never worn a watch or carried a phone since.

Φ   Φ   Φ

At a few border crossings uniformed officers were shocked when I asked the date, and one especially was confused when I didn't even know the month. It simply doesn't matter to me.

Returning to even a small town after a week in the wilderness was often jarring. I had to find my forgotten wallet before being hopelessly confused by the money I found there. Using so many different currencies made it difficult to remember how much the notes in my wallet were actually worth. I often had to look in my notebook to work out if the 10,000 whatever notes I had was enough to buy a tank of gas or just a few bananas. In a few countries I never once used my bank card, and after seven weeks I forgot my PIN. More than once I stared at the first ATM in almost two months while struggling to remember.

Completely letting go of time and money is an alien feeling coming from Australia and Canada. In time it became one of the indicators that let me know I was on a very long expedition away from the developed world. The freedom it brings is powerful, and I've never felt more relaxed and carefree.

First Elephants

Pendjari National Park, Benin
January 2017

W AKING before dawn is a pleasure, and I thoroughly enjoy the chill morning air on my skin. One coffee often turns into two, and today I take the second on the road. I'm eager for my first glimpse of large African wildlife. After six months on the continent I've only once seen hippos in the Gambia river. Unfortunately large wildlife was hunted to near extinction in West Africa decades ago, so sightings are rare.

After paying an entrance fee I'm free to roam the park alone, and soon I'm bumping over extremely corrugated and dusty roads while keeping an eye on the scrubby vegetation. I see scores of monkeys playing in the trees and a vast assortment of colorful birds of all shapes and sizes. Stopping at the many watering holes provides the perfect opportunity to spot hippos, crocs and antelope-like animals whose names I don't know. The midday sun beats down relentlessly and resting in the shade near the water seems like a smart idea.

An hour before dusk I'm skirting the edge of a muddy lake when I see strange grey boulders on the far shore. They're a few hundred yards away and only after I stop for a better look do I realize what they are. My heart jump into my mouth when I realize the grey boulders are moving slowly and I rub my eyes to make sure I'm not dreaming.

I stand on the open drivers window and hood to gain a better vantage point, grinning from ear to ear as I watch the mother

and two baby elephants amble slowly along the lake shore.
I stare open mouthed for ten minutes, knowing I'll remember
the first elephants I've ever seen as long as I live.

Coincidentally it's my birthday, and exactly a year since I
bought the Jeep. My mind boggles thinking about how far
we've already come, and the scale of the adventures that lay
ahead. This adventure has really just begun. My world is
vastly different to the one I left behind in Canada, and I spend
the rest of the night replaying the last twelve months in my
mind.

Φ   Φ   Φ

In the pre-dawn light I meander down a tiny dirt track following
a trickling creek that serves as the international border with
Burkina Faso. There's nobody around for miles, and there's no
fence to stop me wading across into a different country. Only
the hippos and crocs serve as border guards.

In the coming hours I'm treated to three separate herds of
elephants, all much closer than yesterday. Each herd consists
of about fifteen animals of all ages, and I thoroughly enjoy
watching their antics. For hours I watch as they strip leaves
from trees and upend huge clumps of grass before thrashing
them in attempt to separate the edible grass from the dirt.
Their size and power is immense, and I'm fascinated to see
how delicately they can use their trunks when they choose.
Sometimes they pickup an individual stick or leaf, and sometimes they just pat each other in a reassuring way. The big
males glance in my direction from time to time, though they
don't seem to care. I like to think we're friends.

I'm still buzzing as I leave the park late in the afternoon, still
struggling to believe I've driven my Jeep from Canada all the
way to elephants.

Running The Gauntlet

Nigeria
February 2017

N IGERIA is infamous among overlanders and is only spoken about in whispers using indirect language and metaphors that are not helpful at all. One couple who recently drove through can't even describe the country for me. They shake their heads, struggle to form complete sentences and eventually manage to say only "Nigeria is fast," which leaves me wondering what hell that means.

If I could voluntarily skip one country on the entire west coast, I would skip Nigeria.

With over 200 million people, Nigeria has by far the highest population of any African country, and is undoubtedly fast and loud. The mega-city of Lagos is virtually a country unto itself and with a booming economy many believe the future economy of the entire African continent rests on Nigeria's shoulders. Few overlanders spend significant time in Nigeria, probably because bad confrontations are known to occasionally occur. These unfortunate incidents usually involve fake Police checkpoints, spike strips and weapons. Nigeria is also infamous for their Police checkpoints. Both in number and bribery, Nigeria holds the record.

Unfortunately, skipping Nigeria is virtually impossible. By land it means crossing Niger, Chad and Northern Cameroon, all strictly off-limits due to Boko Haram. After hearing Danny and Alice's nightmare shipping scenario I have no interest in going down that path, so if I'm to traverse the West Coast of Africa, I must drive through Nigeria. It's as simple as that.

At The Sleeping Camel in Bamako I met Dani and Didi, a German couple also aiming to drive around Africa in their 4x4 van. After a few days we quickly become friends, and soon the issue of crossing Nigeria comes up. Together we carefully study maps and speak to others before making a plan to cross Nigeria in convoy.

We like our odds better with two vehicles in the event of a breakdown. It will be easier if one needs to get parts or solve a problem while the other waits on the roadside. We also feel that corrupt Police and Military are much less likely to give us a problem with more witnesses. Finally, I'm sure we'll have more fun together.

It's also comforting to know if things go really bad, I won't be alone.

With safety at the front of our minds we plan to drive as far as possible each day, and always stay in hotels at night. Preferably the hotels will have high fences and locked compounds. We won't linger in the vicinity of the Niger Delta, the current kidnapping hot spot where oil field workers are occasionally snatched in boats before vanishing into the maze of swampy channels that litter the region.

Our plan is set and our Benin visas are about to expire. We can delay no more. The time has come to dive in.

Into Nigeria

We've been told repeatedly to avoid the main border on the coast at all costs. Being so close to Lagos it's extremely busy and chaotic, and the officials are notorious for corruption. Instead we aim for the much smaller border at Kétou, just a hundred miles north. Following Didi's van I'm immediately shocked by his perfectly functioning brake lights and turn signals. It's strange to see them actually work, and I realize both have been a very rare sight during the last six months in Africa.

The formalities in the sleepy town on the Benin side are easy enough, and soon we're surrounded by men hounding us to exchange money. Nigeria's currency suffers from severe inflation leading to a thriving black market exchange rate 50% better than official. That means we can actually buy Nigerian cash for half of what we could get it from an ATM. After a huge negotiation I exchange my remaining Central African Francs for 300,000 Nira in a huge stack of small and grubby bills. Thanks to that exchange rate, everything in the country is now half price.

Inside Nigerian Immigration we meet three men, and it's quickly clear the largest is the boss, and he's not to be trifled with. After some pleasantries - which are extremely easy in English - the large man examines my visa. Immediately he exclaims my two month visa is simply not right. He demands to know where and who issued it, and makes it very clear he won't accept it. Purely by chance I still have the business card of the Ambassador in Bamako, and when I hand it over the boss is not happy I've called his bluff.

Next he examines Dani and Didi's passports, and quickly sees they were issued a six month entry window which is also uncommon. He rants and raves about how this is utterly unacceptable and it will simply not be possible to accept these documents. With a lot of careful wording Dani explains they were granted the six month entry window at the Embassy in The Gambia, and it is legit.

Looking grumpier than ever the large man takes to examining our visas in every conceivable way - under different lighting conditions, scratching with his fingernails, and looking through the page from the back. We sit in silence as he spends five minutes per visa looking extremely unhappy throughout. I assume he's looking for forgery or evidence of tampering, or is at least putting on a good show for our benefit. After some gentle persuasion he tosses our passports to the lesser men to enter into the now common giant ledger. In the meantime we complete a document requiring many difficult details. Nigerian Immigration want the name of my employer (... none), my phone number (... none), an address in Nigeria (... hotel Jeep?) and other impossible-to-answer questions for a professional vagabond.

We were warned Nigerian Immigration may only grant entry for a week, regardless of our visas. When the large man asks how long I intend to stay I ask for two months, just like my visa. After a lot of scowling and fretting he says I'm lucky he's giving me a month. Clearly two months was a mistake in the first place, he says, so he must correct it. I'm happy to let him think he won that negotiation - I really only wanted one month.

When all passports are eventually stamped, all paperwork is complete and all ledgers dutifully updated the large man leans back confidently and asks:
"So, what did you bring for me?"

Fully expecting this we have a smart-ass reply ready like "A smile from Australia," and "It's our custom you give something to visitors."
Eventually smiling, he hands our passports back.
"Enjoy your stay in Nigeria. Safe Journey."

Across the gravel parking lot at Customs Didi's Carnet de Passage is quickly stamped, though I hit a snag when I ask for a Temporary Import Permit for the Jeep. I'm repeatedly told I won't need one, and because I'm going to Cameroon that document doesn't apply to me. I really want one to avoid bribery, though I give up after the tenth time he says no. The Customs officer is shocked I think there will be bribery in Nigeria, and assures me that is not the case. I'm not sure I believe him.

With no choice I will drive across Nigeria without any official paperwork for the Jeep. This will be a first for me and I don't like it one bit.

Day One

Minutes after leaving Customs and Immigration we're waved down by men on the side of the badly crumbling road. I've been warned about fake stops in Nigeria that can turn violent, so I have a good look to decide if I should stop. The men wear shorts and grubby undershirts, and one hastily puts on a shirt that clearly says 'Police' across the front. Each man also picks up an automatic weapon, so I decide to stop.

They're extremely friendly, forward and very, very loud. They speak extremely fast in English mixed with pidgin or something similar. One can't stop saying "MY NI**ER" and "NO S**T" at the top of his voice, and is extremely excited to vigorously shake my hand while saying "COOL MAN" repeatedly. After checking our passports and writing the necessary details in yet another enormous ledger, they're happy to send us on. "Welcome to Nigeria. Safe Journey."

A mile further the scene is repeated, though these men look even less legit. It's extremely hard to know if this stop is mandatory, or if we can just keep moving with a wave. We're on high alert for fake stops, and before the men can stand up and pretend to be official, my friends roll through. I see men scramble to grab automatic weapons, leaving me uncertain what to do. Hedging my bets I stop in the middle of the road and leave the engine running. The men are frantic, and I know it's serious when the red faced 'big man' comes to the Jeep. He demands my passport and asks repeatedly why my friends didn't stop. I explain the men were lounging in the shade so my friends didn't know they needed to stop. After snatching my passport he says I must fetch them and bring them back before he will return my passport. He's clearly furious, and I have no intention of arguing.

Our first thirty minutes in Nigeria are not going smoothly.

A few miles further I catch up to my friends who are stopped at yet another checkpoint that looks as unofficial as all the others. This one is apparently Immigration. As I explain what happened the boss of this checkpoint listens intently, curious to learn about these foreigners driving big 4x4s. He demands to see my passport, and becomes furious when I explain the previous guys held onto it. He insists they're not allowed to do that, and I should never give my passport to anyone other than Immigration. I explain I was just following the orders of the large men holding automatic weapons, though he doesn't listen. He and another officer snatch my friend's passports and cram into the front seat of the Jeep before I realize what is happening. With my new friends I turn back to sort out the mess we've landed in.

Before I can even stop the Jeep the two big men begin arguing loudly trying to clarify what's going on. The man from the first checkpoint is mad my friends didn't stop, and the man from the second checkpoint agrees with him. They both turn to me looking for answers. I explain we're worried about fake checkpoints and possible violence in Nigeria so we weren't sure if stopping was the safe thing to do. Both men are clearly shocked, and assure me that won't be a problem in Nigeria. The Police and Military have clamped down in recent months and things are calmer than ever. All are very honest, and nobody will try to bribe us or otherwise give us trouble. Though they seem genuine, I can't bring myself to believe them.

Soon everything is resolved with a round of handshakes and I drive my passengers back to the second checkpoint with my passport. Everyone is now extremely friendly - smiling, shaking hands and posing for photos. They bid us a very warm stay in Nigeria, ending with the already familiar "Welcome to Nigeria," and "Safe Journey."

The next few hours continue in much the same fashion. Men

with automatic weapons at ramshackle checkpoints rise from shady seats, flag us down before writing our details into huge ledgers for who knows what purpose. Every checkpoint is friendly and all the men are eager to shake our hands and give a warm welcome. At some checkpoints the men ask "What did you bring for me?" in a friendly way. I suggest we should trade - I'll give them something and they can give me something in return. I often ask for their hat or shirt, which are both part of their uniform and they'll never give away. This makes the men smile and laugh before waiving me on.

I genuinely feel they appreciate me playing the game, and I realize I'm putting them in a tough spot. They're not so rude as to outright demand something or blatantly steal from me, it's simply against their culture. Once I propose a trade they can't get angry at me - after all I am offering a gift. They're mostly just looking for entertainment and a distraction from otherwise mundane days standing on the dusty and hot roads.

$$\Phi \quad \Phi \quad \Phi$$

In the afternoon we navigate the horribly broken roads and traffic jams through the large and modern city of Abeokuta. There are skyscrapers, a functioning train and infrastructure very different from the West Africa I've seen until now. Abeokuta is the start of a massive expressway that will take us across the entire country. Two lanes of traffic move in each direction at breakneck speeds despite the broken and potholed surface. To increase the danger extremely slow trucks drive as they please and random Police checkpoints force vehicles to stop in moving traffic. It's fast and furious, and I concentrate hard to maintain about sixty miles an hour to keep up with traffic. The odd Mercedes or luxury SUV blows past going much, much faster.

Not used to this driving I'm exhausted after a few hours and just before the sun hits the horizon we find ourselves in a truck stop town clustered around the expressway. Minor roads are severely broken and horribly dusty and after twenty minutes of searching we find a suitable hotel. The price is right at ten dollars each for the night in a rundown room, and we hope the wall around the compound is sufficiently high. The armed security doesn't hurt either.

The city, hotel and room remind me of the developed world more than anywhere else I've seen in West Africa. There are working showers and toilets, air conditioning and sometimes even hot water. Everything is severely neglected and run down, however, and virtually every surface is grubby thanks to the intense humidity. Even in this city I never learn the name of, I see skyscrapers and many modern developments. I learn Nigeria has scores of enormous modern cities I've never heard the name of before or since.

I reverse the Jeep against a wall so the rear can't easily be opened, hoping it will slow down any thief. Conveniently the hotel has a built in bar and restaurant and after much negotiation we manage to order chicken with jollof rice, a Nigerian speciality. It's a kind of fried rice packed full of delicious spices, and it quickly becomes my favourite. The chicken is so huge I have to assume it's turkey, the drinks are cold and cheap and the rice is the most tasty and spicy food I've ever eaten.

When the bill comes we see the agreed upon prices have magically gone up, the total adds up to more than the sum, and the waiter has forgotten I already paid and he owes me change. "Oh yeah," he says, "I'll fix that."

Three more times we have to tell the waiter to correct the bill. Each time he has somehow inserted a mystery item, or has forgotten that three times two hundred is not one thousand. It seems prices are flexible in Nigeria, always going up. Eventually we give up and call it a night, thoroughly exhausted and pouring sweat in the still intense humidity.

Before climbing into bed I drag the desk in front of the locked door and leave the key in the lock, hoping it will prevent someone using another from the outside. I have no idea if that works, but I figure it can't hurt.

Less than thirty seconds after I close my eyes the enormous diesel generator directly outside my window roars to life, literally rattling the window panes. The racket is horrendous, though even still I manage to find sleep quickly.

Day Two

I sleep in fits and spurts, partly happy for the air conditioning and partly hating the world's loudest generator keeping it running. I'm up at six, and after coffee and peanut butter on bread in the parking lot we're on the road soon before seven. The nutty driving and hectic pace on the expressway resume from yesterday, forcing me to wake up before the coffee has kicked in.

We stop to buy gas at a bustling station where the female attendants are extremely friendly and chatty. We strike up a conversation and when I ask to take a photo the lady is clearly embarrassed I've taken an interest in her. It doesn't take much convincing before she's posing and even flirting with me, and soon she ropes in other ladies and customers at the station. She holds a massive wad of money in her hand through she's clearly not worried about theft. For a change gas is half the price of diesel, and I pay just 125 Niara per litre, exactly $1 USD per gallon with the black market rate.

Police, Immigration, Military and 'vehicle safety' officers randomly setup roadblocks on the expressway wherever they see fit, randomly flagging down vehicles. They manage to always setup just over the crest of a hill or around a blind corner, leading to some serious emergency braking on my part a few times. Severely overloaded transport trucks drift between lanes without signaling which makes overtaking a dangerous gamble. When I go for it I just have to hope they don't move over and push me off the road. I'm constantly on the lookout for broken down trucks, potholes bigger than the Jeep tires, rocks, slow moving vehicles, people and animals crossing and every other conceivable danger while frantically racing forward at sixty miles an hour.

I glimpse a partially-clothed man lying in the ditch as I whip by at speed. My brain takes a picture, and I spend the next minute thinking about it. He's face down and lying very awkwardly. A pool of blood surrounds his head, and I notice his upper body is swollen. I realize I've just seen a dead body. Other vehicles can surely see him, though they all speed on, not slowing at all. I ponder that for many hours.

Looking for a distraction I stop to buy fried plantain chips from friendly ladies on the side of the expressway. Not only are they a delicious salty road snack, in a stroke of genius I discover they're the perfect gift to offer at the endless checkpoints and roadblocks. The men often want a gift, and now I produce a bag of plantain chips with a smile. They've probably been eating this stuff their whole lives and clearly detest it. I explain it's all I will be eating for lunch, and they're welcome to have some with me. Again I'm being polite and friendly, while leaving them nowhere to go. Without being downright rude or mean - which is clearly against their culture - they can only smile and laugh as they let me pass.

As the day drags on the frequency of roadblocks increases and I realize the Military and Police here are different than anything I've encountered before. The men are extremely high energy, talk very fast and even yell in their excitement to see a foreigner. They talk about English Premier League Football, American movies, cigarettes and girls. They all ask about my wife, and why I haven't brought her to introduce to them. Often five men rush to shake my hand vigorously, and after some trial and error I learn the knack to these 'Nigeria-fast' checkpoints.

No matter what happens, talk first, talk fast, keep smiling,

and keep talking.
And then, keep talking!

"I'm a tourist."
"I'm visiting Nigeria."
"I'm coming from here."
"I'm going to there."
"I love Nigeria."
"People are friendly."
"I feel safe."
"It's beautiful here."
"I love Africa."
"I'm having a great time."
"People are friendly in Nigeria."
"It's really great here."
"Is this the way to there?"
"Wow, I love it here."
"I'm from Australia."
"I'm driving a Jeep."
"It's really great here."
"Wow, thanks for having me in your country."
"Yes, people are friendly."
"Oh, it's really great."
"I'm a tourist."
"I love it here."
"I feel safe."
"People are friendly here."

After three minutes like this I'm waived through.

Φ   Φ   Φ

Benin City looms large on the horizon and thankfully a ring road skirts the center of the mega-city. Always on the lookout for something tasty to eat I grin when a huge hand-written sign miraculously appears from nowhere:

FOOD IS READY

Needing no more direction we park in a travelers' stop that has about twenty street vendors selling fresh fruit and vegetables outside, and more inside sell plates of food. I'm delighted to see my new favourite spicy jollof rice with chicken on the menu. Nigerians speak perfect English with a heavy accent, so it's not difficult to ask the price and confirm three meals before taking a seat. We're in a large dining hall with many others who are clearly on the road in minivans, busses and trucks.

The meal is delicious and when we try to pay the young man who took our order we find the price has magically increased in just ten minutes. After much discussion we pay the higher amount and agree we've learnt our lesson. From now on we'll pay immediately to avoid the constant price increases we've experienced. As well as prices magically changing, change is often short, mysterious items are added to the bill and 200+200+200 is 1,500 in Nigeria.

We push on and on, putting down big miles. In the early afternoon we approach an impressive new bridge near the mouth of the mighty Niger River in the huge city of Onitsha. We're in the heart of the Delta Region, and very conscious of the need to keep moving without stopping or attracting undue attention. This is the kidnapping hot spot, and we have no intention of experiencing that for ourselves. The bridge is heavily guarded by Military personnel manning the largest artillery I've ever seen. Thankfully vehicles crawl past and we aren't stopped for questioning. Immediately across the bridge we're deposited onto a massive five lane expressway which lasts just half a mile before a dead end mess of roadwork. Evidently the expressway isn't finished, and we become jammed in with hundreds of other vehicles who have blindly driven into the same predicament. Road signs are always lacking, and especially in construction zones drivers are left to find their own route.

We manage a u-turn in the chaos before driving in circles for ten minutes. This is not a place we want to hang around, nor do we want to be roaming aimlessly at nightfall so I make a snap decision. With no obvious way forward, I intentionally drive the wrong way up a curving freeway on-ramp squeezing past oncoming traffic. I fight my GPS to detour the city through an endless street market and one continuous traffic jam. It's here we encounter our first small town Nigerian Police who are much less friendly than their expressway counterparts.

At first they simply yell at us, apparently thinking we'll just hand over money if they can scare us. Now seasoned African overlanders we don't fall for it, and the Police mellow when they discover we don't have a single piece of paperwork they understand. Lacking Customs paperwork I repeatedly give them the Canadian Registration and Insurance while smiling and assuring them it's all correct. Eventually they stop asking and let us go.

Soon before dusk we arrive in another truck stop town, and again find a small hotel not far form the still frantic expressway. I'm happy to see the huge perimeter wall and armed security, and despite this hotel being much cleaner and newer, the price is identical. Having learned our lesson we request rooms on the far side of the building from the generator which earns an ounce of respect from the manager.

Another turkey-sized chicken and jollof rice plate knocks me out, and it isn't long before I collapse into bed exhausted from another massive day on the hectic expressway.

Day Three

I lurch awake to yelling and pounding on my door in the dead of night. My mind races.

They found us, and they're here to kidnap us, I think.
Through the darkness I see the flimsy desk jammed against the door bouncing under the sustained blows. I struggle to control my frantically beating heart. Deep male voices yell

repeatedly in an unfamiliar language and I hear multiple doors up and down the corridor under assault.

Our conspicuous vehicles must have been spotted as we drove into town, I realize. I wonder what they're doing to the Jeep in the parking lot, but quickly realize there's nothing I can do. My safety is much more important than the Jeep and I only hope my friends come to the same conclusion and keep their door firmly closed and locked.

After very little sleep I gingerly leave my room at sunrise and I'm relieved to see Dani and Didi outside with our undisturbed vehicles. We agree a fast exit would be best, and just as I climb into the Jeep a shy looking young man introduces himself. With a warm smile and handshake Vincent explains he's with a visiting soccer team, and after a win last night the team were searching the hotel for people to continue the rowdy after party.

I'm sure he can see we're still shaken, and he apologizes profusely for the loud night and for scaring us. Relaxing a little we decide there's time for coffee after all, and as we chat over steaming cups we see more of the blurry-eyed and confused team stumble from the hotel.

Eventually we relax and even laugh as we realize the whole thing was just a misunderstanding. Vincent wishes us a safe journey in Nigeria and the rest of the team gives thumbs up as we pull away.

The frantic pace on the expressway resumes right where it left off. Days and places begin to blur causing me to drink more coffee and eat more fried plantain chips which only makes things worse. Eventually four lanes dissolve into two when the highway becomes narrow and windy. If anything, the pace only increases. I'm again shocked and disoriented to whip past another dead body lying in the ditch. This person also appears to have been struck by a car, possibly a few days ago. Worryingly, nobody stops or seems concerned in the least.

Police and Military checkpoints become more serious, now they have more firepower and sandbags to block the road. Many have light tanks and large mounted guns that swing back and forth above the line of vehicles. The sandbags limit traffic to one direction, forcing vehicles to move at a crawl when in range of the mounted guns.

A single man waves vague directions, clearly proud of his crisp uniform and automatic rifle held at the ready. Uncertain what a floppy hand wave means I roll forward and instantly know I've done the wrong thing. He's on me like a flash, yelling and waving his arms furiously. I reverse through the sandbag s-bend past the line of waiting vehicles all the way to the back. The lone soldier is clearly satisfied I have now respected his authority, and three minutes later I drive past without incident.

Φ   Φ   Φ

Cresting a hill I jump on the brakes as a jam of slow and stopped vehicles comes into view. I soon see it's not just another Military roadblock. A minivan has rolled into the ditch, and judging by the scene it must have been only a minute or two earlier. Onlookers frantically drag bleeding bodies to a nearby pickup with four badly injured people already in the back. One man holds his head in his hands as blood pools on the bed of the pickup, and another lays unconscious. The consequences of this insane driving are plainly obvious and I can only shake my head when everyone speeds forward and resumes driving with the same frantic pace.

I contemplate stopping to help, but quickly think better of it. I've been warned repeatedly traffic accidents in Africa can devolve into an angry mob, and often any nearby white person will be blamed. The advice is never to linger, so I keep moving and try to focus on the road ahead rather than think about what I just saw.

At midday we arrive in the famous border town of Ikom, only fifteen miles from Cameroon. We've driven clear across Nigeria in just three days. We don't yet have visas for Cameroon, so we can not cross the border yet. Instead we turn south, aiming for Calabar where we hope to get the all-important visa. We can't leave Nigeria until we do.

The road quickly deteriorates into severely broken pavement with pot holes so large they span the entire width of the road forcing us to crawl in and out of each one. Combined with endless Military and Police stops, the last sixty miles to the city takes over four hours. We're sadly unable to find another 'Food is Ready' sign, so we buy a fresh papaya each from a smiling lady on the side of the road who can hardly believe we're real.

When it looms large on the horizon it's obvious Calabar is a mega-city, bigger and more modern than anything I've seen in Africa. We navigate bumper to bumper traffic, street markets and a swarm of tuk-tuks into the fenced compound of a nondescript hotel in the heart of the city. I'm impressed the two security guards are actual Nigerian Military, complete with uniforms and AK47s. They're friendly and eager to chat, though they insist I don't take photos because they're moonlighting and don't want to get caught. One almost lets me hold his rifle, though unfortunately his buddy suggests that too would be a bad idea.

Again we request rooms on the far side of the hotel from the generator, and I'm more than a little skeptical when the manager says their generator is 'sound proof', and assures us we don't need to worry that our windows open directly onto the central concrete yard. The toilet in my room does not flush, the 'hot shower' is freezing cold and the shower head is broken. I don't care in the least. We're inside a locked compound and there's a relatively soft bed. Again it's a mountain of Jollof rice for dinner - this time with beef - before collapsing into bed utterly exhausted.

Day Four

I sleep like the dead, even with the constant drone of the 'sound proof' generator that's anything but. Sleeping until 7:30 is a luxury, and I treat myself to a second coffee in the already hot concrete compound. We wear our best clothes and shoes before gathering paperwork and organizing a taxi with the hotel manager. He takes the name and number of the driver so if anything happens to us it will be OK. Somehow that's not very reassuring.

High above the city in a residential neighbourhood we find a beautiful old concrete mansion with stunning views and a light breeze serving as the Cameroon Embassy. It seems Ambassadors always manage to secure the most expensive and beautiful locations for their Embassies. After a short wait we're ushered inside by the friendly staff who explain a three month visa costs the same as a one month, and paying in Naira is by far the cheapest thanks again to the black market exchange rate. In less than thirty minutes we're issued the all-important visa, and after a brief celebration we find our way back to the hotel with the help of multiple taxi and tuk-tuk drivers.

Our next planned destination is another huge day of driving, and we're happy to take the rest of the day off. Of course, there are no rest days when overlanding in West Africa, and soon we each have a long list of jobs to tackle. We wander the street market in the intense humidity resupplying vegetables, fruit, rice, beans and other essentials. By chance me meet a businessman who can exchange Euros into Central African Francs, the currency we need for the next couple of countries. Curiously West African Francs and Central African Francs are both pegged to the Euro at exactly the same rate - so by definition they're worth the same - though it's not possible to use the wrong one in the wrong countries. Because Africa.

A shiny new shopping centre has just opened not far from our hotel, so we wander over to take a look, thankful for the air conditioning. Walking the aisles of the enormous and well-stocked supermarket is disorienting, and I realize I could be anywhere in North America or Europe. By chance we bump into Liza and Peter, founders of the Afi Mountain Drill Ranch, tomorrow's destination. They immediately invite us to their compound on the edge of the city and we gladly accept.

We're happy to be out of our vehicles for a day, and decide it's more fun to take local transport anyway. The driver of a rusty old tuk-tuk happily agrees to take us for peanuts and I think I know the way, but quickly become lost. The cheery driver repeatedly asks directions from Police and doesn't seem bothered in the least. We soon get to know the young man driving us who introduces himself as Abeo.

He explains the Indian made three-wheeled tuk-tuk costs a fortune, so rich businessman buy and rent them to young drivers who are almost exclusively young men, barely out of high school. Abeo will pay a few thousand Niara every day until he pays off the extremely cheaply made tuk-tuk. He must work enough to make the payment each day, pay gas and maintenance and then hopefully make a modest profit for himself. If he takes a day off work, he still has to make the payment. If the tuk-tuk is damaged or destroyed, he still has to pay off the loan, likely for the rest of his life.

Tearing through the smog-choked streets in the intense sun and humidity it's clear Abeo will be doing this for many decades to earn a tiny living. He's not upset or angry, and has just accepted it as how the world works. I can see he's stressed about taking us so far, and clearly his original price will not cover such a long journey, thanks entirely to my terrible directions. With Abeo's persistence we eventually arrive at our destination where I pay Abeo three times his original asking price as thanks. He is visibly shocked and elated, and can't stop saying thanks.

Inside we're quickly given cold drinks and start chatting about all things overlanding, Nigeria and Africa. Years ago Peter and

Liza were overlanding the West Coast of Africa just like Dani, Didi and I. Arriving in Nigeria they learned of the endangered Drill Monkey, and started a conservation project in the Afi Mountains where they've been working twelve hour days, seven days a week ever since. That was twenty-nine years ago.

They're both extremely quirky, and are literally overflowing with stories of adventure and madness after living three decades in Nigeria. Even after telling outrageous stories about death-defying escapades involving huge car crashes, locals, rifles and the Military, both have a gleam in their eye and use words like 'fun' and 'thrilling'. They clearly love this unpredictable life, and both agree they could never return to live in the USA.

Peter and Liza are a wealth of information on the roads, borders and politics in the area and also have the details on the young couple from New Zealand who were recently kidnapped nearby. The couple worked for a global oil company and had a very predictable daily routine. They were snatched from their car by armed men early one morning as it was waiting to cross a bridge. They managed to escape relatively unscathed a week later, and when the Police caught up to the kidnappers and their driver who sold them out they were all shot on site. No judge, no jury, they were just shot where they stood. It's widely known this is how kidnappers are dealt with, and it's clear Peter and Liza both approve wholeheartedly.

We listen spellbound to many more tales of adventure and Nigerian madness before we call it a night and catch a taxi home. We make it only a few miles before it breaks down so we thumb a ride in another before finishing the last mile of the journey hanging onto a tuk-tuk overflowing with partying locals. I'm always amazed at how disoriented I am when first arriving in a new city and then how quickly I get my bearings and can navigate home by feel alone. Each new city is always daunting, and then just a day later is familiar.

I drift off to sleep to the roar of the generator, now almost comforting.

Day Five

We leave the hotel at 7:30 and battle city traffic across town back to Liza and Peter's house. We load equipment bound for the ranch in exchange for huge quantities of wake-up coffee. I want to take a chimp in the Jeep but Liza says no.

We clear the city to the north, chatting with familiar Police and Military at every stop. Most remember us and are full of smiles and well wishes for our onward journey. Being on familiar ground makes me braver than usual, so I hide my Go-Pro on the dash to film the roadblocks and interactions. For the first time I catch a genuine bribery attempt on film, the one and only in Nigeria. I play my usual long game of wasting time while remaining extremely polite and friendly, and eventually the officer gets bored and waves me on.

Peter warned us about the terrible quality of gas and diesel in the area, so we fill up at the station he recommended in Ikom. I fill my clear stove bottle from the pump before filling the Jeep and auxiliary tank to the brim which takes almost ten minutes. When I pickup the clear container I can easily see an inch of brown muck on the bottom. I've just filled the Jeep with this exact gas and can only hope for the best.

After stocking up on basic vegetables and another deliciously spicy plate of jollof rice we continue north into new territory. When the road is paved, we wish it was not. The potholes and broken tarmac are so bad they force me to crawl forward at a snail's pace in first gear compared to gravel sections where I can cruise in second and even third gear comfortably.

In small villages we encounter roadblocks that are clearly not official, just as we were warned. The men represent a 'community fund' and want trucks to pay to drive through their village. They always have a home-made spike strip that would easily shred our tires so we're forced to stop. The men are always in their late teens or early twenties, and often look like they're up to no good. Keeping a smile on my face and shaking multiple hands always wins through and we never pay, though it's a little tense and I sense things would not be so friendly later in the day after more alcohol. At one stop I see a man holding what looks like a fake rifle. I'm not certain, however, and decide not to find out either way.

Nigeria is certainly a place where things can go wrong quickly, and we keep a sharp eye out for danger and stick together, never allowing more than fifty yards between our two imposing vehicles.

The shadows lengthen and the afternoon drags on as we make painfully slow progress along endlessly broken roads and the occasional tiny village. I'm excited as we drive into thick jungle where fog clings to the low branches of lush trees and the Afi Mountains loom large in the distance. The heat and humidity are more intense than ever, and I feel certain we're driving toward grand adventures.

The vegetation is so thick as we turn into Drill Ranch I'm forced to turn on my headlights. Hanging vines drag across the solar panels on the track that has been hacked through the dense jungle.

We arrive at our destination and setup camp in the jungle just as the light completely fades. I fall asleep to a loud chorus of insects and hear Chimpanzees screeching loudly, obviously very close.

Afi Mountain Drill Ranch

The Drill Ranch was founded by Liza and Peter in 1991 to rehabilitate and breed the endangered Drill Monkey, found only in this region of Nigeria, Southern Cameroon and an island in Equatorial Guinea. They're among Africa's most endangered primates due to habitat destruction and illegal hunting for bush meat. Peter explains that sadly the hunting is mostly commercial - hunters are not just killing what they need to survive, they're killing as many animals as possible to sell. Most of the drills were donated by locals or rescued as orphans and since the project started over two hundred have been born in captivity. This makes Drill Ranch one of the world's most successful breeding programs for an endangered species. In 1996 the first group of drills was released into the wild, the ultimate goal of the project.

Drill Ranch is also home to numerous chimpanzees that have been donated over the years. They weren't planning to host chimps, but Peter and Liza couldn't say no to the highly-endangered animals that also desperately need a home. Enormous effort goes into slowly introducing them to the existing group so they feel comfortable and safe. Unfortunately, there's no chance for re-introduction to the wild for these chimps who are so dependant on humans for their survival. For that reason all the male chimps are fixed to prevent captive breeding.

The huge complex consists of multiple different enclosures, huts, buildings and a common area nestled between mountains in the thick jungle. The vegetation grows at a staggering pace and is constantly trying to reclaim the site. Feeding time is the daily highlight and I find it utterly fascinating for both species. A few of the cheekier monkeys escape from their enclosure during the day, and I often see them sitting near the buildings or investigating the heavily protected banana compound. At feeding time they break back into their enclosure to get their fill of bananas and papaya before enjoying freedom again.

In the chimp enclosure it's immediately clear that each and every chimp has it's own unique personality. Some are extremely chill and laid back as they laze on the grass without a care in the world while plenty of the males are clearly jerks. They hit and bite other chimps, endlessly screech and hurl rocks and sticks at other chimps and even at me. Getting hit actually hurts, and I'm impressed by their consistent aim.

Spending time with the chimps is a once in a lifetime experience, and I spend many hours sitting quietly in the grass near the fence watching and taking photos. It's clear they find me as interesting as I find them, and I honestly think they become used to me over the days I constantly return. The keepers explain chimps are extremely strong and dangerous, so contact is strictly forbidden. Around the world chimp handlers have actually been killed by escapees who turn violent. It's clear they're much stronger than me, and just when play fighting they could easily cause harm.

Φ   Φ   Φ

Throughout West Africa I've often felt as if I'm in Jurassic Park or Indiana Jones, and the feeling is overwhelming on the nearby canopy walk high above the jungle floor. The aluminum boardwalk and rope handrails are overgrown with fungus and moss, and the trees look prehistoric. The expansive views from high in the canopy are nothing less than spectacular. I'm very aware of the hundreds of yards of electrified fence slicing through the nearby jungle, and I catch myself keeping a close eye out for dinosaurs just in case.

Day Ten

For decades the only road from Nigeria to Cameroon was the stuff legends are made of. Endless sticky mud pits so bad it would often take a week to drive just sixty miles. Getting through often required help from tracked machinery when it eventually came along. This road is the sole reason a traverse of the West Coast of Africa is impossible in the wet season, and is the reason I chose a Rubicon Wrangler with factory differential locks. I've been looking forward to this challenge for a long time, expecting it to be a highlight of the entire west coast.
Unfortunately, none of that is true anymore.

In January 2016 a Chinese crew finished rebuilding the entire road and now it can be driven with cruise control, and I'm told it's actually boring. I came to West Africa in search of

adventure, so this new road simply won't do.
It just won't do at all.

Pouring over maps and searching for alternate routes, information is hard to come by. For years The Mamfe Road has been the only crossing used by overlanders, and few ventured elsewhere. Northern Nigeria and Cameroon are off limits due to Boko Haram, so in my search for a more adventurous border I'm mindful of not venturing too far north. It's debatable how far north is safe enough.

One route I investigate was described in 2008 as a 'rough footpath inaccessible to any vehicle'. Tantalizingly, the description also says 'When you reach the top of the escarpment, it seems half of Southern Nigeria is spread out behind you'. All maps I source - printed and online - only show bits and pieces of this potential route, leaving me uncertain. After talking to locals and digging deeper, I come to believe there is a passable road of sorts, and I become fixated on finding out for myself. I've come all this way on the coast of West Africa, it would be a shame to take the easy road now and forever wonder what might be found on that jungle track. If the route is impossible, turning around will be the only course of action.

Always up for adventure, I have no trouble convincing Dani and Didi of the plan, and I'm thankful for the added safety and of course the company. With the route settled, we wonder what we're getting into.
Will locals be friendly? Are Boko Haram in the area?
Is my Jeep up to the tough conditions?

There's really only one way to find out for sure.

Φ   Φ   Φ

We move north from Drill Ranch and soon encounter more and more roadblocks and checkpoints. As has been the case throughout the country, all are friendly and we pass without hassle or incident. "Welcome to Nigeria" and "Safe Journey" really have become the catch-phrases of this country and I've genuinely felt welcome.

After another huge day on the roads we arrive at the town of Takum at sunset, the last for us in Nigeria. We begin the search for a suitable hotel, still not wanting to wild camp, especially this far north. At the first hotel a young man says we can camp inside the compound for just 1,000 Niara total, a bargain.

After we talk for five minutes and agree to stay the price has magically gone up a lot. Now the manager wants 15,000 for us to camp, with no explanation for the sudden rise. Over the next ten minutes I'm in disbelief as the price goes down to 4,000 and then back up to 10,000. After more negotiation it's 8,000 but when I try to hand over the money he wants 12,000. This makes absolutely no sense and I struggle to understand why he can't give me a straight answer. I don't know if he enjoys the bartering, he enjoys screwing me around or if this is just how business is done in Nigeria. I'm exhausted from a long day on the road and I have to remind myself we're doing all of this in English - so nothing is being lost in translation. When we finally agree on 6,000 Niara I quickly hand over the money before he can change his mind again. Soon enough he wants another 4,000 and the negotiations resume.

In any case, we have a place to sleep inside a walled compound, which is a relief. It's intensely hot and humid, and the generator ten yards from the Jeep screams.

Now I understand what everyone meant.
Nigeria is *fast*.

Nigeria to Cameroon

Atlantika Mountains
March 2017

A NTICIPATING an enormous final day in Nigeria we're again on the move early. Gas and diesel are incredibly cheap in Nigeria, so we fill everything we can at the only functioning gas pumps in town. The Niara is virtually worthless outside the country, so we also want to spend our remaining cash. While chatting to the young lady pumping gas a nondescript man asks quietly to see my passport.

The slender young man is wearing blue jeans and a polo shirt, and I'm immediately suspicious. I have no intention of handing my passport to this random character, though I remain polite and friendly as always and when I ask to see his ID he simply waves at a nearby pickup truck. The battered white-and-rust Toyota has large block lettering down the side: 'Immigration', and in the back are six men dressed head to toe in camouflage, each carrying an AK-47.
That's good enough for me.

The officer explains he got word of white people in town, and has come to hear our story. After carefully checking our visas and entrance stamps, he wishes us a safe journey. When I ask about the road ahead he says exactly what I don't want to hear:
"Sometimes there are bandits on that road."
"Is it safe enough?" I ask.
"Don't stop, and you will be fine," he replies before jumping into the pickup and roaring away.

On the edge of town we pass numerous burnt-out vehicles pushed to the side of the road, completely ignored by all. I have no idea if they were accidental fires, or something more sinister. We move through endless Police, Military, Immigration and Community roadblocks, making for extremely slow progress. All have sandbags, logs and home-made spike strips on the road, forcing us to stop. When they realize we're tourists friendly men come forward to shake hands and wish us a safe journey. All smile broadly and talk excitedly.

Scarification of the face is commonly used to identify different tribal heritage in West Africa, and before now I've seen just a subtle line or two above the eye or on a cheekbone. In Nigeria the scars have been much larger and more prominent, and here one officer in particular has huge cat whiskers. The whiskers give the impression of childlike innocence - 'Cat In The Hat' by Dr. Seuss comes to mind - in stark contrast to the automatic rifle he carries.

Only thirty miles along the extremely pot-holed and broken road Didi pulls to the side and crawls under his van. When he emerges with a thumbs down, I too pull off, glancing around anxiously. One of the rear shock absorbers has come loose and is freely swinging around bashing into the auxiliary diesel tank. Didi quickly removes it entirely, relying on the airbags to smooth out the never ending potholes. A few locals stop to offer assistance, and all are extremely friendly. Everyone says "Safe Journey" with a warm smile and handshake before zooming off in a cloud of dust.

Ten minutes further along the road an old man stands guard while a younger man works to repair potholes. Cradled across the elder man's chest is an ancient rifle, a full two feet longer than anything I've ever seen. In pidgin English he explains he's guarding the nearby town from bandits, and we should pay him for his trouble. In the absence of government road crews the younger man has taken it upon himself to repair the road. He's smashing boulders by hand and ramming them into the potholes, extremely hard work in the ever-present scorching sun. Shirtless, he resembles a regular gym-junkie though I have no doubt this is the real thing. After firm handshakes and well wishes, they're very happy with a bottle of cold water each and the last of our Niara coins.

People rush from their houses and follow in the street as we pull into the dusty town of Bissau hours later. I park beside the building with a Nigerian flag and watch as a uniformed Police officer stumbles from a bar. He drops a beer bottle and attempts to straighten his uniform, almost toppling over in the process. Though I can't understand a word of his mumbling, his gestures make it clear he wants more beer. Thankfully I'm soon swarmed by hundreds of people who are clearly excited to see us. Inside at Immigration we're told the townspeople think we've come to fix their broken cell phone tower, though nobody seems at all disappointed when we explain this is not the case. They all stay to watch us and examine our vehicles, clearly enjoying the distraction.

We show the Immigration officer how to stamp our passports, only to discover his stamp doesn't go past 2009. He sheepishly confesses it has never been used. Quickly solving the problem, he stamps the exit date of 2009 in our passports, before crossing it out and writing the correct date with a pen, which he does in a very formal manner, clearly proud of his important position.

Anxiously, I ask about the road ahead.
"Do you have auxiliary drive?" asks one young man.
"Four wheel drive, yes," I reply.
"Do you have a camera?"
"Yes."
"Does it take videos?"
"Yes," I reply, very uncertain where this is going.
"You will take many photos and videos," he says.
Cryptically, he will not answer any more of my questions, though he does volunteer to lead the way by motorbike through the maze of dirt tracks leaving town.

"Safe Journey," says the Immigration officer along with half the town lined up to shake our hands.

What was previously a road now turns into a tiny dirt track, apparently used by motorbikes. Both sides of the Jeep scrape through thick jungle, and we drive through many small rivers. Luckily none are more than a foot deep and don't present any problem. Mud holes are filled with logs and branches, and a few makeshift bridges bend ominously under the bulk of our vehicles.

Hours later while watching my GPS I'm excited to arrive at a much larger river, officially the International Border. There are no buildings, no signs or any indication this is the border. The few men washing motorbikes in the river either do not recognize the significance, or they simply don't care. It's easy to see the fact this is a border between two countries has no impact on their lives.

Now technically - though not legally - in Cameroon, the track winds on through thick jungle, with steep rocky climbs where I use low range first gear and both differential locks. The sun beats down relentlessly, and every time I step from the air conditioned Jeep I'm instantly soaked in sweat. Progress slows to a crawl on the rocky track and we cover less than five miles in an hour. In one climb I get a whiff of burnt plastic, and assume it's just a pile of all-to-common burning trash. When the smell returns five minutes later I decide to take a look around the Jeep, just in case.

To my horror I see thick white smoke trailing from the front grill. In a mad dash I turn off the engine, race around to grab the fire extinguisher and fumble opening the locked hood. A small flame is flickering behind the passenger headlight, and I lean back while blasting with the extinguisher. The burning plastic is stubborn, and requires multiple blasts before I see no more smoke.

When I'm satisfied the fire is completely out I attempt to calm my nerves and take stock of my situation. I have no idea what caused the fire or if I can start the engine. My friends are ahead, and I have no way of contacting them. The Jeep is completely blocking the narrow track and the thick jungle encroaches on all sides. Standing alone with no engine noise it comes to life with insects, birds and maybe even larger critters. I'm drenched in sweat and still shaking from the adrenaline rush a moment earlier.

I down a bottle of cold water in an attempt to slow down and get my nerves under control.

After a careful inspection I dig out tools and get to work, first removing one side of the grill before removing the headlight completely. The anti-flicker harness I installed for the LED headlights is burned and is clearly the culprit. After thousands of hours of use, the harness spontaneously caught fire here and now on this jungle track in no-mans-land between Nigeria and Cameroon. The harness sits directly underneath the power steering reservoir and a major wiring harness. Miraculously, both are just barely singed. If the power steering fluid had caught fire, my little extinguisher would have been no match for the ensuing blaze.

I remove the melted harness and replace the now disconnected headlight. While reassembling the front I unplug the harness on the drivers side for good measure. I would rather have no headlights than another fire, and I'll just have to figure it out later.

I'm immensely relieved to see my companions reversing down the narrow track to find me. With no possibility to turn around they've reversed for about two miles, they explain. I tell my story in one long outburst, happy to share the burden. They're shocked and also happy I appear to have things under control. As usual, the only available course of action is to continue slowly forward.

We crawl slowly ahead through dusk into a moonless night.

After a quick team meeting we decide to keep moving and search for a place wide enough to make camp in no-mans-land. Immigration and Customs will just have to wait. We have no other choice, and we'd rather not block the track on the off chance a vehicle needs to pass in the night. Reluctantly, I reconnect the second headlight and keep moving. I drive with the window down, hyper-alert for the smell of burning plastic.

A collection of tiny mud huts signals the first village in Cameroon, and the first chance we have to get off the track. Before long the entire village swarms out to greet us and the extremely friendly locals shake our hands off before insisting we make camp right there among the huts. We're so exhausted we gladly accept their generous offer with thanks. Children and adults alike stare with wide eyes as we transform our vehicles into houses before I say goodnight and fall into bed without dinner, completely exhausted.

Mercifully the temperature and humidity drop, and I fall asleep quickly.

Φ   Φ   Φ

I wake in the predawn light to the sound of roosters crowing and the tiny village coming to life - pots banging, cooking fires crackling and children laughing and giggling. Again there are many handshakes as we brew a huge pot of coffee to share with the adults of the village. No amount of sugar is enough so heaping spoon after heaping spoon is added to the potent mix. Even the children slowly warm to us, and excitedly run back and forth with home-made toy cars.

Further along the track we arrive at a rural junction of sorts where a bustling market is in full swing. After confirming directions we swing north on a much larger road. In the border town of Abonshie was find a busy crossing for locals making a booming trade moving gasoline, food, clothes and live animals across the border. One look at the massive river and the hand-made wooden canoes plying the shore confirms my earlier research.

With no bridge, it is impossible to get the vehicles across here.

We track down an Immigration officer who is flabbergasted at our appearance. In his three year posting at this border he's never seen a foreigner, and is obviously proud to be the official representative to formally welcome us into Cameroon. My hand is shaken repeatedly while the officer introduces us around and chats excitedly. The entrance stamps we require are no problem, and he even introduces us to the man at Customs to make things easy there. The night we spent in no-mans-land has caused a gap in dates, though neither official sees it as any kind of problem.

Now in Cameroon on roads marked on maps, I assumed the quality of roads would improve. Heavily loaded transport trucks continually work up and down the steep mountain grades and we discover roads are actually much worse. After passing many trucks and 4x4s overloaded with barrels and plastic containers, I'm finally able to flag one down and talk briefly to the driver. He sheepishly explains they're smuggling gas and diesel from Nigeria into Cameroon, where it's more than double the price. Suddenly everything makes sense. The track we drove through the jungle is a smugglers route, which explains why it's passable in a vehicle.

We drive through endless dry mud pits deeper than the Jeep that would be a nightmare with rain, and are forced to squeeze past multiple broken-down trucks on steep mountain passes. Drivers sleep in the dirt under their stricken vehicles, often with a cooking fire smouldering nearby. One group of men working under the cab of their truck motions me to stop and I quickly see they've broken a connecting rod inside the engine. After waiting a week in the dust for parts, the men are now working frantically to re-assemble the engine on the side of the road. I'm amazed at their ingenuity and abilities given their extremely limited tools and dusty working space. After handshakes and well-wishes on both sides, the men ask only for water - which I gladly give.

We're high in the mountains of Western Cameroon, almost certainly with spectacular views in all directions. Unfortunately we've arrived in the middle of 'Harmattan' - the time of year when dust-laden winds blow southwest from the Sahara and cloud the sky with a thick haze, severely limiting visibility. Simply driving on the dirt roads kicks up clouds as fine as talcum powder, which coats everything within thirty feet of the road in bright red dust. Even the midday sun is heavily obscured, creating a constant eerie end-of-the-world feeling.

Over the coming days we slowly sink into life in Cameroon, thoroughly enjoying the cooler dry air in the mountains. Unbeknownst to us we've driven into a massive anti-government protest that's been ongoing for five months. This region of Cameroon is English speaking, and the population are on strike because they're fed up with being treated like second class citizens by the majority French speaking population. This Anglophone region of the country has a pitiful representation in the government, and are forced to travel for days to the capital for any official correspondence. To make matters worse, all paperwork must be completed in French, a language very few people here speak. The strike means businesses and schools are shut, and people openly express their frustration with the government. In response the government has cut off Internet to the region and is bringing in hundreds of troops daily. The troops are all from the Francophone region of the country, and the lack of communication only serves to build tension.

Locals talk in hushed voices about breaking away and forming a separate country, and many plead with my German friends for help. Germany were the first to colonize Cameroon in 1884, and locals here believe Germany played a crucial role in developing their country. Now they want Germany to help with their struggle against the current government of Cameroon. They've clearly reached the end of their rope, and would rather be ruled once again by a colonial master than tolerate the current situation.

We're only a short distance from the regional capital of Bamenda, where anti-government protests have escalated to the point of shootings multiple times in recent years. Tomorrow is supposed to be a massive celebration of Cameroon's independence gained a half century ago and the government has organized a huge parade in the city center culminating with a tribute to the President. With things the way they are locals are refusing to attend or participate and I'm told troops may force the unwilling population to celebrate at gunpoint.

One afternoon we turn off the road at random, and wind to a dead end track to make camp in a huge stand of eucalyptus trees, not far from a small village. Soon after our arrival Francis befriends us and leads the way to the chief of the village to ask permission to camp on his land. After giving the appropriate gift of whiskey the chief not only grants us permission to camp, but also invites us to a huge funeral celebration the following day. Once a year the people celebrate everyone that has passed away during the year and they believe it's a time to be happy, not sad, so we find ourselves in a huge party, full of dancing, singing, and huge quantities of palm wine.

Some of the locals are a little upset we're at the party, though with smiles and handshakes Francis manages to smooth everything over and it all seems fine. After the massive celebration we wander back to camp and fall into bed, thankful for the cool night air and lack of humidity.

I'm awoken by powerful banging on the side of the Jeep.
"Get out of the vehicle."
"Now."
I peer into the darkness and see men surrounding the Jeep. All are wearing black clothes and carry automatic rifles.

"How many people in the vehicle?"
"One," I answer shakily.
"Turn on a light, and get outside."
"Police."

I have the distinct impression a weapon is pointing at me as I climb slowly from the rear of the Jeep. I keep my hands visible and walk towards the man talking, obviously the most senior. "We are tourists, just camping here," I say.
"How many people in total?"
"Three."

Dani and Didi are also forced from their vehicle, and after taking our passports the man instructs us to pack up our things and come with them. It's nearly midnight, and I think it unwise to argue. The leader will not give any further information, but it's clear he's extremely unhappy with us. It's clear this is not a discussion and we must go with them.

While packing the Jeep I notice many men in the thick eucalyptus trees on the outskirts of our camp. All are dressed in black, and their eyes dart around nervously. I don't miss the fact they all carry an automatic rifle at the ready. Twenty minutes later as we're escorted from our campsite I watch as a local man is forced to the ground, rifle to his temple. These soldiers clearly mean business.

As I drive into the heavily fortified Police compound I sense the soldiers visibly relax. Scores of uniformed men amble about, polishing boots or cleaning rifles. Watching the shift in behaviour, I realize these men were scared of us. With the cover of darkness in the trees we were an unknown, and they had no control over the situation. They have no idea why we're here, how many we number and if we have weapons in our obviously well-equipped vehicles. For all they know we're here to stir up protest among the locals during tomorrow's supposed celebration. Here in the well-lit compound, their superior numbers and firepower leave no doubt as to who is in charge, and they're clearly much happier about it.

After waiting an hour the senior man calls us into his office one by one to grill us while he inspects each page of our passports. He's been on the phone constantly since our arrival, apparently calling Immigration and even Customs. When he's eventually satisfied, the mood changes instantly. Warm handshakes go all around, and the senior officer even apologizes for the trouble he's caused while insisting he had to check out our story thoroughly.

We are free to go, and also welcome to camp right here in the compound if we wish, he says. As nice as their hospitality has been, we decide to return to our bush camp and take whatever comes our way.

In the morning the soldiers smile and wave as we pass through town on our way into the heart of Cameroon.

Mount Cameroon

Limbé Region, Cameroon
March 2017

P ART of my personality I'm only just coming to terms with
is the need to test myself. I repeatedly attempt difficult
things simply to find out if I'm up to the challenge. As a young
man I was arrogant enough to think about taking up smoking
just to see if I could quit. Deep down, I'm aware I've chosen
to drive West Africa because I want a bigger challenge than
ever before in my life. I want to push myself to my limits and
see if I can handle it. One way or another I'll find out just
how tough I am.

At 13,250 ft (4,040m), Mount Cameroon is by far the highest
peak in West Africa. The summit occasionally sees sleet and
snow, even though it's practically on the Equator. It's a
popular hiking destination with many people electing to spend
a few days hiking to the summit and back while soaking in the
experience and acclimatizing to the high elevation. Arriving
in town I don't have any plans to hike the summit, though
after only a few hours I begin to get excited. I don't have the
gear for a multi-day trip, and spending hundreds of dollars to
rent it doesn't appeal to me. If I'm going to make a summit
attempt, it has to be in a single day. It's an extremely difficult
thing to do, and I'm half excited and half nervous as I make
the decision to go for it.

By sheer coincidence the annual race to the summit is planned
for two days from now so town is buzzing with excitement
and preparations. Guides for hiking on the mountain are

mandatory and strictly enforced so I visit the mountain guide association and ask around for a guide who can take me to the summit tomorrow. Later in the afternoon Augustine wanders by my campsite and introduces himself as a young local guide just starting out in the business. He's 22, has an ear to ear grin and looks plenty fit and strong. Truth be told I'm a little worried about keeping up with him - all these months sitting in the Jeep haven't done anything good for my fitness.

The single day round trip to the summit is at least twelve hours of slogging, so those who attempt it usually leave by 4:30am to ensure there's time to summit and be a long way down before nightfall. Due to my usual lack of planning there isn't enough time to get the mandatory National Park permit today, so Augustine will collect my permit first thing tomorrow before we start hiking. My hiking poles are one of the only items in the Jeep I haven't used, and I feel good digging them out. I jam my tiny day pack to the brim and put myself to bed early in the hopes of getting enough sleep, though I'm way to excited to sleep much.

I'm up at 4am, and soon Augustine comes to say it's too early to get the permit. With little choice, we settle in to wait.
And wait.
And wait.
Finally we manage to secure my hiking permit and hit the trail at 8:45, many hours later than ideal.

Augustine makes it very clear we'll have to seriously hustle to have any chance of making the summit today.

Right from the start we're walking extremely fast, in fact almost jogging. Augustine and I push each other as we power past everyone else on the busy lower trail through the thick primary forest all the way to hut one at 6,000 feet. It's been a nice steep hike on a good trail through the forest, though I'm already drenched in sweat. It feels great to stretch my legs in the mountains, and I can't stop smiling from ear to ear. At the hut Augustine introduces Mr. Hans, head of the mountain guide association. His small stature, warm smile, greying hair and peaceful presence remind me of kind Mr. Miyagi from The Karate Kid. Mr. Hans is more than double my age, and has hiked the summit over two hundred and fifty times. I'm impressed, though I can't help noticing he moves at the speed of a glacier.

After just five minutes of rest I've just begun stuffing a second PB & J sandwich into my mouth when Augustine announces we must keep moving. I finish eating on the trail as hut one disappears behind us.

Only fifteen minutes later at 6,600 feet we break out of the thick forest onto barren, rocky slopes where Augustine demonstrates the local dance performed to appease the mountain gods. Traditionally albinos were sacrificed to the mountain, and Augustine laughs when I suggest maybe I should watch my back. He explains that yes, in times past people were actually sacrificed, though these days they only sacrifice albino goats. I'm already too exhausted to stop anyone from sacrificing me to any mountain gods.

The trail soon becomes extremely steep and I slog up loose rock and scree which leaves me short of breath. On and on I trudge, with my usual tactic of slow and steady eventually winning through when I arrive to warm afternoon sunshine at hut number two. Two dozen people mill around, smiling widely while enjoying the sun. I learn they're on the way down, which explains why they look so at ease. Everyone is shocked we're pushing to the summit so late in the day and offer many words of encouragement. Underneath their smiles I see deep exhaustion, a hint of what's to come.

The trail beyond hut two is not nearly as steep, though it's a very long way to hut three, and my pace slows to a crawl in the higher elevation. I shuffle forward at a snail's pace, barely able to keep moving. Remembering my strategy from high-altitude mountain hikes in the Andes, I count my breaths, and pause to rest after each hundred count. At first I rest for ten breaths, then twenty, thirty and eventually fifty. I feel weak knowing that I'm resting half as much as I'm hiking, though there's nothing I can do about it. When I reach a hundred I collapse on the ground, trying desperately to suck in the oxygen my lungs can not get.

Twice Augustine gently prods me.
"We must pick up the pace to reach the summit," he says at first. When I'm still dragging forty minutes later, his prodding becomes more stern.
"Dan, if you don't hurry up, we'll have to turn around."
I immediately pick myself up and continue my shuffle ever so slightly faster than before.

Arriving at hut three is a huge milestone, Augustine says it's not much further to the summit. Walking into the hut I'm disoriented to see Mr. Hans sitting peacefully. After all my huffing and puffing, the 62 year old has easily beaten me, and I don't even remember when he passed me. To top it off he grins broadly and pats me on the shoulder with words of encouragement. He looks well rested, like he could easily repeat the whole thing. That's humbling.

Pushing on from hut three I stop repeatedly, trying in vain to catch my breath. At first I double over, though when that doesn't work I simply collapse, gasping for breath on the volcanic rocks. As hard as I try, my lungs are unable to get the oxygen I desperately need. I'm light headed, my legs are screaming, and I can't feel my fingers from the cold. Despite all of this I'm determined to reach the summit and I pick myself up and shuffle forward. I can barely manage to put one foot in front of the other, and seriously think about crawling.

It's times like this I can't understand why I do these things. I wonder what drives me to seek out difficult situations and why I test myself like this time and again. This punishment seems dumb, but somehow I'm drawn to it.

Progress is painfully slow as I climb the final steep slope and

I'm confused when I turn a full circle and can see nowhere higher to step. I've arrived on the summit at 4:17pm, thirteen minutes before Augustine's mandatory turnaround time. Looking around I see we're well above a thick layer of cloud completely blocking any view to town or the ocean. Even so, the scene is spectacular, and I'm happy to see a wisp of smoke and steam escaping from the evidently active mountain. After just a few photos the driving wind gets the better of my hands. Everyone told me it would be cold on the summit and I assumed they meant 'Africa cold', but clearly I was wrong. The gusting wind makes it genuinely 'Canada cold'.

We've barely left the summit before Augustine reminds me of the need to keep hustling. After slowing to snap photos above hut three I scramble and scree-run down much faster than I went up. Although my legs are screaming I don't run out of breath so I can power through. We bid a brief goodbye to Mr. Hans who is settling in to spend the night before we push hard and fast, moving very well. I'm tired, but I don't really care. I still have reserves, and I know I can push myself hard when required. We're hoping to get through the steepest rocky section before dark, so I keep going as hard as I'm able.

This brilliant plan works perfectly, right up until it doesn't.

As the last light fades I find myself staring into the tiny spot of light cast by my headlamp, while Augustine scrambles down with the light of his little cell phone. Time slows and my legs wobble uncontrollably as I struggle down the steepest section of trail. It takes an eternity to reach hut two, and twice as long to reach hut one. I burned all my reserves on the hike up, and have nothing left. Every five minutes I'm forced to sit on the ground to rest my legs, though it doesn't help much. I eat and drink the last of my food and water before we reach hut one, and I can feel my energy levels falling quickly. Without food I can't recharge, a big problem for me. I begin to dream of a chocolate bar, but have no such thing in my pack.

We pass hordes of soldiers hiking up for tomorrow's race, each carrying an AK-47 and literally enough gear for an entire army. All are friendly, and can clearly see how badly I'm struggling. After Augustine explains in their local language we've just been to the summit, they slap me on the back and offer just one word - 'Courage'.

At hut one I'm not thinking clearly and so exhausted I forget to re-fill my water from the stream.

Soon I push past my limits for the first time in my life. I've seen friends in the Yukon and Alaska hit the wall, though it's never happened to me. Never like this. Utterly exhausted, I struggle to function. I stumble on small rocks and begin to slur my words. The trail has a lot more tree roots than I remember, and even my hiking poles can't save me from falling over repeatedly. My toes squash into the end of my cheap and battered shoes and both big toenails are in agony with every step. Stubbing my toe on a large rock does not help, and I crumble to the ground in agony.

I feel terrible about how slow I'm moving and how it must be making Augustine feel, but there is nothing I can do. I repeatedly collapse onto the ground to rest, and when I close my eyes falling asleep in the dirt feels like a great idea. Augustine's gentle prodding always gets me moving again, though only barely.

Augustine first guesses we'll reach the Jeep at 8pm and I set my sights on that, desperately looking forward to sitting down. With my constant stopping 9pm comes and goes and then 10pm does too. Progress is excruciatingly slow, and I can't help stopping repeatedly. Without food or water I can do nothing to recharge, so I simply continue on, staring into the seemingly diminishing headlamp light, trying my best not to pass out. If not for my hiking poles I'm sure I would have given up from sheer exhaustion long ago. As my body screams in agony I again wonder why I do these things to myself. It doesn't make any sense, and it can't be good for me. My stubbornness has once again landed me in trouble and now I have to suffer the consequences and keep going.

Augustine and I eventually stagger to the Jeep at 10:45pm, after fourteen hours of virtually non-stop hiking for a total elevation change of over 20,000 feet (6,100m). We share a beer - Augustine drinks the very large half - before bidding each other farewell. After a freezing shower beside the Jeep I struggle to climb upstairs before I fall asleep the instant my head hits the pillow, the agony of the hike not yet taking over.

In the late morning I stare at the mountain towering above my campsite. Now I know the punishment it can dish out, I see it in a whole new light. I move just a few miles down to a stunning black sand beach, where I make camp for the night. My feet are severely torn with blisters, as are the palms of my hands from using my hiking poles to slow my descent. The backs of my legs are badly sunburnt, and my legs ache so much I can't walk without looking like a cowboy. My two big toenails are extremely sensitive and already turning black.

I spend the day soaking my feet and hands in salty water, and I'm extremely careful to keep all the open wounds clean and covered in disinfectant for weeks to come. The chances of infection in the intense humidity are high, something I really hope to avoid.

It rains lightly overnight for the first time in months turning the thick layer of dust on the rear bumper to mud. While packing camp the next morning in flip flops I stand on the rear bumper to close the roof, and slip on the muddy surface. In a desperate attempt to hold on I reflexively curl my toes, causing them to drag across the corner of the steel bumper as I fall to the ground. Both of my big toenails snag on the bumper and lift up half an inch as they catch on the steel. I silently roll on the ground in agony for five minutes before I manage to dust myself off and continue packing, hobbling the entire time. There's not a thing I can do about it, so I struggle on.

A couple of weeks later both big toenails fall off, and to this day I have scars on both feet from the blisters.

Φ   Φ   Φ

After all of that I'm no closer to understanding why I set out to do these kinds of challenging and punishing things. Maybe it's just a part of my personality I'll have to embrace.
I should probably stop asking questions and just get on with it.

Glorious Gabon

Gabon
April 2017

T RAVERSING the West Coast of Africa requires crossing
a minimum of twelve countries, and up to twenty-four
depending on the exact route. There are many reasons to
skip countries - safety, weather, visa issues and even Ebola
outbreaks closing borders. More commonly, some overlanders
choose to skip a country because they just don't want to go.

On the coast and straddling the Equator lies the relatively
small country of Gabon, which is often skipped. On the surface
it seems too small to explore, and the focus is usually on the
much larger Congos looming large. Virtually no one explores
Gabon's remote corners, so there's little information about
what Dani, Didi and I will find in the dense jungles the country
has in spades.

The mighty rainy season is forecast to start during our visit,
and my now battered and torn Michelin map shows only the
main north-south highway is paved. All other roads are shown
as dirt tracks slicing though dense jungle. There are only
sixteen people per square mile in Gabon which makes it one
of the least densely populated countries on Earth. The vast
majority of the country is wild and untouched, and huge areas
have been set aside as protected parks and wildlife reserves.

Excited to dive into the unknown yet again, we approach the
border of Gabon eagerly. After a final street meal in Cameroon
we drop down into a wide valley where the Aïna River serves

as the physical border between Cameroon and Gabon. We step out of our vehicles where a barrier blocks the road, and Military men write our details into a ledger. Twenty yards on the story is repeated, then again, then again. All along the way everyone is friendly, and genuinely happy to hear we've enjoyed our month in Cameroon. When all is said and done we have exit stamps in our passports and the paperwork for both vehicles is cancelled, so we're free to leave.

On the far side of the bridge is yet another barrier, and I immediately sense the armed man standing guard is having a very bad day, or at least he wants us to. Right away he's short with me in French, and is not happy when I say we're tourists. He immediately announces we can't enter because we need visas for Gabon, and I try my best not to sound like a smart-ass when I tell him we have them in our passports. Again, he's not at all happy.

Once we hand over our passports it's clear he wants to hold onto them, knowing he can wield power over us while he has control of our most important documents. To find my visa he flips through over thirty pages of other visas and stamps, and he repeatedly cuts me off and tells me to be quiet when I try to show and then help him find the Gabon visa. Flipping through page by page is painfully slow, and he repeatedly stops to talk on his cell phone or otherwise do nothing. Not for the first time in West Africa I get the feeling he's intentionally wasting time just to see how we'll react. He wants me to lose my cool and start yelling so he will be justified in *really* messing with me. As usual I keep cool and play the long patience game.

Eventually he resigns himself to doing his job, and insists we go away and wait in the shade by the Jeep. After ten minutes I'm called back, and the man insists on writing the full list of countries I've visited since leaving Australia. Doing as I'm told I rattle off the names of over twenty countries, much to his disbelief. I think he's trying to find a hole in my story, though after country number ten he can't keep track.

Amazingly, this man isn't even Immigration or Customs, and writes these details onto a random piece of paper as some kind of pre-admittance authorization from the Military.

While this is happening I notice a local driving across in the opposite direction. Obviously not willing to waste time he just hands money to the Military man, and the barrier is quickly lifted. Evidently this is how people deal with this irritating and unfriendly man. After driving through the local man walks back and asks in English if we need any help. He explains he's from Cameroon and that we're all in this together. When I insist we will be fine he wishes us well before crossing the bridge and starting the game in Cameroon.

Now finished grilling me, the Military man starts in on Dani and Didi. He can't find an exit stamp from Cameroon in their passports, and absolutely will not let them proceed until he sees one. They explain they've switched passports because their other one is almost full. It's perfectly legal for German citizens to have two German passports, though our new friend thinks otherwise. He convinces himself they're up to no good, and it takes an hour for him to calm down and listen to reason. Now I get the feeling he's just kicking up a fuss about anything he can think of in the hopes we'll pay. Little does he know that's never going to happen. On this point Didi is more stubborn than me, and together there's zero chance we'll pay a cent.

As I've learned time and again, practicing patience like the Buddha and keeping a smile on my face eventually wins through. The Military man finally hands back our passports and the pre-admittance form, and the barrier at the end of the bridge is lifted. We pull forward to another barrier less than a hundred yards later where the entire process is repeated. This time the men are friendly and the whole process is actually pleasant. After more similar stops we find Customs where the vehicles are also easily granted entry.

In the first town we come to is Immigration where we get

multiple copies of documents before we're finally given entrance stamps in our passports. After roughly four hours we're legal to explore Gabon for the next month.

Φ   Φ   Φ

In the morning at our wild camp we smile over coffee, knowing we're in for a good day. For the second time in my life, very far from home, I drive my Jeep across the Equator. Years ago I drove across in Ecuador, and I'm grinning like mad thinking about where I'll be next time. We trade out posing for photos at the sign, and I can't help noticing my GPS says it's in the wrong place by about thirty yards.

Soon after we turn east off the major highway, aiming for Lopé National Park in the heart of the country. National Parks in Gabon have been setup exclusively as a playground for rich foreigners, with prices around five hundred US dollars per day. The steep price means we're not determined to visit the actual park, but are just looking forward to the adventure and beauty we're sure to find along the way. An hour later when the landscape is dotted with small grassy mountains I know we've made the right decision.

The dirt track winds along the twisty shoreline of the monster Ogooue River, alternating from dense jungle to open plains, forests and grasslands. At night we simply pull off the road and make camp anywhere we please, and over three days and hundreds of miles we see only two other vehicles. Late one afternoon we cross the river above boiling whitewater on a monster bridge before stumbling on a magnificent high bluff with commanding views to make camp. While cooking dinner we're treated to an incredible lightning show many miles away, with the wall of lightning slowly inching closer. Sitting outside transfixed we hear the trumpet of a wild elephant that makes my hair stand on end. Later we're scamper into our vehicles as the monumental downpour begins, and once again I'm staggered by the amount of rain that can fall in just an hour.

Φ   Φ   Φ

In the morning we find the enormous luxury lodge at Lopé
National Park and immediately feel very conspicuous. The
manager is extremely friendly and happy to show us around,
even though we're a bit muddy after a few days without a
shower. The lodge is five hundred Euros per night, meals are
about thirty each and a morning safari into the park is well
over a hundred. There is no denying the lodge is extremely
beautiful, though these prices are simply outside our world.
We wander the manicured lawns to the river, past the pool,
a bar and luxury cabins with electricity and air conditioning.
Meals are prepared by an internationally trained chef, we're
told.

When we explain our travels and situation, the manager is
honest and kind, explaining the park only permits guided
safaris and it's forbidden to drive our own vehicles. He adds
that if it's gorillas we're hoping to see, this is not the best
place and we need to visit a different region of the park. He
suggests a man who might be able to guide us, so armed with
only a vague description we set off to search for this mystery
gorilla man.

At a Military checkpoint on the edge of town we meet Ghislain,
an extremely polite and gentle man who has just been picking
wild lemons with his six smiling children. Ghislain is tall, quick
to smile and patient while I butcher the words in French to
explain what we're looking for. He's happy to tailor a trip to
meet our tight budget, and he appreciates we want to cook our
own meals and camp in our vehicles. After thirty minutes we
shake hands on a deal for Ghislain to guide us into the park
in search of wild gorillas and I simply can not wait.

Later in the Afternoon with Ghislain in the Jeep we venture
further towards the center of the country, and it's immediately
clear the road is much less traveled and in desperate need of
repair. Until just last week it was completely blocked by a

washout, a continual problem in this part of the world due to the torrential rains and dirt roads. Ghislain and I discuss life in Gabon, his children and his perspective on life. He has always lived in this part of the country, and worked for many years at the gorilla research station before it closed. For three years Ghislain hiked alone into the jungle hoping to just glimpse the gorillas, who would immediately leave when he got within a hundred yards. After years of adjustment the gorillas eventually came to tolerate his presence, and after five years he was able to sit for ten minutes within thirty yards of the gorillas. Because of his years with the wild gorillas he knows where they will likely be and how best to find them. I had no idea we hired The Gorilla Whisperer as our guide, and I'm all the more excited by his skills and relationship to the gorillas.

After paying a small fee to the local community we branch off onto a seriously overgrown jungle track and drive a further five miles to the abandoned research station. Enormous fallen trees have been cut and moved off the track, and vines hang down low enough to scrape across the solar panels. Thousands of insects and small birds make their presence known, keeping up a constant chorus in the background. I can't help but feel sad about the lack of maintenance at the research station which comprises about ten buildings slowly being reclaimed by the jungle. With just a little work it would be nothing short of magical, and could easily be the overgrown set of Jurassic Park. After cooking a mountain of pasta for dinner we crash into bed just as the jungle chorus really comes to life.

Φ   Φ   Φ

At sunrise we set out hiking into the steamy jungle with stomachs full of butterflies. Ghislain explains there was an extensive network of trails in this region of the park used by researchers studying the gorillas. Most are overgrown or abandoned, and others are now only used by the forest elephants that live here. By carefully inspecting broken twigs, footprints in the mud, half-eaten fruits and stopping to listen every five minutes, Ghislain tracks the gorillas and leads us deep into the thick jungle. He takes turn after turn on the muddy tracks and soon I'm completely disoriented. When Ghislain assures me he knows the way back I trust him completely.

After hours on the muddy tracks we find a large pile of leaves crushed onto the ground and after carefully inspecting the area Ghislain finds a gorilla hair, and even a few pieces of half-eaten fruit. This is where the gorillas slept last night, Ghislain explains. His mannerisms change, and I sense he's now determined to find them.

We continue forward, dropping elevation to a small creek were we find fresh gorilla tracks in the wet sand. Ghislain doesn't say anything for ten long minutes while he stares at the far bank and paces up and down with his senses on high alert. When we scramble up the far bank Ghislain jumps up and down with excitement before punching his fist into his hand in frustration. After making it abundantly clear we must be completely silent he motions for us to follow up a small riverbed. I haven't seen or heard anything yet, though Ghislain's behaviour makes it clear we're extremely close.

We wait for five minutes without moving before retreating and approaching from a slightly different angle to gain a different vantage point. When I hear the gorilla's deep rumbling call I'm shocked. Judging by the noise they're extremely close, and enormous. Ghislain says the alpha male is agitated, and doesn't like us being so close. He will soon lead the troop away, and they will continue to move if we follow. Instead Ghislain puts distance between us, guiding us backwards to high ground so we can watch how they react.

After only a minute one of the female gorillas approaches to investigate, and I get a clear view of her clinging to a huge tree high above the ground. I'm immediately struck by how massive she is - much, much bigger than the chimps I'm used to. Her face and expressions look even more human and I can clearly see the inquisitiveness and intelligence behind her eyes as she studies us.

For five minutes we watch each other through the jungle until the big male calls her back to get the group moving. Instead of climbing down she simply relaxes her grip while hugging the tree, sliding to the ground. I'm struck by how much she looks like a large child doing exactly the same thing on a fireman's pole.

We move back a hundred yards and sit on a large rock to eat a snack. If we're lucky the big male might bring the troop to have a closer look at us. They clearly know we're here, and don't seem too alarmed, so there is a chance. Over the next forty-five minutes we hear them grunting and calling as they move around, though it becomes clear they're making a slow retreat, and we never see them again.

I'm tingling with adrenaline from the encounter, and Ghislain confesses he's feeling the same. He honestly didn't know if he could track them down in a single day and he's clearly proud to have done so. He's also elated the gorillas remember him, and his connection that took years to build is still intact. If they didn't remember him the gorillas would have fled long before we ever saw them, he explains

We retrace our steps through the dense jungle, and Ghislain never once hesitates at a single junction. After an hour on the wider trails he stops to point out our footprints in the mud, and the elephant prints that now cover our boot prints.
"Oh sure," he says, "Forest elephants are all around us."
I can't stop thinking about mighty elephants walking through the dense jungle behind us and I realize how badly I want to see one up close. Ghislain is constantly on the lookout and listening so we don't accidentally stumble into one, however. They can be extremely unpredictable and dangerous when startled, especially in this dense jungle where they feel trapped.

Almost on cue we hear an elephant trumpeting loudly and

Ghislain estimates it's less than five hundred yards away. We freeze and listen for a couple of minutes before Ghislain explains this is a very bad situation. Because the elephant is repeatedly trumpeting loudly he thinks it must be injured or distressed, and we absolutely must not approach any closer. In fact he doesn't think we're entirely safe now, so we walk a huge semi-circle to give the animal a wide berth. I'm disappointed to miss seeing the elephant, though of course I listen to Ghislain's expertise and do exactly as he says. Each time the elephant trumpets my hair stands on end and I freeze in place. Even for a little forest elephant he sure sounds mighty big.

On the drive back we're both buzzing, and continue to chat about our experience, Ghislain's family, his religion, his experiences in the park and everything else that comes to mind. He misses his family who all moved to the capital city, as most Africans inevitably do, though he knows city life isn't for him. He wants his children to grow up close to nature as he did, and besides, he hates traffic. In time we get around to the recent Presidential election which was marred in controversy. West African countries are not renowned for peaceful elections, and I've been careful with my timing to avoid them altogether. For fifty straight years Gabon has been ruled by only two men, a father and son duo widely believed to be bleeding money from the country.

Just a couple of months ago eight of nine states in the country voted for a new leader, but shockingly the President's home state turned the tide and pushed him over the line to victory. Amazingly, voter turnout in his home province was 99.9%. This is particularly staggering given the national average was only 59%. It's also jaw-dropping that 95% percent of his home state voted for the President *and* the total number of votes cast in this crucial province was thousands more than the actual population. It could not be more obvious the election was rigged.

The election itself was peaceful, orderly and even open to

International observers. Shockingly, after these clearly fictional results, the incumbent was announced the winner. Because the President controls the loyal Military, there is nothing regular citizens can do about this corruption. Burning cars, rioting and general unrest were met with closed borders and the Internet being cut off so the outside world couldn't learn what had transpired. Now just a few months later life has returned to normal. Locals simply get on with it, accepting voter fraud as part of life. Mr. Bongo will be President of Gabon until the next election in 2025, though with no term limits and rampant corruption he could easily win office again.

Ф   Ф   Ф

After bidding farewell to Ghislain we spend two days re-tracing our steps to the main highway and further south. I slow to a crawl to enter an enormous pothole that stretches the full width of the badly broken highway just as a heavily loaded truck enters at high speed from the other direction. I have just enough time to flinch as a huge rock flicks up and smashes into the windshield. Thankfully it doesn't come all the way through, though it gets close. Tiny shards of glass shower me, the dash and the front passenger seat, and the windscreen is now spongy where it hit. Luckily my sunglasses protect my eyes and it's easy to brush everything off.

I'm thousands of miles from Jeep parts, so there is little I can do. Hopefully tape will keep out the worst of the rain and I layer it thick inside and out. To add insult to the injury I find a flat tire during my morning walk-around of the Jeep the next day. A screw is buried deep in the tread, though it's easy enough to plug the hole and air up using my on-board compressor.

Ф   Ф   Ф

Wedged against the South Atlantic Ocean, Loango National Park hit International headlines when wild hippos were seen playing in the ocean and even surfing in the waves. In this extremely wild and untouched landscape, elephants too can be seen on the beach and swimming in the ocean. Both of these occurrences are extremely rare, so we set our sights on visiting the area, eager to explore.

Simply getting to the park turns into an adventure in itself when maps and GPS show a tangle of small tracks that lead nowhere. Guide books and locals mention roads under construction, though nothing is certain. In our usual fashion we stop in every small village to ask directions, and fumble along in no particular hurry. Eventually we come to a guarded gate, which marks the entrance to an active Shell oil field. The security guards are extremely friendly, and it's no problem to radio for an escort vehicle to lead us across. On the far side the driver gives directions, which I mostly understand in French.

Again we simply camp on the side of the road wherever we fit, and night after night we're surrounded by enormous trees, vines and bright red earth. I know we're getting close when the track turns to deeply rutted white beach sand, littered with monster puddles. On a brilliantly sunny day we break out of the dense and humid jungle onto a spectacular beach complete with perfect breaking waves and a grassy bluff. It doesn't take long to appreciate the paradise we've found, so we immediately setup camp. We have the entire place to ourselves, though we do take note of the elephant dung on the grass around us. A light breeze in camp and swimming in the ocean directly in front provide the perfect way to cool off, and a stunning sunset caps the perfect wild camp.

Gabon is deceptively big, with towns extremely few and far between. After hundreds of miles getting into Loango on sand, dirt and mud, I wonder if I have enough gas to get out again. We venture further south just to look around, and in the small coastal fishing town of Omboue I'm given directions to the local gas station. An enterprising man has bought gas and diesel from who-knows-where and is selling it from drums on the side of the road. The gas looks very clear, though I think it smells more like paint thinner than gasoline. Before I can get out my syphon hose the smiling guy sucks on the hose and manages to keep grinning when he gets a mouthful. I wonder why it's cheaper than the official price in Gabon, and it all makes sense later when I'm warned not to buy that because it has a reputation for destroying engines.

Late in the afternoon we roll into Loango Lodge uncertain what to expect. It's obvious this is a five star lodge, and is much fancier than anywhere I've set foot in my life. Jan the manager introduces himself, and we soon discover he's the friendliest person in the world. Originally from South Africa Jan has been building and running this extremely remote paradise for many years. He invites us to camp right on the grass of the lodge and insists we're welcome to hang out and use the facilities and pool. Jan doesn't get out much, and he's eager to hear about our adventures and the wild places we've visited, and we're just as eager to learn more about life in Gabon and this paradise he's built. He smiles constantly and insists that nothing is a problem while showing us around the impressive complex. It's a full time job keeping the jungle at bay, and the intense humidity and monsoon rains play havoc with the equipment and buildings which require endless maintenance, especially the uncooperative generator that demands constant care.

The following afternoon we catch a small boat across the tidal river and within five minutes spot forest elephants out for an afternoon stroll. We roam for hours with the majestic creatures before moving down to the sandy beach where we spot many herds. None are actually walking in the ocean, though it's clear they'll spend the night on the beach sand.

At night we take a boat tour upstream into the dense mangrove swamps in the pitch black. Deep in the mangroves I'm stunned when our guide jumps into the waist deep water and snatches up a baby crocodile with his bare hands. When the baby squeaks loudly for it's mother I get downright uncomfortable. "Where's Momma?" I ask while scanning the pitch black water. "Oh, she's around here somewhere." He replies with a grin.

I'm usually not afraid of large reptiles with teeth, though I've never been swimming in crocodile-infested water in the pitch black before. He assures me no local has ever been attacked by a crocodile here, though I feel certain he's pushing his luck. I'm relieved when he releases the baby croc and climbs back into the boat, and thankfully everyone makes it back in one piece.

The skies let loose the following afternoon with a torrential downpour that doesn't stop for many hours. Jan explains the rains are a month late, and everyone in Gabon has been holding their breath. Again I'm staggered by the volume of water pouring from the sky, and before sunrise the earth is completely saturated until it's all one big shallow lake dotted with much deeper lakes.

Φ Φ Φ

Reluctantly we bid farewell to Jan and pry ourselves away from the paradise at Loango Lodge, a truly unforgettable place. The non-stop rains in the last couple of days have changed the already sketchy access track considerably, though Jan assures us the water crossings should be manageable, if not a little sketchy. He reminds us not to walk any to check the depth on account of the large toothy reptiles that infest the entire region. I squirm in my seat as I drop into a couple of the deeper ones, wondering just when I'll hit bottom. Water does slosh over the hood a few times, making me extremely thankful for the snorkel that ensures the engine does not suck in water. Thankfully the bottom of these monster puddles are always solid, so I have no trouble maintaining forward momentum and no water comes inside.

We backtrack to the oil field and after being escorted to the far side we take a different road through the dense jungle and over rolling hills. I round a corner and am startled to see an elephant standing directly beside the road. I stop and stare, not believing my eyes as he stares right back. Driving my own Jeep this close to an elephant on a regular road is surreal, and I'm transfixed for ten minutes. At first the big guy is a little uneasy and keeps a close eye on me, though he quickly calms down and settles into stripping leaves from a tree. I'm shocked by how much power he has in his trunk, and how much noise he makes while snapping branches and eating.

Years ago when I dreamed of Africa, this was exactly what I dreamed of!

Φ Φ Φ

A week later on our last night in Gabon I feel as if we've just barely scratched the surface in our month of exploring. It's a surprisingly large country with huge tracts of untouched wilderness that provide unlimited opportunities for exploration. Locals are extremely friendly and laid back and are always quick to smile and shake hands. Gabon's spectacular wildlife, wilderness and National Parks stand out as a highlight from all of West Africa.

I wave goodbye to Gabon and drive into a county I'm very excited about.

It's Congo time.

Gas Crunch

Republic Of Congo
May 2017

T HERE are actually two separate countries in Africa called
'Congo'. 'The Republic of Congo' lies to the north of
the mighty river of the same name, and is the smaller and
less famous of the two. The capital of each country is usually added to the word Congo in an attempt to clarify this
naming confusion. It's capital is Brazzaville, and to avoid confusion this country is often called 'Congo-Brazzaville' while it's
much larger and infamous neighbour to the south is commonly
'Congo-Kinshasa', which we'll get to in good time.

After just a few hours in Congo-Brazza we learn the country
is suffering from massive gas and diesel shortages. We're told
the only oil refinery in the country has been shut down, and
supplies across the country have run dry. Some say it's for
maintenance and others say it's a battle of politics. Whatever
the reason, it means I have a problem. The enormous diesel
tanks on the sportsmobile allow Dani and Didi to travel over
twelve hundred miles before needing a fill up, while I'll be
lucky to make half that. Congo-Brazza is a massive country,
and I'm going to need gas at least three or four times.

Every regular station displays a 'sold out' sign, and I quickly
realize I'll have to get more creative. In one small town I
learn enterprising men have smuggled gas from Cameroon and
are selling it from plastic containers. The smiling young men
clearly know it's in high demand, and their twenty-five percent
price inflation is fine by me given the convenience they offer.

As always they're curious about the Jeep, and ask about the nearby countries they've never seen. One young man slowly pours each container through my filter funnel, and towards the end he says

"You don't want the last half gallon."

I agree when I see the nasty black sludge on the bottom of his plastic container. Running out of gas is a problem, though I'm sure running that sludge through the engine will cause bigger problems.

After exploring the far north we retrace our tracks and continue south, aiming for Brazzaville where we must secure the final visa. I ask in literally every station, and all are completely empty. About half way to Brazzaville I transfer the thirteen gallons in my auxiliary tank from Gabon into the main tank. I'm running out of options, but I'm not worried yet.

Wild camping is hard to find in Congo-Brazza because the dense jungle prevents us pulling the two vehicles off the road even fifty yards. Eventually we squeeze them end to end on a tiny walking track that dead ends at a gated farm and though not ideal, it will work for one night. At dusk a couple of old farmers leaving the farm stop to shake hands and say hello. I ask for permission to camp in French, and they immediately wave me down. I soon realize these two old men don't speak a word of French, and after looking closely I realize they're pygmies. Both men must be well over sixty, and both have the build and height of ten year old boys. In fact they barely reach above my waist, which is extremely confusing. They seem extremely happy and friendly, and after using hand gestures to show we intend to camp they both nod and smile before again shaking hands and wandering on.

Φ   Φ   Φ

In the morning we continue towards Brazzaville and the gas gauge slowly sinks to empty, and then lower. Always the optimist I reason there must be gas in the capital, and I become determined to make it there. Thankfully the last twenty miles are all downhill because Brazzaville lies on the banks of the mighty Congo River. We take a road directly on the shore of the monster river, so large it's difficult to easily make out the other side. When I hit traffic lights and stop signs the gauge goes further below empty than I've ever seen. The computer said empty was thirty miles ago and I have to think it will die any minute. Every gas station is packed with vehicles in long and rambling lines, yet none have a single drop. When I stop to ask locals think I'm trying to cut the line and soon become unhappy with my being there. I say thanks and move on before anyone can get angry and it's very clear tensions are running high in the big city.

In the stop and go traffic I seriously worry about the Jeep conking out, so I kill the engine at every red light and inter-section, hoping to squeeze another few miles. I'm relieved as I drive through the gates of Hippocampe, a famous overlander hangout on the West Africa route. The kind and friendly owners of this downtown restaurant have offered free camping in their parking lot for decades, and everyone driving this side of the continent make a stop here.

I've driven 569 miles without a gas station, and I'm sure there is less than a gallon in the tank. For ten minutes I wind down after the stressful drive before the reality of my situation sinks in. I'm in the heart of a massive capital city that doesn't have a drop of gas. The Jeep is completely empty, and I wouldn't dare try to drive anywhere. One way or another, I will have to find gas before I can leave Hippocampe and Brazzaville. I have no idea how I'm going to do that.

Φ   Φ   Φ

I've been in Africa almost a year, and I'm starting to under-stand how locals manage the constant challenges like the one I find myself in. There are always problems and difficulties, but locals simply don't let them impact their happiness. These minor issues and inconveniences are endless, and it's not worth getting upset. Anyone that does will be a very grumpy person the majority of the time. The only sensible way to tackle these problems is to stay happy and slowly chip away at whatever problem arises today. I've come to learn Africa will always provide a solution for every problem. It's really just a question of time.

Trying my best to channel that attitude, and realizing I'm perfectly safe and comfortable at Hippocampe we order cold beers and food from the restaurant. Trying to relax into it, I remind myself that as long as my visa doesn't run out I'm in no particular hurry.

Later in the afternoon while chatting to the owner I mention my gas problem and we start throwing around possible solutions. He orders diesel in bulk for his generator, and he's fairly confident that if we order a big enough quantity of gas from his supplier, they can probably fill the order.
"How much is enough?" I ask, already scared of the answer.
"Oh, something like two hundred and fifty gallons should do it," he replies casually.

Because his vehicles and generators all burn diesel he has no use for regular gasoline. He also has no interest in buying such a large quantity and then trying to sell it off in small lots at a profit. As much as I want gas, I'm not sure buying two hundred and fifty gallons is a good idea when I can only carry thirty-five. We decide to shelve that idea and order another round of cold drinks. Even though it will be outrageously expensive it's nice to know if I get *really* stuck there is a backup plan that might work.

The man working security on the gate overhears our discussion and springs into action. He makes call after call while assuring me he will eventually find gas, it's just a question of price. He explains how enterprising locals all over the country fill containers whenever they can before biding their time until the stations inevitably run dry. The official price is 595 Central

African Francs per litre, around $USD3.40 a gallon. Given the massive shortage crippling virtually the entire country I will undoubtedly pay more, and I shudder to think how much more. Late in the evening he swings by the Jeep to say gas can be delivered in the morning and it costs three times the official rate, $USD10 a gallon.

At first I'm shocked at the price. After thinking about it for ten minutes I put it in perspective. The entire country has virtually no gas and nobody can say if it will continue for weeks or even months. Hippocampe and the Republic Of Congo overall are very nice places, though I'll go crazy if I'm forced to sit still for an entire month. I have the chance to buy gas this minute, and I have no idea how long before it's sold to someone else.

When I really think about it, paying two hundred dollars for the convenience sounds very worthwhile. I try to negotiate on the price, though the seller won't budge an inch.
She knows her gas is in high demand.

After struggling to sleep in the intensely hot and humid concrete parking lot my saviour arrives first thing in the morning. With three plastic containers of seven gallons each, I can virtually fill the main tank. I ask for more, but there isn't any. The liquid in two of the containers looks clear and smells about right as it go through my filter funnel, though the third is cloudy with a layer of brown muck on the bottom. It again smells more like paint thinner than gas, which is concerning. My man assures me repeatedly it hasn't been watered down, and all I can do is trust them. I can only hope that mixing the bad container with the two good ones will dilute it enough not to cause trouble.

I thank my saviour and the security man, and the Jeep fires up without missing a beat. Eager to solve our next problem, we move across town to the Angolan Embassy, desperately needing the final visa. At the door we're denied entry before we can even speak to the Ambassador. The smiling secretary is adamant we won't be issued a visa, so there's no point wasting time, she says. This is not good.

Back at Hippocampe thirty minutes later we assess our options. None of us has much interest in spending another night in the hot and sticky concrete parking lot, and it's still early in the morning. Staying in Brazzaville doesn't help us get the visa we need, and our next - and only - chance is in Pointe-Noire on the coast, three hundred and fifty miles away. If I drive carefully I should be able to make it with the gas in the Jeep and I'll simply have to find more there.

After spending less than twenty-four hours in the big city we drive north out of Brazzaville, nervous about the road ahead. Three hundred miles to the west we're relieved to find a perfectly normal station that has plenty of gas and diesel. While filling everything to the brim we strike up a conversation with the chatty attendant. He tells us they were completely dry two days ago and it might dry up again tomorrow for all anyone knows. When I explain our planned route he just smiles broadly, claps me on the shoulder and says *"Bonne Route!"*.

Flush with gas I have enough to leave the first Congo, though nobody can say if Congo-Kinshasa is suffering the same supply problems. I'll just have to find out.

Before ever setting foot on Africa I was convinced gas would be exceptionally hard to find and therefore a diesel vehicle was an absolute must. After a few months on the ground I saw African countries are swarming with cheap Chinese scooters and motorbikes that vastly outnumber four-wheeled vehicles by ten or even one hundred to one. Because they all run on gas, it's often more readily available than diesel. Diesel transport trucks have huge tanks and drive mostly on major highways, so the distance between diesel stations is many hundreds of miles. On the other hand scooters with tiny tanks need gas regularly so it's available much more frequently.

On the whole, regular gas stations were a lot more common and gas was much easier to find than I planned. Across Africa development is marching ahead at a staggering pace, and both gas and diesel availability in every country has improved vastly in just the last five years. On less than a handful of occasions I had to go out of my way to find gas and I always managed. With both the Jeep main tank and the auxiliary I drove over five hundred miles on multiple occasions which was always adequate.

Congo Bongo

Democratic Republic Of Congo
May 2017

A T over 905,000 square miles, The Democratic Republic
of Congo (aka Congo-Kinshasa, aka the DRC, previously
Zaire) - is the stuff African legends are made of. Countless epic
tales like *Heart Of Darkness*[5] by Joseph Conrad are set in the
Congo, and Africa was often referred to as 'The Dark Continent'
because so much of Zaire went undiscovered and maps showed
the interior as a solid black blob of unknown. Modern-day
DRC is widely believed to hold the richest mineral reserves
of any nation on Earth. Trillions of dollars of diamonds, gold
and rare earth metals lie undiscovered, and it's estimated to
contain over five billion barrels of oil. Despite this immense
wealth - or because of it - the DRC is one of the most dangerous
and least functioning countries on Earth.

King Leopold of Belgium first enslaved the region in 1884,
setting the scene for a long line of violent figures who pillaged
and exploited in increasingly creative and depraved ways. The
infamous President Mobutu ruled with a brutal iron fist for
over 30 years and is estimated to have personally pocketed up
to $15 billion. While his family flew on Concord for weekend
getaways in Paris, millions of his countrymen suffered and
died as a direct result of his cruelty. In 1997 Mobutu fled
the country, leaving behind 'a feral state of lawlessness and
brutality', as it was once famously described.

---

[5] *Heart Of Darkness* - Joseph Conrad, 1899

Recently the capital of Kinshasa rates among the top five most dangerous places on the planet caused by citizens protesting the lack of a promised Presidential election. Knowing he will be voted out, President Kabila is indefinitely pushing back the election. Protesting in Kinshasa typically means burning cars and rioting in the streets.

There is no getting around it, traversing the West Coast of Africa requires crossing the DRC, the challenge is to find a safe way to do so. While the DRC is certainly not the safest place to explore, it contains vast swaths of the most remote and least-explored regions on the planet. For this reason I've long felt drawn to the DRC, and I plan my crossing with a mixture of awe, respect, fascination and fear.

Usually a river as big as the Congo forms the International Border between two countries, though this is not the case with the Congo River. Downstream of the two capital cities Brazzaville and Kinshasa the river is completely contained within the DRC, so even if I successfully cross to the southern bank, I'll have hundreds of miles remaining in the DRC.

Φ   Φ   Φ

Enjoying beach-side paradise in Pointe-Noire in Congo-Brazza one afternoon, Pascal the owner gives us the good news we've been waiting for. We must get to the Angolan embassy as fast as possible. We've been waiting for our Angolan visas for a week, desperately hoping it will be granted. This is the final visa we require, and is also the most important and most difficult to secure. Without the Angolan visa we will be stranded in the DRC, or might even have to contemplate driving across the heart of the country, an enormous and dangerous undertaking we seriously hope to avoid.

After paying at the bank nearby we're handed our passports at the Embassy, and are elated to see we've been issued one month double-entry visas which give us options for the route ahead. On the way home we buy ice cream to celebrate our success at this final piece of West African bureaucracy. We're not out of the woods yet, but we're getting very close.

Our double-entry Angolan visas means we have two viable options to safely cross the DRC from north to south:

South of Pointe-Noire we can enter a small and separate region of Angola called Cabinda. This part of Angola has virtually all the oil reserves, and is completely isolated geographically from the rest of Angola, similar to Alaska from the USA. I'm told it's a friendly and clean place, if not a little dull. From Cabinda we would continue south and enter the DRC, only crossing a couple of hundred miles before reaching the bridge over the Congo River at Matadi. The border with mainland Angola is not much further, and we would use our second authorized entry there.

I'm told these roads are in good shape, and to expect some bribery in DRC, especially near both Angolan borders. I've been warned repeatedly the DRC is not a place to mess about, and that I should alter my usual anti-bribery strategy and simply pay up.
There is no doubt about it, this route is the most conservative way to cross the DRC.

The other option is a lot more adventurous.

It involves hundreds of miles on virtually non-existent roads, a ferry that may or may not operate to cross the Congo River and then many more miles of still nightmare muddy roads. If it rains, all bets are off. It's entirely possible no vehicles can move in either direction for months during heavy rain. The dangers are real and the chances of recovering the Jeep if it becomes seriously stuck or suffers a major breakdown are for all intents and purposes nil.

This is a heavy decision, the DRC is no joke.

I've been weighing up this decision for a long time now. On

one hand I came to West Africa for adventure and to explore the most remote places on Earth. On the other hand I'm well aware this route is at the upper limit of my capabilities - and that of my Jeep.

I have enjoyed West and Central-West Africa immensely, and it's almost over. Angola has shopping malls, fast food joints and cinemas, and by the time I reach Namibia I'm told the development will make my head spin. I'm sure there will still be plenty of remote places to explore, but it won't be anything like the West Africa adventure I've enjoyed so much.

That realization makes me a little sad, and I'm not ready for the massive adventures to end yet. I want one last adventure into tiny villages with nasty roads, and I want to explore the DRC at least a little, instead of just racing across as fast as possible. Whatever comes my way, I'm going for it.

Traveling with Dani and Didi for the last couple of months has been a pleasure, and I've really come to appreciate their willingness for adventure, their company and their cool-headedness. We very much enjoy each other's company and we make a great team - always using our heads rather than the proverbial bull at a gate. Like my Rubicon, their beefy 4x4 Sportsmobile van is equipped with a winch and front and rear lockers. Given what we're certain lies ahead, their massive 37 inch mud-terrain tires look very appealing.

Knowing we're driving into the worst conditions we've ever encountered, Didi and I think it wise to put the lighter Jeep in front. If I get into trouble he can probably winch me backwards to safety. If the tables were turned, however, we both fear the Jeep would have no chance winching the heavy Sportsmobile. The plan certainly makes sense when we say it out loud, and I can't help wondering if it will actually work.

We backtrack over the mountains to Dolice where we camp at 'Mess Gaps', a restaurant run by a quirky Frenchman who has lived in the Congo for forty years. Now well into his eighties,

Gaps has lived a wild life of adventure all over the Congo, and tells stories that make my jaw drop. He has an incredible collection of masks, voodoo dolls and other artifacts, and explains locals believe very strongly in voodoo and witchcraft, and that putting a curse on one's enemies is serious business in these parts. Feeling particularly brave and on Gaps' advice I order a large bush rat for dinner. It's much bigger than any rat I've seen and comes cooked on a plate, completely whole - head, teeth, tail and all. I struggle to eat the dry brown flesh, and I force myself to be polite. It tastes like dirt and is the most gamey meat I've ever eaten. It's utterly disgusting, and I decide on the spot to stop eating exotic creatures.

Overnight the skies let loose with another impressive thunder-storm and hours of torrential downpour leaving me to wonder about the roads ahead.

I'm relived to have friends with me for the biggest challenge of my life.

Day One

In the morning we stock up with our usual supplies, fully expecting to be alone for up to a week. At the only functioning station we fill will every last drop of gas and diesel we can possibly carry, thankful that Dolice is not currently suffering shortages. Leaving town to the south we make good time on what are at first good gravel roads. Evidently this road is traveled frequently, and doesn't present any problem for our well-prepared vehicles. Once or twice in the deepest river crossings water laps at the hood of the Jeep making me squirm. As long as I keep moving, no water comes in the door seals. River crossings are no time to get stuck so I use both differential locks and don't hang around.

We tick off the miles at our usual slow and steady pace while the intense heat and humidity beat down relentlessly. Even after applying sunscreen four times and wearing a hat for the entire day, I still get sun burnt and I'm drenched in sweat. Our route parallels the border of Cabinda, and we're amused to see a fork in the road and even a border crossing we didn't know existed. We stop on the side of the track to eat bread and avocado for lunch, and we're entertained by a group of young boys who are clearly fascinated, but are too timid to approach.

Late in the afternoon we roll into the dirt street town of Londela-Kays, stopping at the Police station on the near side of town. Quickly a group of smiling kids assemble, all eager to see photos of themselves on our camera screens. After a short wait a Policeman writes our details in a very familiar looking ledger and a Customs man arrives on a scooter to cancel the paperwork for our vehicles.

Town is just a few hundred yards long and we easily locate Immigration on the far side where we wait for an exit stamp from the friendly chief. The sun slowly inches closer to the horizon, and when all the paperwork has been shuffled and we have legally exited the country we step outside to catch a brilliant sunset. The chief immediately gives us permission to camp right there in the Police compound on the edge of town.

For the second time in my life I setup camp in no-mans-land, legally in no country.

Day Two

Mercifully the heat and humidity drop overnight, allowing me to sleep soundly less than fifteen yards from a Policeman. In the morning we share a huge pot of sugary tea before bidding farewell to our new friends who are clearly proud to have helped in our journey. Within fifty yards the road deteriorates until it's nothing more than a thin muddy track sliced through the jungle.

We climb up and onto a slippery mountain ridge and see mud huts dotted throughout the landscape. A local man is eager to point the way and his jerky hand gestures clearly show very steep uphill. I'm not disappointed when I round the hairpin turn to find an off-camber climb around a corner on extremely slick clay. In low range first gear with both differential locks neither vehicle has any problem, though I wonder about our chances with more recent rain. I'm close to the traction limit of my tires on the slick clay, and I'm happy to see trees big enough to winch off.

A few hundred yards later as the dense jungle completely closes in on both sides a stricken Land Cruiser pickup entirely blocks the track. The driver explains the Cruiser runs fine, but it doesn't have a starter motor and he stalled on the incline. If we can just get him running, he'll be fine to continue on his own. We barely manage to push the overloaded Cruiser forward a few yards so I can squeeze the Jeep past and hitch to the Cruiser with my recovery strap.

My thumbs up is answered with two honks, so I gently ease off the clutch. The slack goes out of the tow rope and I barely notice the additional dead weight the Jeep is hauling, low range first gear in the Rubicon is just that low. Slowly but surely I climb with the Toyota and it's passengers and cargo looming large in my mirrors. I can't help but smile as we crawl across the dotted line on the GPS showing the International Border between the two Congos.

A Jeep Wrangler is towing a stricken Toyota Land Cruiser from one Congo to the next. I'm sure the hundreds of people who told me to sell the Jeep and buy a Toyota didn't see that coming.

At the crest of the hill we glide downhill for a second before the driver pops the clutch and his engine rumbles to life. We disconnect the vehicles before bidding farewell and watching the young men tear ahead into the dense jungle. I feel certain we'll see them again, though we never do. I have absolutely no idea where they go, but somehow they manage to disappear. With butterflies in my stomach we dive deeper into the no-mans-land. I've been dreaming of the DRC for so many years I'm excited and nervous to be all-in. We don't have a double entry visa for the previous Congo, so there is literally no possibility of turning back.

For a few miles I guess the way through grass taller than the Jeep, constantly on the lookout for invisible logs and holes. Eventually we stumble onto what could be called be a road and slowly creep through muddy gullies and up slick inclines, trying to pick whichever track leads in a southerly direction. In one such gully I crawl gingerly up a steep and slick incline. With it's narrow track and no wheel spin, the Jeep is able to just barely skirt a major washout in the centre of the road. Didi, however, is not so lucky.

The combination of wider track and increased weight proves his undoing, and the rear of the big van slides sideways into the washout. Watching in my mirror at first I'm horrified and then relieved when the Sportsmobile wedges into the washout on a 45 degree angle rather than flopping right over.

After calming our nerves and a quick team meeting we make a plan and get to work. Using my winch we secure the Jeep to a small tree - the only one in sight - and Didi secures his winch to the rear of the Jeep. We use all of our combined six traction mats in an attempt to bridge the washout and create a level surface the Sportsmobile will have to climb through. We're soon pouring sweat in the scorching sun, and each of us is thankful for the endless supply of cold water we have stockpiled in our fridges. A small crowd of locals begins to materialize from dense jungle, clearly enjoying the show while smiling and waving happily.

When we're all set I take a moment to evaluate our situation. Legally, we're in no country. We're way off the map and GPS, somewhere in the no-mans-land between the two Congos. I'm stamping on the brake pedal so hard my leg is cramping, and the Jeep cooling fan has not turned off once, the engine is so hot just at idle. Behind and below, the 12,000lbs Sportsmobile begins winching off the back of the Jeep causing it to buck and squirm under me. I watch anxiously in the mirror as a front tire rises dangerously high into the air, and I worry the Jeep will be pulled backwards causing who-knows-what damage.

Slowly the big van inches forward while Didi keeps a very close eye on progress. Unbeknownst to him the far rear tire is extremely close to sliding back into the washout, dangerously close to disaster. One very observant local man very loudly and clearly shouts "Stop," to our great thanks.

When the van is finally free and we're putting away equipment the helpful man comes forward to introduce himself. We thank him repeatedly for his timely intervention, to which he simply replies *On Ensemble* - We Are Together.

I knew the DRC was going to be an immense challenge, but this is ridiculous. We're not even there yet! Deep down I wonder if we've bitten off more than we can chew. With no choice we must continue forward.

Φ   Φ   Φ

We tread gingerly through more deep mud pits, washouts and ruts before arriving at a sizable mud-hut village. At the edge of town we stop at a large log laying across the road, apparently the Immigration post. Soon a crowd of smiling children and adults gather, and after looking around I sense the DRC is different than anything I've experienced in Africa. Children and adults alike openly display child-like glee, barely able to contain themselves. Their openness and welcoming manner radiates from them as a kind of unspoilt innocence, and they are clearly fascinated by us and our vehicles.

Even the village looks and feels different - the main street is wide and airy, and the mud buildings are well maintained and spotlessly clean. Most strikingly of all, and for the first time in Africa, I can not see a single piece of trash.

A smiling man steps forward to declare himself the Immigration representative, proud to welcome us to his country. We talk next to the Jeep in the shade of a large tree. The slender man is nervous and shy, and I sense he's concerned about the long and detailed Immigration forms he hands each of us. After he spends a painfully long time explaining how and where I should complete my form, and after seeing his confusion and watching him point to the wrong line on multiple occasions, I realize this man can not read or write. Though he is the official and it's clear he needs the forms to be completed correctly, it becomes very clear he can not do so himself. I now completely understand his concern and repeatedly assure him we're following his instructions to the letter.

After many false starts and three identical and time consuming explanations he's finally satisfied and grants permission for us to enter the country with a firm handshake. Although he proudly carries a small stamp, he's unwilling to mark our passports, explaining we'll be given entry stamps at a later checkpoint.

Very concerned about bribery in the DRC, we have no intention of entering without the correct stamps. The always-prepared Germans produce an ink pad, and with the help of the gathered crowd we're able to sway the opinion of the official. I've learned I only need to convince a couple of bystanders of my point of view before they enlist the gathered crowd, and finally the person in charge. All I have to do is stand back and nod agreement until the official can't hold off any longer. There is no Customs here, so we'll just have to deal with vehicle paperwork at an unknown future location.

Multiple men from the village assure us there is an actual road in the direction we're headed, though they all disagree on the distance. With little choice we continue on the small track, completely ignoring the GPS. Five minutes later and still hotly pursued by a crowd of playful children we stop to write today's date across the fresh stamp. It's not every day you get to write in your own passport.

After a simple lunch crouching in the shade we continue south through the jungle on the severely overgrown motorbike track. Mile after mile both vehicles tear and scrape through the tangle on both sides, and when I snag a guard flare on an unseen tree stump it tears in half, almost completely coming off. I ask locals on foot if this is the correct way, and a young boy of fifteen climbs aboard to ride into the bigger town. He assures me this is an actual road used by vehicles and we will get through. I want to trust him, though I've never seen a road anywhere on Earth as small as this.

When we finally reach the east-west road children again sur-round the vehicles, smiling, cheering and jumping on the spot as if they might burst with joy at any moment. My passenger spots his sisters in the crowd who are clearly impressed he's riding in a 4x4 instead of walking today. I can't help noticing the town is again spotless, without a single piece of trash in sight. I realize this is because the people here can't buy any-thing that would make trash. There is no store, there are no cokes or plastic bags for sale, and I doubt anyone has money for them anyway. For the first time in my life I'm so remote there is simply no possibility for trash.

It's clear this east-west road has more traffic, and it soon be-comes clear more traffic means deeper ruts and longer, churned up mud pits. The ruts are deeper and wider than the track of the Jeep, leading me to suspect only the largest 4x4 trucks pass this way. Progress is slow as we bump along the severely washed-out track through deep mud and the occasional river crossing that laps at the hood of the Jeep. The sun beats down relentlessly long into the afternoon and I realize after a full fourteen hour day we haven't seen a single vehicle in the DRC.

Soon before dusk we turn onto a spur track and make camp in a small clearing a few hundreds in. A crowd of curious onlookers soon materializes from the jungle to begin a fierce staring ritual. The thirty-odd children and adults stand a few yards away and watch our every move with intense curiosity. They giggle and squirm with excitement when I answer their questions and ask questions in return, though it's clear I will never satisfy their curiosity in us and our vehicles. Not a single person takes their eyes off us until it's pitch black more than an hour later.

After a stunning sunset of boiling clouds it's still staggeringly hot and humid when I climb into bed and search for sleep, my first night officially in the DRC. I'm utterly exhausted after the biggest and most difficult day on expedition in my life, and I barely manage a broad grin before exhaustion penetrates to my bones and wins over.

Day Three

We're on the move soon after sunrise, eager to beat the heat of the day and before our curious neighbours can return. The major east-west road picks up where it left off - sometimes a decent gravel road, sometimes a series of deep washouts to be carefully navigated, and sometimes a mud pit hundreds of yards long. Thankfully none of the water crossings prove too deep and we're able to continue our slow and steady march forward.

We pass through more tiny villages with eagerly waiving kids and spotlessly clean huts and dirt paths. My GPS shows a village on a junction in the road and I assume it will be larger, and might even have a store where I can buy bread. Though marked as 'bigger' on my GPS, the village is nothing more than ten or fifteen mud huts on either side of the muddy road. Clearly, there is no store here.

The sun beats down and the mud and potholes on the track are endless, so we move forward at the only speed the road will permit - crawling. Late in the afternoon I'm encouraged to see a truck in the ditch which I take to mean the road from here is passable, and bridges will support our weight. Didi correctly points out the truck is abandoned, and we have no idea how long it's been there.

Enormous storm clouds have been building in the near distance since midday, and the first huge spots of rain splatter on the windscreen just as we come upon a battered old pickup stuck in the mud blocking our path forward. Evidently about twenty people were riding in the back, and now they all mill around, eager to get underway. I step out of the Jeep into the mud and immediately everyone stares at me. They can't believe I've chosen to walk in the mud, and insist I should get back in my Jeep. I assure them repeatedly it's fine, and soon I sense they accept me as one of them. Because I'm out of the Jeep and helping with the stuck vehicle they see I'm just another person battling the harsh conditions. Without realizing it, I've just discovered an extremely effective way of breaking down any gap between myself and locals.

I walk through the knee-deep muck to the driver who explains the pickup runs, though again it doesn't have a starter and he stalled in the thick mud. We form a plan and the driver almost shakes my arm off with his enthusiasm and thanks. We'll winch the pickup backwards and squeeze past before pulling it through the mud and starting it on the dry road beyond.

Eager men dive into the mud to search for a suitable point to attach Didi's winch, completely unfazed about getting covered head to toe in mud. The gathered crowd is clearly entertained with our antics, and while we work entire families traveling on small motorbikes squeeze by, their riders showing expert skill in the slick mud.

When the pickup is running on dry ground each and every person is overflowing with thanks, and all repeat the mantra *On Ensemble* - We are Together. I'm surprised and happy they use this informal conjugation in French while speaking to us. This way of speaking is usually reserved for friends and family, and not the formal address I've become used to. Throughout

Africa people often call me 'sir' and use the same respectful language they would if speaking to the President. It's clear the people here don't see me as anything special or different from themselves, and I really like it a lot. We really are all in this together. With more than twenty people in the back of the pickup they dive full speed into the next mud pit and I can't help wondering when we'll run into them again.

Afternoon has turned to early evening, so two miles later we pull off behind a couple of large brick buildings hoping to make camp before the light fades completely. The buildings have a familiar feeling I can't quite place, though somehow it doesn't seem important with the thunderstorm bearing down. The minute I finish cooking dinner the skies let loose with a downpour of monumental proportions and I bail inside the Jeep and soon feel comfortable and relaxed. I'm extremely happy with my Jeep-house and the modest interior living space it affords. Escaping the weather at times like this helps to maintain a small measure of sanity, and I move around inside eating dinner and reading a book, perfectly dry and mosquito free.

I wake multiple times in the hot and sticky night to the sound of thunder and heavy rain pounding the fibreglass roof, and I wonder how our friends in the pickup are making out.

Day Four

In the morning I finally understand the buildings we're camping behind when children in school uniform arrive. Again they gather around to stare in silent fascination as I make coffee and pack up camp. Soon a man I take to be the teacher wonders over and is very proud to welcome us before assuring me repeatedly it really is no problem that we camped in the school yard. Everyone waives excitedly as we pull away, and I think the children are disappointed we're not sticking around to provide entertainment for the day.

The small town of Lwozi is perched on the high banks of the Congo River, famous in overlanding circles for having one of the only functional ferries across the river. I'm still in disbelief as I bounce along the potholed and muddy main street, hardly able to accept I'm really crossing the mighty DRC. We find our way to Customs where paperwork for the vehicles is easily completed by a friendly young man in just ten minutes. Back on the street we're searching for bread and vegetables when a very large man wearing an immaculate Military uniform strides over and says in no uncertain terms we must go with him.

I have no doubt he's not making a request, but rather giving an order. He's at least 6'5", barrel chested and speaks in such a way I'm certain his orders are followed like gospel. With his appearance, stern manner and deep scowl, he embodies the B-Grade movie role of 'Nasty African Warlord'.
He does not smile.

Across town we're forced to wait while the big man very obviously yells at his off-sider and assistant before storming around the Immigration building, making his huge presence felt. Something feels off to me, and I wander if it's all just a show for our benefit. My French has improved leaps and bounds so I understand everything he says. I'm careful not to let on and we all pretend to speak only English until we learn his intentions. When finally calm, he begins with a meticulous examination of every single page of our passports. Finally he questions Dani for her personal details before writing them painfully slowly onto a very familiar Immigration form.

When he finishes questioning Dani he rocks back in his chair with a triumphant grin. Clutching her passport and the newly completed form, he says an entrance stamp will cost $10 each. Thinking he has the upper hand, he leans back further and grins wider. In English Dani very politely explains we already have entrance stamps, and therefore do not require his services today. A flicker of shock passes over his face and I see him hesitate, unsure how to proceed.

To demonstrate we don't need him, Didi reaches across the table and takes his passport back, making ready to leave. Calmly, and without raising his voice, the big man demands the passport be returned before lecturing us that all passports are under his control. We will get them back only if and when he says so, and not a minute sooner. West Africa runs on authority and respect, and we have clearly not satisfied his need today.

When all three Immigration forms are complete, the big man again demands we pay $10 each. Now very accustomed to this game, all three of us smile and sit back in our chairs without saying a word to each other or our friend. We make it abundantly clear we have all the time in the world, and we're perfectly happy to spend it crowded in his small office. After just a few minutes and with no choice the big man hands back our passports before dismissing us with a wave of his hand. He's clearly not happy, but as we suspected he won't take it any further.

I'm eager to poke around Lwozi, and it's always nice to explore on foot and wander street markets looking for supplies. The local money changer is easy to spot and we strike up a conversation as I change $20USD into Congolese Francs. I need some to buy supplies, and I also want to add a note to my growing collection of African money. When I ask where I can buy bread he tries to explain but says it's too complicated and insists I should just follow him. He drops a huge stack of cash on the table before walking into the market. He walks a full block away from what must be $10,000 USD in cash lying in the open and is clearly not concerned in the least. When he sees my shock he explains with a grin that theft is simply unheard of here. Everyone knows everyone, and they're all in this life together. If someone were hungry or needed help, they would just have to ask and it would be given. This is extremely refreshing and at odds with everything I've been told about the DRC and how dangerous and lawless it is. It's fantastic to know that even in the harshest of African conditions treating each other well is still a priority.

We buy lunch in a road-side restaurant and laugh when we realize it's just a tin of canned soup poured over pasta, a first for me. Outside I chat to men furiously betting on a fast-paced card game. They're as curious and interested in us as we are them and it's exciting to spend even a little time in a town getting a feel for the DRC.

A stone's throw from town the mighty Congo River is staggeringly big and looks more like a lake than just a river. From a distance it appears peaceful and clean, though up close it has a strong current and smells like a sewer. Men wash motorbikes on the muddy banks while fishermen repeatedly pull up nets with nothing but plastic as reward for their efforts. It's difficult to believe I've driven my Jeep all the way to the mighty Congo River, and I try to take it all in as we sit in the shade with a handful of locals waiting for the ferry to return.

From the second the ferry lands on the muddy shore a furious scramble begins with people, motorbikes, food sacks, chicken cages and even a dog moving off and then onto the ferry. The massive Sportsmobile is first and I'm relieved to drive up the steep loading ramp to find just enough length for the Jeep. Nobody asks or seems to care about our combined weight, so I just go with the flow and hope for the best.

The instant the Jeep is on board the ferry lurches into gear causing last-minute foot passengers and motorbikes to scramble aboard however they can. On close inspection I see the ferry is nothing more than two pontoons welded together with scrap steel and a big diesel engine belching clouds of thick smoke. A talkative guy writes me an official-looking receipt for the $14 ticket for the Jeep and I, and I'm impressed there isn't a hint of bribery or price inflation.

The big diesel engine screams loudly, and soon I'm chatting to the foot passengers, ferry crew, and even the captain who is proud I want to climb into the bridge to chat with him. Huge storm clouds bubble on the horizon, and I see the odd bolt of lightning hit land. The wind in our faces swings from stiflingly hot to pleasantly cool, a sure sign of the storm we're quickly approaching.

Twenty minutes later the smiling ferry crew deposit us in a dilapidated shanty-town on the southern banks of The Congo River. Hoards of children run to the road and thrust out their hands, screaming in English at the top of their lungs - 'GIVE ME MONEY!' - and are clearly furious when we do not. As always in Africa, it is blatantly clear where the influence of foreigners has left it's mark.

I take a long look around and savour my position on the globe. I'm not out of the jungle yet, though it feels great to know nothing major stands between myself and the southern tip of the continent. As the small town fades in my mirror we're once again crawling forward on a severely pot-holed and muddy track. We know with certainty we've left town on the right track because it's the only one.

After many more hours negotiating endless mud pits we find a tiny spur road to make camp on a stunning high bluff with commanding views and a light refreshing breeze. Soon a very withered old man comes by to shake our hands, and is delighted to explain the women with him are his wife and daughters. All carry huge bundles of firewood they've collected and they all smile from ear to ear, though the women are extremely shy and scared to actually approach. I can't help notice the very stooped old man has absolutely no teeth, though it doesn't seem to curb his enthusiasm in the least. Content just to say hello they wander off along the dirt track, all barefoot. As the light fades we enjoy yet another stunning display of thunder and lightning that slides by to the east. Thankfully the sheets of rain remain on the distant horizon.

Day Five

Mist blankets the rolling green hills at sunrise, and I thoroughly enjoy walking in the cool mountain air. I feel fantastic to be walking and not pouring sweat for the first time in the DRC. The day plays out much like the others - scorching heat and humidity, tiny villages with mud huts, friendly waving people and virtually endless mud pits to negotiate.

Where the mud is most severe deep trenches have been dug with walls well above the roof of the Jeep. The tire ruts are so deep the entire Jeep underbelly and two diffs scrape along the bottom, though with the lockers at least a couple of wheels are able to maintain traction and we keep scrambling forward.

Vehicles are still few and far between, and the ones we do encounter are literally falling apart and severely overloaded with food sacks and people hanging on anywhere they can. Around midday we find a heavily-laden transport truck hopelessly stuck on the uphill side of a mud hole. We're just able to squeeze past before we stop to offer assistance. The driver explains he stalled on the steep uphill leaving the mud pit, and the truck won't fire back up. It's so heavy and the mud hole so steep the ten men travelling on it have not been able to budge it. They've simply been lying in the shade for three days in the hope help would arrive.

Didi and I both suspect the truck is too heavy, though we spool out the winch cable and try anyway. Immediately the men rush from the shade to help and offer encouragement, obviously excited at the prospect of rescue. As Didi loads up his big winch we hear all kinds of nasty noises before the truck has even moved. Unfortunately we're out-gunned on this one and I feel terrible explaining to the driver and assembled men we can't help.

Each and every man takes the time to shake hands individually and convey their thanks. It's clear how much they appreciate the effort, and I feel certain they would have helped if the tables were turned. Although they return to the shade looking dejected, each man was sincere with his thanks for our efforts - *On Ensemble*.

On and on we crawl through the endless mud, slowly putting down the miles. I've been traveling with Dani and Didi for so long we're able to communicate without words and can sense feelings with just a glance. Each day around midday we do our best to shelter in the shade cast by our vehicles while eating our meagre supplies.

Almost imperceptibly the road gradually grows in size and traffic. Finally, after days on the most horrendous roads I ever imagined, we arrive at a major paved highway. Just for the novelty I set cruise control at 55 mp/h, and I'm happy to see the computer reported distance to empty actually go up, even after covering forty miles. To complete my disorientation, a Porsche with DRC plates whips by at high speed.

We planned to stay a night in the final town in the DRC, though as we enter Songololo I quickly see we need to change our plan. Trash covers every possible surface and an overpowering stench hangs in the air and sticks to my skin. Grubby and desolate people mill about in the trash and broken-down vehicles litter the roadside. This is clearly not the kind of place we want to spend a night. The DRC has suddenly changed from stunning wilderness with smiling faces to a kind of industrial wasteland, and I'd much rather not linger after dark.

I pull into a clean and functional gas station where the friendly guys are happy to give me the rate of the day for my cash US dollars. Gas is much cheaper in Angola, though I want to be absolutely certain I'll make it.

Leaving town towards the border we're soon stopped at one of the DRC's infamous 'Traffic Control' checkpoints. A large boom gate blocks the road, and an armed Military man lounges in the shade watching us. I intentionally block the road with the Jeep, and Didi wedges me in to create our own impassable barrier. We both kill our engines and step out, bracing ourselves for what we know is coming.

We're quickly told me must buy a transit ticket to use this road, and we're directed to a price sheet posted on the wall. Regular cars pay a few dollars, transport trucks pay ten, and foreign vehicles must pay fifty US dollars. There is no explanation for why, and it's clear everyone standing around is happy they're about to part us from our money. Sooner or later we knew this would happen in the DRC, and I laugh at myself for thinking we were going to make it out unscathed.

We're exhausted, and we've had enough of this price gouging crap. Having practiced different approaches in many different situations, Didi takes the lead on this one. He grabs the most senior man by the arm and leads him to our vehicles. Didi explains our international registration includes these kinds of fees and that's why we pay so much. Our government has an agreement with the government of DRC and they will pay the appropriate fee directly. After all, he says, that's how we're allowed to drive here in the first place. It's clear the senior man doesn't want to hear it, though we give him no choice. We repeat this story over and over to the point it's nauseating, and eventually we see it's having an impact.

Slowly but surely we chip away at the gathered crowd, and eventually even the senior man sees our point of view. Finally he completely agrees with us, and instructs everyone we don't need a ticket, and they should let us pass. Reluctantly the Military man raises the boom gate, and we're free to go. I don't know if he actually believes it or just wants to get rid of us, but I'll take it. After a nod to each other and a very quick round of thanks we quickly move on before anyone can change their mind.

A few miles later we hit another checkpoint, and I know immediately it's a bad scene. The men are armed and wear uniforms, though their casual attitude and the look in their eyes tells me this is not official business. These men are clearly off-duty and are simply trying to get whatever they can from anyone that will give it. Along with a bunch of onlookers for moral support they demand I give them this or that from inside the Jeep.

Normally I'm not worried about my safety or that of the Jeep, though I've been warned multiple times the DRC can be an entirely different animal. I need to tread carefully here, these men are clearly not following any rules. Feeling intimidated I manage to remain polite and firm, and repeat time and again I simply have nothing to give. I've run out of food and water and I have none for myself, I explain. Hearing this one very young and heavily armed man leans in my window and snatches for things on the dashboard. This is a first for me, and I don't feel comfortable, so I improvise my response. I open my door to force him back before raising my window and jumping out while locking the driver's door.

Now I'm outside and the doors are locked, the men see they can't get anything. I rest in the shade and try to be as uninteresting as possible and soon they all ignore me and forget there is anything inside the Jeep they might want. Happily Didi's window is much higher off the ground so the men can't reach in. He has left the enormous diesel engine rumbling which makes conversation impossible and drowns out the men's pleas for gifts.

When the men have completely lost interest they wander back to their shady spot, apparently giving up. I jump in the Jeep and we quickly drive on without paying or giving anything.

Driving into the border town of Luvo I'm sure I've wandered onto the set of Mad Max - the only thing they got wrong in those movies is the trash. It's literally knee deep and covers every surface while revolting muddy puddles line the street creating an overpowering stench. Thousands of people walk back and forth across the border, buying and selling whatever they can and pulling it in overloaded hand carts. Loud motorbike taxis tear up and down, and hundreds of wooden shacks line the narrow road selling the stuff that has apparently just crossed the border. The flow of people and goods is immense and hard to comprehend. I soon learn it's trivial to buy the kinds of consumer goods in Angola I've never seen in West and Central West Africa which fuels the trade here. I see heavily loaded carts with everything from soda and food to flat screen TVs, fridges, stoves and microwaves.

Still in the DRC we stop to get our Customs paperwork cancelled by men sitting in the shade who enter our details in a huge hand-written ledger. After changing money and receiving a huge stack of Angolan bills we drive forward to a fenced Immigration compound, where I'm happy to park inside. We wait ten minutes in the scorching heat while the friendly officers fight with their computer to swipe us out of the DRC.

I'm stunned, and find it difficult to understand what I'm seeing. The last time my passport was swiped in Africa was entering Mauritania, fourteen countries and twenty thousand miles ago. Adding to my disorientation I watch a man casually walk across the parking lot carrying a full-size fridge on his head. He balances it with one hand, and doesn't appear to be having any major difficulty. The whole scene doesn't even look real, and I have to ask Dani if the heat is causing me to hallucinate.

Eventually we're clear to leave the DRC and drive through enormous steel gates and across a one-lane bridge over a small river, officially the International Border. We're immediately stopped at a checkpoint less than ten yards from the bridge, the first of many in Angola. There's a lot of confusion about what to do with us, so we settle in to wait. Eventually an officer asks to look inside our vehicles before waiving us forward. Less than fifty yards further is the next checkpoint where exactly the same thing happens.

Again there's a long wait and confusion until we can move forward another fifty yards to yet another checkpoint. It's now late in the afternoon, and exhaustion takes over. Trying to explain ourselves to the officials it becomes clear how difficult life is going to be speaking Portuguese instead of French which I've come to rely heavily on. All I can do is drink cold water and try my best to communicate in a Spanish / French / English mix.

Finally we move forward through even bigger steel gates and park in front of Angolan Immigration and Customs. Now I realize everything up until now has just been a preamble. When I step out of the Jeep I notice an immense change - there is no trash, concrete buildings are large, solid and well maintained and a group of men play basketball nearby on the first court I've ever seen in Africa. I sense I've entered an entirely different world.

Our passports are quickly stamped, though there's a problem at Customs. I must pay for my Temporary Import Permit at the nearby bank, which has just closed for the day.

In my exhaustion it takes a full two minutes to understand the ramifications. We're stuck here for the night.

For only the second time in my life - and the second time this week - I setup camp at an International Border.

Malaria Round Two

Angola
June 2017

F IRST thing in the morning I pay $32 at the bank before I'm issued a two month Temp Import Permit at Customs. I've been told repeatedly Angola is simply stunning, so in anticipation of extending my stay I've made the Jeep legal for two months. I can always leave before then if I want.

Away from the border Angola looks and feels similar while also different to previous countries. There is modern development, but there are also mud huts and road side vendors selling vegetables and cheap Chinese plastic stuff. This close to the border many people speak French which makes stocking up on groceries straightforward. Ready to fill up with extremely cheap gas and diesel we wait in a long line at the only station we can find. I don't understand the hold up until a French-speaking man is kind enough to explain. The underground tanks are full, but a city wide power outage means it can't be pumped up and out. We wait two hours without moving an inch, and after carefully checking maps we give up and leave town without getting a drop. My splash and go in the DRC means I have enough to reach the next town, and we can only cross our fingers there will be gas and power there.

Angola's brutal civil war raged almost non-stop for twenty-seven years, and it's not long before we see destroyed bridges and buildings riddled with bullet holes. We're extremely careful not to drive truly off road, and we must never walk through long grass. There are still millions of buried landmines in

Angola and more than two people every single day are still injured or killed by them. Gravel roads are apparently safe enough, but we must always follow tire tracks and not venture off into the unexplored. If the tire tracks stop, so must we.

Angola has been at peace since 2004, and the efforts to rebuild and modernize are clear to see. Money is being spent on much-needed infrastructure repairs and upgrades, though progress has slowed in recent years due to the low price of oil, Angola's main source of income.

I'm aware of all this, but still get a huge shock driving into the capital of Luanda. In the city center I see development like never before on this continent. I drive along a wide and beautiful boulevard with the glistening ocean on one side and glass-fronted sky scrapers on the other. The picture is complete with palm trees, perfectly manicured grass and wide walking paths. The city center is extremely clean and modern, and I feel disoriented and unable to grasp where I am. Suddenly the view outside the Jeep looks more like Miami than the Africa I know.

I've been told the manager of the Luanda Yacht Club loves to host overlanders, and he welcomes us warmly on our arrival around the bay. We're invited to camp directly on the water's edge with million dollar views past anchored yachts to the city scape beyond. Free camping with a shower and wifi means the manager risks having us as permanent guests.

We spend an entire day taking in the National Museum of Military History perched high on a hill overlooking the city. The museum is extremely comprehensive and explains every step of the civil war from the factors that led up to it to the lasting impact on modern day Angola and the national psyche. It's heart wrenching to see the devastation caused by almost thirty years of civil war, and it's clear nobody wants a repeat. Famously it was a proxy war between the US and Russia, with each country arming their favored side - Democracy versus Communism. All the Military hardware was either American or

Russian, and it's clear there was never a shortage of equipment or bullets, only young Angolan soldiers to man them.

Local overlanders who spot our vehicles stop to chat in the Yacht Club and share their secret spots and highlights around the country. So far many locals understand my Spanish, though I can't understand a word of reply. I get a crash course in Portuguese and after adjusting my accent and pronunciation I learn there are hundreds of words I can use directly from Spanish. Chatting with regular people on the street is going to make Angola a lot more enjoyable.

Tearing ourselves away from the paradise at the Yacht Club we explore far and wide. I'm staggered to find Kalandula Falls, a monster waterfall nearly as impressive as Niagara Falls. There are no tourists, no fences, no signs and certainly no entrance fee. I'm able to stand on the very edge with water surging past me and over the falls. Nearby at the stunning *Piedras Negras* (Black Rocks) the story is repeated. Both sights would undoubtedly be packed with tourists if they were anywhere else in the world but here in Angola we have them all to ourselves. Each night we find a secluded place to wild camp, immensely enjoying the thunderstorms that constantly boil on the horizon after sunset. On the rare occasion a local wanders into camp they happily give permission to stay, and are content to wander home after a round of handshakes.

In the stunning and harsh Namib Desert one morning a local man and his teenage daughter wander into our campsite. They're both barefoot, wear traditional colorful clothes and apparently herd cattle in this region. We don't share a common language but manage to communicate regardless. He would love a cup of coffee, but after tasting my best brew he spits it out with a frown. I've forgotten the all important heaping spoonfuls of sugar and soon he's nodding and smiling happily as we crouch together on the ground. The young daughter is very shy, though her father is clearly bursting with pride and tries his best to show her off. After ten minutes we shake hands before they walk into the barren desert. I can't help wondering if they know humans have walked on the moon or even about the Internet.

I think they probably don't know, and I'm sure they don't care.

Φ   Φ   Φ

Driving down out of the mountains one morning I begin to feel strange. I feel tired and washed out, even though I slept well, and just finished my usual breakfast of two egg, lettuce and tomato sandwiches. I feel shaky like I drank too much coffee, or haven't eaten for days. Half an hour later the feeling deepens, and soon I also have a headache and feel vague. My usually dependable body is off balance, and I don't like it. Dani and Didi are happy to call it a short day, so we find a small clearing in the trees to make camp. I immediately lie down in the shade to do nothing, and two hours later my symptoms feel very familiar. I try to deny reality, but that doesn't help. I'm weak, shaking slightly and feel disconnected from my body, like I'm an outside observer.

"I think I have malaria again," I announce to Dani and Didi. I don't want to believe it, but the feeling is just too familiar to deny.

I gobble down the 'cure' pill from my fridge, hoping it will work miracles again. As my symptoms worsen everything feels even more familiar, and I watch from outside my own body as I begin to say loopy and morbid things. I tell Dani she can have the Jeep if I die, and maybe that would be best anyway. I'm fully aware how inappropriate this is, but I can't stop myself. The hot afternoon drags on and on, and all I can do is lie in a puddle of sweat in the shade before putting myself to bed early without eating. I desperately hope I can sleep it off.

Soon my head is splitting open with the worst headache of my life and I can't bare to have it touch even the pillow which has transformed into solid rock. For hour after hour I kneel instead of lying, resting my weight on my elbows and forearms in an attempt to keep my head from touching anything at all. I'm pouring sweat and feel utterly horrible. My joints ache, my fingers tingle and my headache is so excruciating I can't imagine I'll ever function again.

I finally drift off to a restless sleep before waking what must be many hours later. I'm elated when I realize I've been asleep, and relief washes over me to have made it through the night. When I see it's only 9:45pm I'm utterly devastated. The pain in my head does not let up, and I toss and turn all night, never sleeping more than fifteen minutes at a time. At 2am I take another 'cure' pill, hoping beyond hope it will rescue me from the agony.

I lie awake through the night, pouring sweat and feeling desperately sorry for myself. I have no choice but to persevere through what turns into the longest night of my life.

Φ   Φ   Φ

In the morning, my situation has not improved.
In fact, it's much worse.

At 10am I sit in the full sun wearing my thick jacket from Canada while shivering uncontrollably. My teeth chatter and small convulsions rock my body. I'm pouring sweat and freezing cold at the same time. A small part of my thinking brain begins to feel genuinely scared for my life.

Knowing we were diving into the deepest jungles of West Africa we planned for this possibility months ago in Cameroon. The more potent version of the 'cure' medicine is an injectable, and we each bought a course along with many disposable syringes. This is the medicine I would be given if I could get to a clinic, and I'm relieved we planned for this outcome.

I feel so weak I'm not sure I can inject myself, so I ask my friends for help, never more thankful not to be alone. I barely manage a smile at the hilarity of getting a needle in my backside from a large German mechanic on the side of the road in Angola. As I crumple to the ground with exhaustion I wonder which of my life decisions led to this outcome.

Φ   Φ   Φ

For two more days and nights the pain does not let up. During the day I lie hopelessly in a puddle of sweat before tossing and turning for hour after hour at night hoping the pain in my head will subside enough to let me sleep. Each morning and night Didi injects more medicine, and I continue to take the pill form of the drug. My joints ache, my fingers tingle and I'm so weak I can barely walk, talk, eat or drink. I must be scaring Dani and Didi half to death, and I try to reassure them as best I can.

I watch all of this from outside my own body, and I begin to ponder my own mortality. I never actually think I might die, though it does occur to me a few times.

To add insult to injury, another medical problem surfaces at the same time. Large red welts appear on my arms and legs, and I have no idea why. The welts look horrible, like some kind of infection or almost burn, and I begin to wonder if I have something like leprosy from a cave full of bats we visited. At first there are only a few, though they soon multiply until I have about eight of them, mostly on my forearms and thighs. Thankfully they don't hurt or itch at all, so I try my best to ignore them while struggling through malaria.

As the days slowly pass I begin to see light at the end of the malaria tunnel. One morning I even manage to eat a small breakfast, and realizing we've been stuck in the same place for days I make the call to move on. I concentrate extra hard on driving which is a good distraction from the endless headache. Thankfully we find a great place to camp near the town of

Benguela on the beach next to a restaurant, and the helpful owner calls his friend who speaks English to translate. He guides me back into the city to a clinic where he's certain I'll receive good care.

The staff at the clinic establish my Portuguese is utterly useless for conveying medical problems, and miraculously there is a single doctor who speaks Spanish. After explaining my story the friendly doctor orders a slew of blood tests, which take a couple of hours.

Looking over the results she explains I have essentially no red blood cells because the malaria ate them all. Maybe I'm still delirious from the fever, or maybe I'm really desperate about my possible leprosy which is getting worse by the day.
"I don't care about the malaria," I say.
"What about my skin?"
I'm scared and the doctor can see I'm not messing around.

After carefully examining my arms and legs the doctor looks puzzled.
"I've never treated a white person before."
"What color is your skin normally?"

I'm shocked by this, and feel more desperate than ever. Running out of composure I lift up my shirt, point to my less-tanned stomach and say
"I don't know, this color. Please just help me."

The doctor isn't certain what the problem is, though she's not too worried about it, and is sure it can be fixed. She prescribes an immense amount of tablets and creams, the schedule for which I go over three times before I'm reasonably confident I understand. After visiting multiple pharmacies I begin taking twelve different tablets three times per day, as well as applying two kinds of cream to my red welts all while continuing the twice daily injections to be sure the malaria won't resurface. I feel like a walking illness.

Back at camp I concentrate on resting and recuperating, which is to say I sit and lie around doing absolutely nothing. As my headache subsides I'm able to sleep soundly and two days later I'm much improved. After another two days I feel almost back to normal and even manage to cook my own food and go for a walk into town with Dani and Didi. They tell me they were watching very carefully during the malaria to make sure I did drink some water and eat at least a little food in the hopes I would regain my strength. They were also trying to keep good thoughts in my head and helping me keep a positive state of mind. If my situation had not improved on that final day they planned to take me to hospital. Didi was going to drive my Jeep while Dani drove the van with me lying in the back. They explain they were so concerned they don't have the words in English to explain it, and we're all relieved I'm back on my feet.

For the final night at our beach camp we splash out for dinner where we finally get an explanation for the red welts. At the restaurant many small flying ants litter the table and a nearby customer warns us to be careful. Though they're only tiny, he explains, the red-and-black striped insects are quite nasty. Commonly called a 'Nairobi fly' or 'acid bug', these little insects are essentially made from acid. If one gets squashed against skin it will leave a nasty burn for a few weeks.

With this new knowledge I inspect the Jeep and find a handful in my sheets and sleeping bag. In the days following I see the bugs are attracted to the condensation on the canvas each morning, and evidently a few found their way inside. I must have been rolling over at night and squashing them onto my arms and legs, causing the nasty looking acid burns. To my immense relief the welts slowly fade and a few weeks later they completely disappear, and I put the whole incident behind me.

Φ   Φ   Φ

I *really* hope there is no round three when it comes to malaria.

Chinese Construction & Enslavement

T HE more time I spent in Africa, the more I saw the immense scale of Chinese construction all across the continent. In virtually every country I encountered teams of Chinese workers building roads, deep sea ports, bridges, hydro stations and other enormous engineering projects. Many thousands of workers drive Chinese construction equipment, speak Chinese and live in entire cities of temporary housing. They're complete with road signs, shops and restaurants all in Chinese. In many countries the jungle is being cut down faster than I can comprehend, and I was often stuck behind an endless procession of massive logging trucks carrying trees bigger than I've ever seen.

People often ask if this kind of Chinese development is good or bad for Africa. As usual, the answer is complicated.

Before I answer the question we need to understand the history of modern Africa and how things got to where they are today.

$$\Phi \quad \Phi \quad \Phi$$

Towards the end of the 1800s the major powers of Europe were vying for control of various parts of Africa. They each wanted their own slice so they could extract resources and expand their empires, and if possible they wanted to avoid fighting with each other. In true 'gentlemanly' fashion they sat down in 1884 in Germany and divided Africa into the regions they each wanted. Often called the 'Scramble for Africa', this period resulted in rapid invasion, occupation, division, and colonisation of Africa by the European powers.

By 1902, 90% of the African continent was under European control.

This carved Africa into more or less the map we see today and explains why modern Africa has more straight-line borders than anywhere else on Earth. No attention was paid to the regions local people already recognised because what the locals wanted was irrelevant. To this day it's common for family members with the same last name and who all speak a common language to live in three separate countries because borders were drawn through their homelands.

Things remained this way until Roosevelt and Churchill sat down after World War II to decide how they wanted the post-war world to look. There was mounting pressure to allow African nations to self-govern, and most of the European powers were hurting for money after the war and didn't have the time or energy to run their far-flung colonies in Africa. After stealing an immense amount of African resources for five decades they were losing interest.

In 1957 Ghana became the first sub-Saharan African country to gain independence from European colonisation, soon followed by nearby Guinea in 1958. Once the trend started many countries in Africa fought for and won their independence, and by 1977, fifty-four African countries had seceded from their European colonial rulers.

Exactly how this was done has crippled Africa economically ever since.

Because these regions had been ruled by European masters for so long, when it came time to establish their own countries it was decided they must have the same pompous bloat and wasteful expenditures their colonial masters had. Creating a country costs an astronomical amount of money, so the newly formed governments were generously lent money by the International Monetary Fund (IMF) and the World Bank. Loaning these vast sums of money to new countries with inexperienced leaders virtually guaranteed the terms of the loan would never be met, but the newly elected leaders were eager to start their nations and accepted what was essentially forced on them if they ever hoped to stand on the International stage. It's estimated less than a handful of people in each of these countries even had a degree, yet they were lent billions of dollars and given the reigns of new nations.

To this day many African countries carry so much debt from independence they have no hope of ever paying it back. African countries pay tens of millions of dollars in interest every year, though their debt continues to grow. From time to time the IMF and World Bank wipe away a few billion in debt here and there, though interest means it just grows right back.

Although we no longer enslave African nations in the physical sense, we keep them enslaved through our global financial policies.

Φ   Φ   Φ

This global financial enslavement runs much deeper than just simple debt. Coffee was first discovered in Ethiopia, and is now the world's second most exported commodity after oil and is such big business it's traded on all the major financial markets. This should be good news for Africa, because the primary export of many African countries is coffee. Unfortunately the world doesn't work that way.

Virtually all processing of coffee into packaged final products is done in western countries, and it's the processing that makes coffee so profitable. In fact coffee growing countries only receive about 8% of total coffee revenue globally. African countries don't process the coffee themselves to reap the profits and lift themselves out of poverty because we don't let them.

For decades the World Trade Organization (WTO) enforced high tariffs on processed coffee coming from Africa into the developed world which means processed coffee directly from Africa would be many times more expensive than coffee from western nations. This allows Germany to buy the raw beans from African nations for pennies before they process and mark it up astronomically before they sell it on the global market and keep virtually all the profits. This system is so perverse that Germany is the world's third largest exporter of coffee to the tune of $2.5 billion dollars annually, despite never growing a single bean[6]. Switzerland is forth, and together they capture 15% of global coffee exports.

Of course the African nations don't like these rules and tariffs, but there's nothing they can do because we hold the crippling debt over them. If a country doesn't play by the rules, the IMF and World Bank just threaten heavy sanctions and to crush their currencies and economies which would send them back to the dark ages. Because of this many African nations today are forced to sell raw resources to Western countries like oil, bauxite and precious metals for a fraction of the globally-recognised price. This means Africans must do all the hard manual labor but can not make a reasonable profit by processing their raw materials.

Make no mistake about it - Africa is not poor because the people are lazy. Africa is not poor because of corruption - though that is still a big problem in some countries - or because the people are not intelligent. A major reason Africa is poor is global trade and monetary policies keeping them poor. Western countries want to buy Africa's resources for peanuts then make their own economies strong by reaping the profits.

The IMF, World Bank and WTO ensure African countries will never be paid a fair price for the resources, leaving them no chance to build their economies and lift themselves out of

---

[6] *Coffee Exports by Country*, worldstopexports.com

poverty. If things continue this way, nothing will improve for regular Africans, and they'll be our slaves forever.

Φ   Φ   Φ

In recent decades China has offered African nations an alternative. China very much wants the resources Africa still has in abundance, and rather than forcing the African countries to cooperate via physical or financial enslavement like we do, China offer a mutually beneficial deal with their 'Road and Belt' initiative.

China offers to build extremely expensive and complex infrastructure in exchange for the rights to extract and buy raw resources. All across the continent I saw Chinese built hydro power stations, bridges, train systems, roads, shipping ports and electricity grids that help everyday Africans live a better quality of live. These kinds of projects require immense engineering expertise that is currently beyond the reach of many countries. With this deal African countries get a boost to their quality of life and China can buy the resources they want.

It's also important to see the deals with China are completely optional, and African countries are free to take it or leave it. That's an option we've never offered.

While the immense stripping of resources isn't good for the planet, we need to remember downtown Seattle and Vancouver once looked like Redwood National Park with towering old growth forests thousands of years old. We certainly did our share of environmental damage to develop our own countries and economies that allowed us to climb to the standard of living we now enjoy. Clearly it would be hypocritical of us to demand Africans stop development and building their own economies. Obviously we can encourage and assist them to do so in sustainable ways, and hopefully they can learn from our mistakes and grow in smarter ways than we ever have.

Of course the western media is very quick to paint this new

Chinese deal for Africa as a terrible thing. By helping Africa, China are taking away the ability of western countries to profit so grossly from economic slaves in Africa.

China are currently helping to improve the quality of life of hundreds of millions of Africans rather than physically or financially enslaving them like we have.

It's very possible China are doing more good than we ever did.

One of the chill chimps relaxing at Drill Ranch

A broken bridge in the mountains of Cameroon

Celebrating on the summit of Mount Cameroon with Augustine

Crossing the Equator in Gabon

With Dani and Didi in the DRC

The mighty Congo River in the DRC

A man and his daughter who wandered into camp one morning

An abandoned Russian tank in Angola

Changing money was always an experience

Smiles and handshakes are key to deflecting corrupt Military

Buying gas on the side of the road

Familiar Corruption

B RIBERY in Africa is nothing like the Hollywood version. There is no violence. There are no threats. People are not dragged from vehicles at gunpoint and beaten senseless until they pay up. In fact, I was never threatened even once. I never had a gun pointed at me and nobody ever used words like "or else." It's almost never scary, and it's something I got used to, and very good at deflecting. In ninety-nine percent of cases bribery is so subtle it's easy to miss. A friendly conversation simply turns into

"What did you bring for me, my friend?"

Though I had no idea at the time, Latin America and the corruption I experienced there served as the perfect training ground for Africa. The roadblocks in Honduras, Peru and Colombia taught me tactics I put to good use deflecting over three hundred bribery attempts across Africa. In many countries there was never a hint of corruption, though in others it happened almost hourly.

This chapter is a collection of my most memorable bribery stories from the continent and I hope they're entertaining and educational.

Old Memories

I had been in Morocco less than a week and was quickly readjusting to make-it-up driving, street markets, wild camping and learning a new language. Driving with the flow of traffic is much safer, and often intersections and speed limits are not signed so I simply drive however I think is safest. The Jeep is bigger than most - but not all - vehicles, and with steel bumpers I feel confident pushing in like a local. While re-learning all that stuff, I had forgotten there was something else I needed to reacquaint myself with.

Though I drive safely, I completely ignore speed limits and other road signs when they do exist. Extremely slow farm machinery and horse-drawn carts are a regular occurrence on good paved roads, and after zipping around one I'm surprised by two Policemen who wave me down. This is the first patrol I've seen in Morocco, and it hadn't even occurred to me I should be paying attention to speed limits.

A uniformed man extracts himself from the vehicle and slowly strides over to my window. He's short and stern, wearing an impeccable uniform with the kind of pomp and flair I imagine of English Policemen in the 70s and there are so many stripes, badges and shiny things it's difficult to tell what color the fabric is. He has a strip of a moustache that is probably supposed to command respect, but instead brings to mind B-grade movies and shady pool boys.

He checks and re-checks my passport, temporary import, drivers license and vehicle insurance. His disappointment is obvious when he realizes everything is correct. I fumble through in terrible French, betting my horrible accent will dissuade further conversation. To my complete surprise he asks me to step out of the Jeep and follow to his cruiser. Damn.

The other officer sits in the cruiser with his feet on the dash, smoking a Marlboro Red. Huge reflective aviators cover most of his red round cheeks, and he barely glances in my direction. This is clearly the boss. Still speaking French the lesser man shows me a photo of the Jeep on a radar gun and explains I was speeding. I try to explain the lack of signs, painfully slow truck, and the stream of other vehicles that also overtook. Not surprisingly, they're having none of it.

I must pay a fine, they say, and everything will be OK. Not to worry. Don't be afraid. No problem.
It's just 600 Dirhams, about $60USD.

Of course I must pay right now, they say. Here. In cash, on the side of the road to these two characters. They must think I'm new to this game, but for me the bribe couldn't be more obvious.

With the most concerned look I can muster I gravely nod, accepting my fate. My voice trembles and I surprise myself with my acting abilities.
"Can I pay with VISA?" I ask.

They both grin from ear to ear and the mood lightens up.
"You can go," says the boss. "Pay attention next time."

As I hop back in the Jeep it dawns on me I wasn't the only one playing - he said that in perfect English.

Oh how I've missed these games!

Seat belts save lives

A couple of months later I'm driving the length of The Gambia, paralleling the mighty river of the same name. There are scores of Police and Military checkpoints, and all the men with automatic rifles are friendly and welcoming, genuinely wishing me a good stay in Gambia. A few ask repeatedly and are determined to get a small 'gift' from me, so as a distraction I hand out my business card and accumulate Facebook friends.

Rich with slave-trade history I detour towards Jufureh, directly opposite the infamous Kunta Kinteh Island, a UNESCO World Heritage site. My GPS leads me down a rough dirt track that has clearly been more river than road in recent years. Although rock hard and dry now, the path has deep tire ruts from when the road was pure mud. These ruts cause the Jeep to pitch and bounce wildly so I take off my seat belt and lean forward away from the seat. This means the seat jostles around behind me while I sit in relative calm. There are no other vehicles on this track and I'm crawling forward almost exclusively in first gear, so I decide it's safe enough without my seat belt. Ten minutes later on the edge of town I roll through a Police checkpoint and they pounce on me in an instant.

Quick as a flash one uniformed man is demanding to know why I'm not wearing my seat belt, another says he's a narcotics officer and must search the Jeep, and a thrid says it's an offence to film in The Gambia and I'm in big trouble for the GoPro attached to the mirror.

Here we go.

I explain it's simply not possible to talk to all three men simultaneously, and quickly the narcotics man steps forward to claim first rights to his victim. For almost an hour he searches every corner of the Jeep, opening almost all the lock boxes and hidden compartments, thumbing through my documents and painstakingly checking every tablet and item in my first aid kit. He eventually finds my stash of hidden cash which he hands to me to ensure there is no funny business. When he finds my second passport he demands to know who I am and why I have two passports. Immediately he suspects I'm some kind of government spy or I'm lying about who I am. I have to give this man credit, he finds almost all the documents and money hidden throughout the Jeep and he almost pulls off the intimidation act. Almost, but not quite.

When the narcotics officer is finally satisfied he confiscates my spare engine oil. He explains that because it's in a coke bottle it might be engine oil like I say, or it might be something more sinister like drugs. He can't be certain, so he must confiscate it. I pour some on a rag and let him smell it, but he's not satisfied and even after I offer to pour some into the engine he still won't change his mind. Though he's putting on a good show it's obvious he just wants to keep the oil for himself.

Playing the game I suggest we pour it on the ground for safety. He quickly snatches the bottle from my hands, very unhappy with my suggestion. A small crowd of locals has gathered and it occurs to me he wants to save face and make it appear that he did find something to justify the long detention and search. It's important for these men to feel they have a purpose, and if they can detain and hold something over a white man like me, their authority in the eyes of the locals will rise.

After this lengthy process we move inside where the other Policeman says I must pay a fifty Euro fine for not wearing my seat belt. The third officer quickly adds that I must pay a further fifty Euro fine for the GoPro that is still recording on the mirror.

All three men clearly saw my hidden cash, so they know I have it. Gambia doesn't use the Euro as it's official currency and to me it's blatantly obvious this is a scam. We go back and forth for twenty minutes with me trying to negotiate while being as respectful as possible and them trying to part me from my cash. We're speaking English so I have no trouble implying this whole thing is nonsense without saying it outright. Even still, they're clearly determined to get my money.

Falling back on my old tactics I stubbornly ask for a ticket, saying I'll pay at a bank to make sure it's all official. Of course they say that's not how it works in Gambia and I must pay right now in cash. Furthermore, they refuse to write a receipt. Again the whole situation couldn't be more clear - they're going to pocket any cash I give them.

The afternoon sun beats down, and while I'm trying to be respectful, I've also had enough of going around in circles. Speaking English makes me a little cheeky, and I press my luck. I raise my voice just a little as I say:

"I'll make you a deal."
"We're going to watch the next vehicle drive past. If the driver is wearing a seat belt, I'll pay your fifty Euro fine."

"If he's not, I'm leaving."

The narcotics officer cracks a huge smile before he can turn away, so I know the game is up. Another officer yells that I'm being disrespectful by telling him how to do his job, though I know he's just putting on a show and he will calm down soon enough. I've made it clear I won't play their game, and they reluctantly give me back my documents as they slump their shoulders.

Another day, another shakedown and bribery attempt avoided.

International Training Institute

Roadblocks and shakedowns have been very common throughout Guinea, and I slowly get a feel for them. As long as I remain polite and friendly, the officers don't push it too far. With my terrible French and endless friendly questions I make it clear I'm not an easy target, and the corrupt officials soon see they should spend time on an easier victim. I often see locals slow down just enough to hand over cash before zooming on - clearly paying off the local Police is a regular occurrence.

At one remote stop I see the determination in the Policeman's eyes and know I'm in for the long haul. In my usual style I stop the Jeep on the road and kill the engine before settling in for a ten minute round of handshakes and greetings. I don't make his life too easy, so I pretend to speak just enough French to be friendly, but not a word more.

The stop is routine with him asking where I'm going and where I'm coming from before asking to see the Jeep paperwork and my license. As he examines the documents written in English and looks around it's clear he's trying to think of something to catch me out.

I get a nagging sense of déjà-vu when he asks to see my safety triangle and my head spins when he asks for my fire extinguisher before carefully checking the expiry date. I'm tens of thousands of miles away, on an entirely different continent and speaking a different language, though the steps are identical. If I didn't know any better I would think this man and the numerous corrupt Police and Military I delt with in Latin America went to the same school for bribery. Apparently they were all taught by the same teacher and follow an identical prompt card to part foreigners from their cash.

Almost on cue he asks to see a reflective safety vest, a jack and then he even checks the spare tire before asking me to prove the headlights actually work. I find it difficult not to ask the questions before he can, and struggle not to laugh. Many words are similar in French and Spanish, and I begin wonder if I've taken a wrong turn and somehow I'm back in Honduras. I can hardly hide my grin when he finally asks to see the windscreen wipers functioning.

I know exactly what's coming next so I study his face for every emotion. At first he's disappointed they work perfectly, and three whole seconds later I see the pure excitement pass across his face as the obvious next question pops into his head. Certain he's finally found a defect with my Jeep, he asks me to demonstrate the water jets. Many vehicles in this part of West Africa don't even have glass or any lights, so functioning wipers *and* water jets are almost unheard of.

I almost feel bad for the guy as two perfect jets of soapy water spray the windscreen before the wipers clean it away, leaving the glass spotless. I'm enjoying the game so much it's almost disappointing when he can't come up with anything else to ask and waves me forward. The poor guy spent over thirty minutes on me while his buddies collected their fee from local traffic.

I had no idea corrupt officials the world over attend the same training school and follow the same prompt card. It's hilarious and it sure makes my life easier.

The Captain

I aim for the smallest border crossing from Mali into the Ivory Coast, not entirely sure what I'll find. After wild camping a night in the scrubby bush the formalities leaving Mali are quick and easy before three shabby men approach the Jeep and introduce themselves as 'The Authorities' at Ivory Coast Customs. They setup a rickety table in the shade and invite me to sit for a conversation. They want me to believe they're officials, though I can't help noticing they don't have ID badges, or uniforms, or guns. In fact none of them are clean-shaven and I see one doesn't even have shoes. I'm already fairly certain this is some kind of scam, though it never hurts to be polite and see what they have to say. In a very serious manner they explain they're conducting a very important medical check, something I was not expecting.

After examining my Yellow Fever vaccination - mandatory to obtain a visa to enter the country - they ask for my Meningitis vaccination. There's a very serious outbreak in the country and they can't let me proceed without one, they explain and if I can't prove I have this important vaccination they will give me one here and now for just $50 USD. To emphasise the point they display a shabby collection of needles filled with an unknown clear liquid. There are no bottles or labels anywhere in sight, so there's no telling what might be inside the needles.

There's no way in the world I'll let them inject me with anything, and I enjoy watching their faces drop when I produce my proof of an up-to-date Meningitis vaccination. All three men slump their shoulders in obvious disappointment before I walk across the dirt road to Customs. Inside I'm issued a hand-written Temporary Import Permit for the Jeep and the friendly lady explains I must get a computerized version at the nearest big city.

The ten mile track to the Immigration shack is one endless mud pit and I use low range first gear just to get through. The minute I step from the Jeep a rotund Immigration officer is outwardly hostile, something I've never before experienced in Africa. Almost immediately he identifies a problem with my new paperwork - the start date on the Temporary Import is tomorrow, which is apparently a huge problem. He becomes more hostile as he explains that under no circumstances will he allow this gross violation of the law. He spotted it so quickly I suspect it's all a ruse, and he's betting I'll just slide some cash across rather than drive all the way back through the mud. Unfortunately for him I'm a lot more stubborn than he realizes, so I backtrack to Customs, have the paperwork corrected and then drive through the mud pit for the third time. An hour later when I arrive back at his shack he doesn't look any friendlier and he's called in support.

Now I must talk to an even rounder man who wears a freshly-ironed Military uniform and proudly displays a pistol on his hip, a rare sight in Africa. As if there was any doubt, he announces loudly to the masses he's the boss. This man struts around like a king, and it's immediately clear he has nothing but contempt for me even when I remain calm and polite.

After checking my documents multiple times and wasting my time, the boss explains I must 'give' him money. He emphasises repeatedly this is just a simple gift between friends, and is nothing sinister at all. Because we're friends this is something I want to do, he says, and I should be happy to give it. Between them the men barely speak a word of English, so I fall back on my old faithful routine of pretending not to speak French while remaining calm and wasting their time. I pretend to try my best to understand while remaining completely oblivious to the requests for cash. Because they think I'm a moron they speak freely in French and I have to be careful not to laugh out loud when I catch the following:

"The whites always have the right paperwork," says a junior officer while checking my insurance.

"Why do the whites make it so hard to get money?" replies the big boss.

Now I'm *really* determined not to give them any money.

In English with the occasional French word I explain over and over the Ambassador said I must not pay any money at the border because I've already paid for the visa. Of course I'm making that up, but these men don't know it. Apparently it's a convincing story and soon the other men try to convince the boss to let me through, causing his frustration at my lack of French to bubble over. He realizes if he can't communicate with me he can't get any money out of me, and that bothers him.

After my passport is stamped the boss leads me to the Jeep, away from everyone else. He tries his best one last time to ask for 10,000CFA (about $20USD), clearly still determined. He's disgusted when I use my favourite trick and explain I have no cash and need an ATM while showing my VISA card. He rants loudly about how this is not Europe and there are not ATMs everywhere, and I try hard to keep a blank look on my face, still playing the village idiot. Unable to communicate with me he waves his arms wildly while asking if I can see any ATMs nearby. He's clearly angry, though I don't think he'll take it any further. After all I'm being very polite and cooperative, I'm just too stupid to understand his request for a gift. At his wits end he hands back my passport leaving me free to drive into Ivory Coast without paying a cent.

The hold up at the border means it's late in the day, so I pull into the first mud-hut village at dusk. I ask to speak to the chief, who proudly grants permission for me to camp in his village, directly in front of his house. With the chief's permission I could leave the keys in the Jeep and all the windows down without a worry in the world. Nobody will go against the chief, and I feel extremely safe and welcome. It's been a ten hour day to cover less than a hundred miles, and I'm exhausted after another scorching day. Much to my surprise the friendly villagers insist I take a plate of delicious food and water before they sit to chat while I eat. They're extremely curious about the outside world, and though my French is far from fluent they don't seem to mind at all. A small army of children with bright and curious eyes assemble to watch my every move.

When I lay down to sleep I think about my day and the bribery attempts I've experienced in just the first hours in the Ivory Coast. I wonder if bribery here is more serious than elsewhere, though I dismiss the thought as I pass out. At sunrise I'm delighted to see at least thirty smiling and eager children again surrounding the Jeep. They stare at my every move as I make coffee for the adults, fascinated by my stove, utensils and anything else I dig out. I'm completely surrounded until I excuse myself mid-morning with a huge round of thanks.

Φ   Φ   Φ

A few days later in the larger town of Man I pay a visit to the main Customs building to get a computerized permit for the Jeep. My first mistake is parking inside the Customs compound where everyone can see my nice 4x4 Jeep and where they have a degree of control over it. My second mistake is asking for directions in French, taking away my chance to pretend I don't speak any.

Soon 'The Captain' is called, and after making me wait another ten minutes I'm introduced to a very smartly dressed man who clearly gets what he wants. He doesn't wait for replies to his questions, and is clearly unhappy I've come to waste his time today. After he invites me to sit in his office I politely ask if I can please have a computerized copy of the Jeep permit. Without missing a beat he looks me square in the face and says that because I'm white and have a lot of money I'll pay him 50,000CFA ($100 USD).

Something about his attitude has me rattled right away. I'm not sure if it's because I'm tired, because I'm not ready for this, or because I'm speaking French and only understand about half of the conversation. I have a tendency to nod and smile along and say "yes...yes" when I'm listening in a foreign language and then ten seconds later I fully understand what was said. In this case I've already more-or-less agreed with what he just said before I understood.

Now I'm in trouble. I know it, and he can sense it. He seems like the kind of no nonsense man who will impound my Jeep without a second thought, and that worries me. He just laughs in my face when I ask for a receipt and I can't just leave because he holds my paperwork I need to legally drive through the Ivory Coast.

This is a new one for me, and I honestly don't know how to proceed. Out of ideas, I try something I've never tried before. I explain I'm traveling Africa with very little money, and I sleep in the Jeep every night. I show him my dirty shirt and scruffy beard and explain I haven't had a shower in a few days, which is actually true. After five minutes he lowers his price to 30,000 CFA ($50 USD), and I don't know what else to do. When I pay he casually drops the stack of bills into his top drawer while an underling types the details into an ancient desktop computer.

After a quick round of thanks I leave as quickly as possible, thankful to still be in control of the Jeep. I'm extremely unhappy to have paid that bribe and I try to notch it up as a learning experience.

I didn't know it at the time, but that was the only bribe I ever paid in Africa.

Respect is everything

The Republic of Congo, Cameroon and Central African Republic all meet in a triangle border with some of the most remote and unexplored jungles in all of Africa. Each of the three countries has declared a National Park, which effectively combine to one massive region of projected wildlife and jungle.

Dani, Didi and I have been told repeatedly it offers some of the best gorilla and elephant viewing in all of Africa, so we're on a mission to reach the area.

Arriving in the Northernmost city of Ouésso is very different to anything I've seen so far in Congo-Brazza. This is a large border outpost bustling with people and commerce flowing in from neighbouring Cameroon. The intense heat and energy-sapping humidity are off the scale and as soon as I leave the Jeep I'm drenched in sweat just standing in the shade. When we sit for a delicious meal of spicy street food we're told the humidity is perfectly normal for the northern Republic of Congo.

The Nouabal-Ndoki National Park lies across the massive Sangha River, which partly forms the border with Cameroon. There is no bridge, so we explore the dusty riverbank until we find a huge industrial ferry that services an endless stream of heavily-loaded logging trucks. A small collection of huts serve as the ferry terminal and as I park I see many people sitting in the shade drinking beer at a makeshift bar. Because I speak the best French in our group I'm nominated to begin the negotiations with the man in charge.

Nothing is ever straightforward in Congo-Brazza, and negotiating prices in French is always difficult when the prices change every fifteen seconds. There's a separate fee for our vehicles versus the people, a loading fee and some other kinds of fees I don't quite understand. I'm concentrating hard in French trying to calculate the total price when a Policeman interrupts and asks to see my papers. I saw him stumble from the bar earlier, and his slurred speech means I don't have time for his drunken nonsense.

I make my first mistake when I tell the drunk Police Officer I'll finish in the ferry office then come to see him. I make my second mistake when I brush off a Customs Officer in the same way, and then a third with a Military man in full camouflage uniform.

The price negotiation drags on and on, and about every five minutes one of the three officers demands to see my paperwork. Each time I repeat that I'll finish here and then come over, a reply they are less and less impressed with. Eventually I calculate the ferry will cost at least $100USD return, and the National Park probably costs double that. As much as we want to explore the area, that's more than we're willing to spend. Now we know the price, it's an easy decision not to cross the ferry.

I walk back to the Jeep to get my paperwork and the drunk Police officer corners me at the driver's door. I try to explain we're not crossing the ferry, but he won't listen. He's convinced I'm trying to drive away, something he simply will not allow. To reassure him I give him my passport, registration, drivers license and import permit - literally all the important documents in my life. He stomps away with the documents just as the other two officers arrive and demand to see the same paperwork. No matter how many times I politely and calmly explain I just gave them to the Policeman they won't listen. Repeatedly they demand to see my papers, and soon they get angry when I don't obey.

I'm thoroughly confused about why this has gone so horribly wrong, and it's clear that talking to these men is not helping so I walk away and sit in a shady patch of dirt to think it through. Now the sun is not frying my brain, and with a cold bottle of water I quickly realize my mistake.

Respect is everything in Africa and I didn't show these uniformed officers even a little. By dismissing them I violated the most important rule of authority figures in Africa.

Especially with so many onlookers it was extremely rude of me to dismiss them so blatantly. I basically told them to go away, and they lost face in front of the crowd. If a white man can brush them off so easily with no consequences, the locals might start to think they can do the same. Clearly the officers can't tolerate that, so now they must demonstrate they're in charge of everything and everyone - including me.

After more than half an hour of raised voices and arm waiving, I begin to get a handle on the situation. The Policeman writes my details into a huge ledger and hands back the two documents he still has. He has given the rest to the Customs man, and when I catch up with him I'm not surprised to learn he's found a 'problem' with the import permit for the Jeep.

He says it's not valid in The Republic of Congo, and he demands money. It was issued at the border of this country, and clearly has the name of the country and multiple stamps on it, though he doesn't care in the least and sticks with his story. He refuses to even listen to my explanation, and with my patience wearing thin I make a big show of writing down his name from his uniform and take a photo of his face with my big camera. Everyone clearly sees me do this, which I was counting on.

The man is shocked into silence and sensing my advantage I politely ask for my papers before going to see the Military man. In the usual course of things he writes my details painstakingly slowly into yet another huge paper ledger and before I can leave an extremely polite female officer also needs to write my details in her ledger, so I sit with her. After another ten minutes she asks my destination, and is utterly shocked when I say Brazzaville. After watching all the yelling and arm waiving she's flabbergasted we're not even crossing the ferry. All I can do is agree.

Back at the Jeep the Customs man again corners me and it's plain to see he's both scared and angry. He obviously doesn't want anyone to know about his behaviour here, and is not happy that I have his name and photo. Especially when it comes to demanding money, trouble with a tourist would be very bad for him. He knows it, and so do I. Hoping to just leave I make a show of thoroughly scribbling out his name and deleting his photo from my camera, and again everyone can see.

He stares at me for a solid ten seconds, trying to decide how to proceed. Eventually we shake hands before I jump in the Jeep and drive away without looking back.

I won't soon forget this lesson in respect

An unexpected twist

After a year exploring the least developed regions of the planet in West Africa I got a huge shock driving from the DRC into Angola and then into even more developed Namibia six weeks later. It takes weeks to get over the array of things for sale, and how much more development surrounds me simply because I drove across an imaginary line on the ground. I stop at the first rural gas station in Namibia and can't help but marvel at the array of items for sale I haven't seen for the last year. Car batteries, jumper leads, rope, tools, frozen meat, ice-cream, hats, sunscreen, oil, grease, chips and even salty snacks.

These are all simple things you expect to find at any gas station, but these are things I haven't seen for a very long time. Even though I'm in the middle of nowhere I feel as if I'm in a Developed country compared to the DRC and what came before. I can't help walking the entire store to carefully check every item, and I realize everything looks and feels just like rural Australia.

I freely roam the stunning wilderness of Namibia before crossing into Botswana at the smallest border I can find. Though I ignore road signs and speed limits, I'm sure I always drive safely and carefully. Because speed limit signs have been extremely rare for the last year, I simply drive at whatever speed I think is safe for the conditions.

Only an hour into Botswana I'm driving in my usual care-free manner when a very eager Policeman jumps onto the road and waves me down. After a friendly hello he escorts me to his cruiser, where I'm flabbergasted to see what must be a radar gun on a large tripod. Having just come from the Congo I suddenly feel like I've stepped into the future, and the feeling intensifies when he rewinds the digital recording to show me footage of the Jeep in motion with a speed superimposed below. I've barely seen a digital screen for the last year, and this one looks extremely high tech. I'm absolutely certain this gadget is from the future.

My inner child comes out and I get caught up in the moment, just wanting to play with this cool piece of tech. The officer is happy to oblige and even points the radar at a few passing cars to demonstrate how it works. Once I get over the shock of the radar gun, the Policeman explains I was driving in a thirty zone, and I see the problem when the speed on the screen underneath the Jeep shows forty-seven.

I'm so caught up in the novelty and shock of seeing an actual radar gun I completely forget my usual anti-bribery tricks, and it isn't long before he says I owe twenty dollars for a generic ticket and another thirty for the amount I was speeding. With no other options up my sleeve, I decide to tell the truth for once. I honestly did just cross the border an hour ago, and I honestly don't have any local money.

"Sorry, I don't have any cash," I say. "I only have a visa card." I'm feeling pleased with myself, thinking I'll get off even though I'm actually telling the truth.

Suddenly, my plan crumbles.
"No problem," he says while taking out a wireless credit card machine, stunning me into silence.

To all appearances we're in the middle of nowhere, and I'm shocked to see the wireless machine has two bars of 3G signal and it even accepts my chip credit card. I'm excited to be in the future, but suddenly I'm not feeling so smug.

On the side of a dusty road in rural Botswana I pay the second speeding fine of my entire life.

Φ   Φ   Φ

While Hollywood likes to show the violence and the worst of human-kind in an attempt to suck us in, they've completely ignored the fact these men and women are professional soldiers, just like our soldiers at home. They're well trained like our soldiers, and they take their jobs just as seriously. Being a soldier is their chosen profession, and it's how they put food on the table for their families. Never mind the fact they don't want to hurt another human being, the simple fact is they would go to jail for a very long time if they hurt a foreign tourist.

Keep in mind the stories above are only the most outrageous and memorable, and they don't give an accurate representation of the thousands of roadblocks, checkpoints and borders around the continent. Almost always I was welcomed with warm handshakes and smiles, and was rarely inconvenienced for more than a minute or asked to give a gift. Somewhere along the way I began to treat the corrupt stops like a game, always trying to be the most friendly and happy version of myself. I killed the officers with kindness, and it almost always led to me leaving without trouble.

When you treat people with kindness and respect - even corrupt ones - they'll invariably do the same.

Halfway

Cape Agulhas, South Africa
January 2018

D RIVING the last few miles I struggle to understand the significance of where I am. After 32,885 miles through twenty-one African countries I've driven to the extreme southern tip of the continent and the official halfway point of the expedition. I park the Jeep on the water's edge where it's literally impossible to drive further south and can't help pose for a few photos with fist pumps.

I try to wrap my head around my achievement and can't fully comprehend what it all means. On one hand I'm elated to have reached this point successfully, and on the other hand there is a long way to go.

Less than three hundred yards after leaving the parking lot a tourist reverses into the front of the Jeep. He's driving a little rental car, and apparently forgot to check his mirrors before backing up for a photo. I bury the horn and try to get the Jeep in reverse, but it's too little too late. This is my first 'car crash' in Africa, and I don't miss the irony of it happening in sight of the halfway point. There is a huge dent in the tailgate of the shiny rental car, though I can't find even a scuff on the Jeep's front bumper. The guy is severely embarrassed at his clumsiness and apologizes profusely, and I smile as I tell him not to worry. Given today's achievement, it's simply not important. I just hope his insurance will cover it.

Cape Agulhas is a beautiful ocean-side town, and sits on a

bluff overlooking the mighty Indian and South Atlantic oceans coming together. The coastline is rugged and windswept, and the difference in color between the two oceans is clear to see. I'm reminded strongly of isolated coastal towns across Australia so I decide to stay a couple of nights and rent a surfboard. With a thin wetsuit the Indian Ocean is plenty warm enough and the waves are beginner friendly which is perfect for me.

I camp in the parking lot of a hostel, and immediately after visiting the southern tip I eagerly update the hood map with a yellow paint pen. I want to send photos to my family as quickly as possible, and I've been dreaming of the line touching the end for months. I usually balance on the front bumper to get a photo of the hood, but here in the parking lot I'm next to a large palm tree so I climb one handed while holding my camera. I snap the photo just as bark breaks off the trunk and I come tumbling down, barely missing the front bumper with my face. Trying to protect my camera means I land heavily on my elbows and knees, which really hurts. I quickly dust myself off, hoping beyond hope nobody was watching.

The Jeep

When I bought the Jeep to live my African dreams a friend christened her 'Sandy', partly for the sand color and partly as a companion for Rusty, the rust-bucket Subaru I drove all over the Yukon and Alaska. Sandy and I are friends, but I don't think of her as my girlfriend like the Jeep I drove through Latin America. She's so much bigger and more capable, so she's more like an adventure buddy, or even teammate.

Sandy herself has been extremely strong and reliable, overcoming every obstacle without complaint. The West Coast has been a battle of sand, mud, rocks and severely broken pavement, never mind the intense heat and humidity for thirty-two thousand miles. In the deeper river crossings water came over the hood a handful of times, and I pushed Sandy hard for hours on end through the endless Congo mud. Make no mistake, West Africa has some of the worst roads on the entire planet and the Jeep performed flawlessly, never once letting me down or failing to go where I wanted.

I talk to Sandy regularly to discuss routes and wild camp locations, and I have a few other friends inside too. 'Kevin the Cobra' is a wooden cobra on the dashboard who provides security. Africans are often terrified of snakes and refuse to go near the Jeep the second they spot Kevin. In fact I've seen hundreds of people jump back in fright, even big Military guys carrying automatic weapons.

A friend knitted me a sloth named 'Sid' because I've always wanted to see a sloth and somehow have never managed to. Sid perpetually smiles while swinging from the roll bar over the fridge, and he often helps me pick what to cook for dinner. Finally, I nicknamed my GPS 'Nagging Nelly' because of her British accent and insistence I'm always driving the wrong way. These friends of mine don't often talk back, but I'm sure they love the adventure as much as me.

After all the time I spent planning, designing and building Sandy into a literal house on wheels, I'm also very happy with how the upgrades have functioned and enabled the expedition. I've wild camped and cooked the majority of my own meals so far, and the fridge and drinking water system have been absolutely essential. I rely on them so heavily I have no idea how I managed without them previously. I've fallen into my old habit of buying lunch from street vendors most days which is a great way to get out of the Jeep and interact with locals. Street food is almost always delicious and extremely cheap.

Everything else on the Jeep from the pop-up sleeping area and interior living space to the solar panels, air compressor, lock boxes and 4x4 upgrades have been brilliant, and I wouldn't change a single thing.

Jeep Maintenance

Early on the West Coast I made a couple of upgrades and alterations that proved essential. I originally installed lightweight flexible solar panels which failed in Senegal from all the twisting and vibrations caused by the horrible roads. At the Sleeping Camel I mounted two solid panels which have been flawless and essential.

Under hood temperatures were scorching through Morocco and Mauritania and the engine occasionally experienced 'heat soak'. When I turned off the engine the temperature was normal, but starting the engine twenty minutes later it would be sky-high. Because the heat couldn't easily escape the engine was actually getting hotter while turned off. Aiming to prevent failures from this intense heat I cut holes in the hood and installed two air vents, and I added a mechanical cooling fan in addition to the electric fan. From the driver's seat I see waves of hot air escaping the engine bay, and I'm happy with how much cooler everything feels.

Otherwise I've only been performing my own tire rotations and oil changes every six thousand miles. I crawl all over the Jeep at those times and I've never seen anything amiss.

Φ   Φ   Φ

After thirty-two thousand miles, however, it's time for more serious maintenance. When I researched the expedition I learned Southern Africa has plenty of Jeep dealers and 4x4 outfitting shops, and I planned to take advantage of that from the beginning. I setup camp on a working farm, and after telling my story over a cold beer the owner is happy for me to use his massive farm shed. The huge workshop has every tool I could ever need and even a pit for oil changes. South Africa and Namibia both have well-stocked auto stores similar to NAPA so I have no trouble buying the supplies I need.

I take my time to do the work properly, and over three weeks

I complete the following maintenance:

- I replace the filter in the drinking water system. The flow rate has slowed significantly since a few questionable fill-ups in northern Angola, and the old filter is dark brown compared to the bright white replacement.
Clearly it's been doing it's job.

- I replace the front & rear brake pads, which are looking low.

- I install new U-Joints in the front axle shafts. My grease gun doesn't have a nipple small enough to grease them, so it's my fault they've worn out prematurely from all the river crossings. From now on I'll grease them during regular maintenance.

- I replace the starter motor in the hopes of fixing an intermittent issue. The problem comes back, and after careful inspection I see the trigger wire is almost broken through. A new piece of wire permanently fixes the issue. From now on I'll carry the original starter as a spare.

- I perform oil changes in the front & rear differentials, transfer case and transmission. Buying the correct Mopar oil from a Jeep dealer feels great, and I'm happy to see a minimum of iron filings caught on the magnetic drain plugs. None of the oils show signs of water ingress, so my breather hose extensions have been working.

- I spend an entire day rebuilding and packing new grease into the electronic sway bar disconnect that is chock full of Congo mud. My efforts are rewarded when it works perfectly and the light on the dash stops flashing.

- I have a new clutch installed in a very impressive Jeep aftermarket workshop in Johannesburg. Because I bought the Jeep used the clutch has always been a question on my mind and I'd rather replace it as preventative maintenance now than deal with a possible failure later.

- When I designed the Jeep I chose a modest 2.5 inch suspension upgrade. The manufacturer warned me it wasn't designed for my additional weight, but I didn't listen. After

the worst roads on the planet it desperately needs an upgrade, and I have a 3.5 inch upgrade installed which makes
an enormous difference.

- I finally have the windshield replaced, badly cracked since
  Gabon.

- I have the constant velocity joint on the front drive shaft
  replaced. The rubber boot tore on a rock, causing all the
  grease to spit out. Without sufficient grease the old joint
  was destroyed and recently started clunking loudly.

- I have new tires installed. The old ones have life remaining,
  though I don't want to be low on tread for the harsh rocky
  conditions in Ethiopia and Sudan. Also it's easy to get the
  size I need in South Africa and might not be later.

- I flush the radiator, replace the coolant and pressure wash
  the muck caught between the radiator and air conditioning
  condenser. Mud and grass pour out, and I'm satisfied the
  cooling system is back to peak performance.

With all of that, I'm confident Sandy is ready to tackle whatever conditions East Africa can throw at us.

On Long Term Travel

Tofo, Mozambique
March 2018

L ONG term travel differs from shorter trips in a few very important ways and I've discovered issues and nuances that aren't obvious until months of continuous movement turn into years. One such problem is that because Im always on the move the stream of incomming experiences is endless and I never get time to process them properly.

Every day on the road I meet new and interesting people who have insights and different perspectives on life. I see the kinds of wildlife I used to dream about - elephants, lions, giraffes, hippos and countless more playing and doing quirky things. I see hundreds of people waving, smiling, dancing and singing, virtually bursting with joy. The landscapes and weather are unlike anything I've ever experienced before and just driving in Africa is always eye opening. Almost every day I see horrendously overloaded and decrepit vehicles making all kinds of insane maneuvers.

These are experiences I want to remember as long as I live, but with so many coming in every day I have a problem. New information I desperately want to remember is coming in faster than I can process it. And it never stops.

I've come to think of long term travel like drinking a large glass of water while it's being filled. As long as I drink faster than water is being poured in, it won't overflow and I can enjoy all the water. Once I'm full, however, it doesn't matter how delicious that water is, the glass will start to overflow because I can't drink as fast as water is coming in. I've come to realize if I keep traveling and having new experiences, the glass representing my memories will continue to overflow and I'll lose experiences because I can't process them as quickly as they're coming in.

In hindsight I realize this is a big part of the reason I needed to stop in Ecuador for five months, and I've been feeling the same way lately in Africa. The new experiences are pouring in so fast I can't process them quickly enough, and I'm upset they'll be lost forever if something doesn't change.

Φ   Φ   Φ

I'm thoroughly enjoying Mozambique, learning it's unique culture and speaking terrible Portuguese again. Locals are ecstatic when I stop at their small road-side stalls, and everyone wants to say hello and show me what they're selling. Watermelon, mangoes, avocados, pineapples and all manner of roasted nuts are abundant and so cheap they're virtually free.

In one stretch of road I see rows endless rows of bright red bottles and have to stop to investigate. A friendly lady with a smile big enough to change the shape of her face explains they're home made piri-piri sauce - the local hot sauce. Even with my basic Portuguese I easily understand her warm greeting, and the explanation she gives. She made the hot sauce herself, and there are two to choose from, 'spicy' and 'very spicy'. Even with hindsight I'm sure I got this right - the words are identical in Spanish so I have no trouble understanding. I love spicy food and usually choose something towards the hotter end of the scale, though something about the setup here makes me think twice. The bright red liquid is almost glowing and certainly looks like the good stuff.

I buy a 'spicy' bottle from the delighted lady who bids me a safe journey and later that evening I get the shock of my life when I crack open the very full bottle. Even the tiniest drop on the end of my finger is more than I bargained for, and soon tears are rolling down my cheeks. For dinner I put one small drop into an entire pot of pasta sauce only to discover the meal is unbearably spicy. I can barely eat it, and only while drinking a half gallon of water.

I firmly believe there is no second, third, or even tenth place when it comes to hot sauce, this is by far the hottest bottle I've ever experienced in my life. In town I feel a kind of deep fear watching locals heap the stuff on everything, even at breakfast. I try again, and again, but it's simply too much for me and I realize the bottle will last a decade at the rate I can eat it. Finally admitting it's just not for me, I give it to a local family. At first I feel bad and try to warn them in my basic Portuguese before I realize they surely know better than I. Incredibly, they're overjoyed, and look like they might drink the stuff straight. I walk away shaking my head, happy to be free of the red bottle that has tormented my dreams.

It's these quirky experiences I don't ever want to forget, and I become determined to slow down so I can process all my memories.

Ф   Ф   Ф

After a quick look at the main beach and small town of Tofo nestled among palm trees on white sand I know I've found beach-side paradise. I setup camp just outside town at Turtle Cove, a kind of surfer's hangout/campground run buy a friendly South African who discovered this slice of paradise twenty years ago. In town I rent a surfboard from another ex-pat, and soon I'm surfing twice daily at sunrise and sunset. Even when the waves aren't great I paddle out just for the relaxation and calm.

The water is always crystal clear, allowing me to see through to the sandy bottom. Dolphins often come close to investigate, and I sit in the warm water for hour after hour. Directly in front of town the beginner point break is the perfect place to hone my skills and gain confidence with slow and friendly waves that are just the right size for me. Five minutes outside town at Tofiño the waves are much bigger and more aggressive, well above my skill level. Towards the end of my stay I graduate to the smallest part of this break, and manage to catch a few waves in between rounds of getting pummeled by the monster swell rolling across the immense Indian Ocean. I sit on the sand after one particularly good thrashing and realize these waves have been building since Western Australia.

The sun beats down, the water is warm and the sand perfectly white. It doesn't hurt that the beers are huge, cheap and cold, and it only takes an afternoon to find the friendliest local lady selling heaping plates of delicious food for a dollar. I'm always quick to say no hot sauce, and each and every day she laughs heartily at my obvious fear of the stuff.

I plan to stay a week, which turns into two and then three. I thoroughly enjoy being out of the driver's seat, and I walk everywhere in town just for the change of pace. I digest all the experiences and conversations I've had during the previous months on the road, and I feel happier for it.

With my visa running out the time comes to move on, and I feel rested and ready for a host of new experiences.

Φ   Φ   Φ

Everyone travels at their own pace, and there is no magic one-size-fits-all approach. After experiencing it twice now I see how important it is to take time out to process the thousands of experiences that build up during long-term travel.

I can think of nothing worse than pushing on, fully aware my glass is overflowing. Those memories and experiences would be lost forever, defeating the entire purpose of leaving home in the first place.

Zimbabwe - Let's Make a Plan

Zimbabwe
April 2018

A CROSS Africa it's obvious the colonial powers didn't want to actually live in the lands they were conquering and colonizing, but only wanted to pillage as much as they could before abandoning the region. In Zimbabwe, however, it was clearly different. The British built enormous stone estates, impressive bridges, railroads and infrastructure, clearly planning to stick around. The mountain climate provides perfect fresh air, the soil is fertile and the landscapes are stunning. As evidence of how this particular colony was regarded, the British Royal Family have vacationed in Zimbabwe on numerous occasions. Clearly this is a very special place.

While all of that's true, Zimbabwe also has enormous problems. Just six months before my visit the Military removed infamous President Robert Mugabe from power in what was possibly the best-executed bloodless *coup d'état* of all time. After ruling for thirty-seven consecutive years, Africa's oldest leader was finally kicked out after his mismanagement and corruption brought the country to it's knees.

Rampant corruption and greed caused Zimbabwe to begin a steady decline in 2000 that went into free-fall in 2008. Mugabe was helping his friends and fellow ministers embezzle money and profit from the black market, which lead to an official inflation rate of 79,600,000,000% per month. Inevitably the world's largest bank note was soon printed - a whopping 100 trillion dollars. Inflation was so high by the time it was printed and distributed it was already worthless, and now locals have stacks of them.

Given all this good and bad, and the very recent ousting of the President, I'm curious to discover Zim for myself and to learn how everyday people manage to live under these incredible conditions.

ɸ   ɸ   ɸ

Leaving Mozambique I climb steadily into scraggly mountains, and after yet another easy border I soon experience the dysfunctional government of Zimbabwe first hand. After the spectacular crash of The Zim Dollar it was replaced with the 'Bond Note' which look like regular paper money and are supposedly locked in value to the US Dollar to prevent the same run-away inflation. Bond notes are in very short supply and locals are forced to wait at the bank for hours to get their daily ration of a single $20 bill.

I see a bank with an ATM, complete with the usual uniformed and armed guard. I walk over intending to use my card, and the guard smiles broadly while explaining I'm wasting my time. Because bond notes are so scarce all ATMs in the country are empty. I can't help wondering why he's guarding it, but I don't bother asking.

Not only are bond notes in short supply, they're worthless outside the country. This creates a demand for US dollars so Zimbabweans can buy products from the outside world, or even just visit another country. I raid my emergency supply of US cash which I exchange for bond notes at better than face value. In theory they're supposed to be one to one, but the reality in Africa is always different. My $100 US bill buys $125 in bond notes, and I learn the bigger US bills are worth more than smaller ones. As crazy at it sounds, a single $100 bill is worth more than five $20 bills. With this black market exchange rate everything from food to gas is now 25% cheaper.

I quickly become hooked into 'The Zim Network', a group of friends spread across the country who offer a hot shower, a place to camp and plenty of fascinating conversation. I'm immediately treated like a relative and I quickly see the unique perspective and insight these people have after decades of living under insane conditions. In each town there's another friendly and smiling face to welcome me and engage in endless thought provoking conversation.

Through the network I meet Nigel, a fascinating entrepreneurial Zimbabwean who runs various ventures around the country. I soon learn Nigel and his family were at the heart of the farm invasions during the collapse, and his jaw-dropping first hand account is documented in the stunning book *House of Stone*[7]. Nigel's relationship to the local workers is central to the story and outcome because the workers are much more like family than just hired help. When things fell apart some local workers tried to protect Nigel and his family while others were simultaneously trying to kill them.

Over cold drinks Nigel tells jaw-dropping stories about how it all went down and I find myself captivated. During the very worst days Nigel feared for the safety of his family and after friends were killed nearby they decided it was time to flee to Australia, a very common choice even today for Zimbabweans and South Africans. Zimbabwe's currency was decimated and they lost literally everything from the family farm except the clothes on their backs. Even their children's toys were never seen again.

They were quickly granted residency in Australia in a town that many consider beach paradise and even lived close to friends and relatives. Life was good and in fact Australia is commonly nicknamed 'The Lucky Country'.

At this point in the story I see Nigel is very uncomfortable,

---

[7]*House of Stone: The True Story of a Family Divided in War-Torn Zimbabwe* - Christina Lamb, 2009

and I have to coax him to continue. Eventually, and only after I promise not to take offence, Nigel continues.

After only six months in Australia, Nigel and his family decided to return home to Zimbabwe. Of their own free will they chose to leave one of the safest and most comfortable countries on the planet to return to Zimbabwe which was hardly functioning, and where they had been issued face-to-face death threats.

I can't understand why a thinking person would make such a choice, and Nigel explains it concisely as such:
"Australians don't know how to truly live, they just die slowly."
He watches my reaction carefully before continuing.
"They're so caught up in following rules, saving for retirement, insurance, careers, accumulating stuff and everything else, they've forgotten the point is to have a good time."
"I can't live like that, and I wouldn't wish it on anyone," he finishes.

Just like that they turned their backs on a very comfortable life in a beautiful beach town in Australia to start again in the ruins of Zimbabwe. The economy was decimated and there was very little food or gas in the entire country. Still, they choose Zimbabwe. With stern faces they both proudly say they've never once regretted that choice, and I believe them completely.

It's clear Nigel was afraid of offending me, talking so bluntly about how he'd rather live in a country literally falling apart than my home. This is a shocking thing to hear about your own country, and I managed to offend many friends and family re-telling the story in Australia. To this day they refuse to believe anyone would not willingly choose Australia, comfortable and safe as it is.

Nigel's story made it abundantly clear there are thinking people who want more from life than just a stable job and a retirement plan, and it left me wanting to dig deeper into the Zimbabwean psyche.

Φ   Φ   Φ

A week later in the capital of Harare I meet Phil in a bustling café when he asks to share my table. Soon we're chatting back and forward like a couple of old friends and everything is on the table.

Phil was born and raised in Zim, must be around sixty and has a short white beard that blends so seamlessly it's difficult to tell where the beard stops and his hair begins. Phil is well spoken, concise and polite and his eyes sparkle like a mischievous teenager. Phil also has jet black skin.

When I give Phil the cliff notes of my life he surprises me with his response.
"Oh yeah, I've seen that life."
"Lived it too. My two kids went to University in America and still live there," Phil tells me.
"I lived there for fifteen years, but man, I was happy to leave. Everyone is so focused on money and careers and buying more junk, they don't have time for anything else. Even when they have kids they don't have time to spend with them, and they pay other people to raise them."
"What's the point in having a bunch of money and stuff when you don't even have time to spend with your family?"
I can tell from the look on his face he really means it, and has spent a long time thinking about this.

"I know tons of people like the comfort and easy life in Europe or America or whatever, but that life just isn't for me. I grew up wild in Zim, running around without shoes and doing what I pleased. Even today I thumbed a ride here in the back of a pick-up just because I wanted to feel the wind on my face. I could have driven my car, but it's more fun meeting new people and relaxing in the sunshine."

"Sometimes I think of myself like a lion who grew up in the wild but was captured and caged. Because I know what true freedom feels like I'll never be happy living with so many rules and restrictions. Like the wild lion I would die a painful death under those conditions, always dreaming of real freedom. I understand why someone born into it might like being fed on schedule and having their cage cleaned everyday, but man, I'd rather be free."

"I don't have nearly as much money as when I lived in America, but I have all the time in the world to spend how I please."

"So Dan," he says before standing up to leave, leaning close across the table. "What kind of lion are you?"

Φ   Φ   Φ

Still in Harare I meet young and energetic Greta at a music festival. She moved to Zimbabwe a few years ago from Germany, is tall and confident and speaks perfect English which she learned at University.

"After my last trip, I asked my boss to relocate me here permanently."
"I'll never live in Germany again," She says with a serious look on her face.

I'm again fascinated to meet an intelligent person who has consciously chosen to live in a country struggling to function when she could so easily choose a more functional - and much safer - one.

"When you really think about it, the life back there only makes people less happy," she begins.
"Let me explain." "People in the developed world have every comfort a person could ever want - electricity, running hot & cold water, air conditioning, fast wi-fi, good roads, supermarkets. . . the list is endless."
"Not only do they have all of that, they have it all 24/7."
"It's accepted as the normal state of things, so it's just the baseline. Because everyone has become so used to all of that, it doesn't make them happier, it's just the everyday normal."

"Now think about what happens when one of those services doesn't work." Greta says, clearly excited.

"Imagine you're in Canada or Australia and the water stops running in your house. No shower, no dishwasher, no drinking water and no washing machine for the clothes. It's not clear why or for how long it will be off. Through no action of your own you're unhappy because the status quo has been upset and your expectations have not been met."

When the unexpected happens, it makes you unhappy.

"Now let's compare that with Zimbabwe," she continues.

"Here, we all assume the water doesn't work, the electricity is spotty, the roads are terrible and there is never money in the ATMs. Dysfunctional is our baseline, but the important part is we're still happy despite all of that crumbling stuff."

"When those systems do sometimes work it only increases our happiness because it's a nice surprise."

"So in the developed world an upset to the status quo will only make you unhappy, whereas in Zimbabwe an upset to the status quo actually makes us happier. Expectations in the developed world are sky high, and happiness is tied to those high expectations."

She loses me with her next statement "Supermarkets are the same."

After seeing my confusion, Greta goes on "Here's an example."

"Imagine you're baking a cake for your friend's Birthday. You drive to the nearest supermarket expecting it to have butter, because it always does. When there is butter, you don't think much about it, you're just impatient waiting in line for the one open register. The store having butter doesn't make you happy, it just *is*."

"Now think about what would happen if there wasn't any butter in the supermarket. It's an inconvenience to drive five minutes to the next supermarket simply to get butter. If *that* one also didn't have butter you'd be furious about wasting all this time driving around town just to get stupid butter."

"Again, when your world works as expected it's not a reason to be happy, you're just running around town getting jobs done. But when that supermarket suddenly doesn't have the precise thing you want, you're unhappy and it's a big inconvenience."

"Your expectation that a supermarket will have everything all the time means they can only make you unhappy when they don't."

"Here in Zimbabwe, we assume stores don't have any butter. In fact we assume they have almost nothing, which is often true. We just have to work around that and find other ways, which we've become extremely good at."

"A few weeks ago a friend organized a family member to buy butter from South Africa so she could bake a cake for my birthday. I know how much effort went into just getting the butter from another country, and it was the best gift of my life."

"Because our expectations are set correctly, we know how to appreciate when things do work, and we're happy regardless of everything around us being dysfunctional. We don't allow little things outside our control to negatively impact our happiness, because then we'd constantly be at the mercy of external things, and we'd be unhappy all the time."

This really makes me stop and think, and what Nigel and his wife had said about Australians just dying slowly hits me.

"Landing in Germany after two years living in Zim I was sure zombies had taken over. People have this glazed-over look on their face as they stand around waiting. Nobody smiles, nobody laughs. It felt like everyone is just waiting for the next minor inconvenience so they have something to complain about. It's almost like these negative things are the only events in people's lives worth talking about."

Greta's parting words really make me think about where I want to spend my life.

"Tens of millions of people in the developed world now live in this state of waiting to be unhappy about some minor thing. They're just one little inconvenience away from being upset for reasons completely outside their control."
"Is that who you want to surround yourself with?"

As if by fate when I visited Australia the following Christmas the electricity went out. Maintenance was scheduled and everyone was notified weeks in advance and the outage was over faster than expected. Even still I spent the next week listening to people complain about it. With no real problems in Australia it feels like people invent drama and things to be unhappy about just to fill the time.

I couldn't help thinking about Greta consciously choosing to live a happy life in dysfunctional Zimbabwe while I listened to Australians who have everything a person could ever want complain about a four hour power outage.

Φ   Φ   Φ

Zimbabwe takes me completely by surprise as one of the most fascinating countries I've ever spent time in. I enjoy myself so much I explore far and wide, and extend my visa so I have time to digest all the unique perspectives and thoughts running through my head. At every turn I see people choosing to live a happy life despite the chaos and dysfunctional system around them. Time and again I hear the following slogan which has almost become the national catch-phrase:

"Let's make a plan."

Even without a functioning monetary system, unreliable electricity, terribly potholed roads and a raft of other failing services, Zimbabweans simply get on with living a vibrant and enjoyable life. Even though they have every right to complain I never once hear a single word of complaint. People here have an impressive way of turning a negative into a positive and enjoying themselves regardless.

After sundowner drinks with locals high on a stunning lookout I ride home clinging to the outside of a pickup with a few teenage kids having a riot. When we get onto the highway I lean out so the wind rips through my hair and I can't help grinning and feeling like a teenager myself.

It's hard to believe that back in Australia the driver would immediately go to jail for letting us ride outside the vehicle like this, and such a simple activity gives me a strong sense of living rather than just dying slowly.

Zimbabwe and the amazing attitude of it's people helped me understand I shouldn't tie my happiness to the reliability of electricity or the speed the government processes paperwork.

I choose to be more like Zimbabweans who are happy regardless of all that unimportant stuff.

On Foreign Aid

FOREIGN aid in Africa is an extremely complicated situation fraught with tricky nuances and unintended consequences. After six months on the ground I thought I was an expert. After twenty-four months I realized I knew just enough to know I knew nothing at all.

The unfortunate reality is that giving money to an enormous international aid agency is extremely unlikely to make a lasting or worthwhile difference. Because those agencies have such massive overheads studies have shown less than 10% of donations actually reach the people it is intended to help. The rest is spent on marketing to attract more donations, administrative fees and employee salaries. In the most outrageous case the Red Cross raised half a billion dollars to help Hati in the aftermath of the deadly 2010 earthquake. With that enormous amount of money they only managed to built six houses[8]. Miraculously, the Red Cross still celebrates their achievement in Hati and continue to ask for more dontaions.

The big international aid agencies are most interested in 'quick wins' so they have good news stories for their glossy brochures and marketing campaigns. They often dump money into solutions that look good on the surface but don't genuinely solve any underlying problems.

The classic example is the aid agency that buys tractors for isolated villages so they can farm more efficiently. Tractors

---

[8] *How the Red Cross Raised Half a Billion Dollars for Haiti and Built Six Homes*, ProPublica.org, June 2015

helped in the development of the west, so surely they'll help in rural Africa too. Nobody sitting in their air-conditioned office in Geneva or Atlanta stops to think about the enormous supply chain required to keep a tractor running in harsh conditions, they just ship them over. Of course there's no diesel anywhere near a truly remote village, no spare parts and nobody capable of swapping in spare parts anyway. Money isn't even allocated for more diesel or upkeep of the tractor into the future.

Photos of the modern tractor in a remote village with smiling locals are posted to websites and printed in marketing brochures and the agency declares a win. Unfortunately after the first tank of diesel runs dry the shiny tractor sits in the field to rust, never to be used again.

Even worse than a rusty tractor going to waste, the sad reality is that aid often does more harm than good, especially when viewed in the long term.

One such story is the international reaction to famine in Somalia. When hundreds of thousands of people don't have enough food to eat, the aid organizations go into full panic mode, drawing on their immense resources to collect vast sums of money from donors. Rich countries give hundreds of millions of dollars in aid each year, which sounds extremely generous on the surface. What most people don't know is those countries mandate the majority of government aid money must be spent with companies from their own country. So when France donates $50 million, virtually all of that must be spent with French companies. The transport trucks, planes and labor are all French. While the French government wants to help hungry people in Somalia, they also want to pad their own economy when possible.

Not only is the labor and equipment all purchased outside Africa, but the food is too. When vast quantities of rice and grains are required to feed hungry people, thousands of tons are flown in from developed countries around the world. The French government buy tens of thousands of tons from their own farmers to send to Somalia. This is great for French farmers, but unfortunately it has disastrous long term consequences for the Somalian growers and economy, because the market in Somalia becomes flooded with an unlimited supply of literally free food. This causes the local price to plummet. As a consequence no local farmer can afford to grow grains, so next year the local market produces none, and the need for foreign grains is even higher than in the first place. This cycle repeats until the local economy is decimated, and Somalia is utterly dependant on foreign aid to feed it's people. Any local who tries to grow their own grains will soon go bankrupt, making the situation even worse.

So with the best of intentions to feed hungry people, foreign aid causes horrible long term dependency, and only makes the situation worse year after year.

Φ   Φ   Φ

This paints a very bleak picture, but there is a lot that can be done if aid is allocated thoughtfully by people who have a clear understanding of what's needed.

In the case of the useless tractor it would be much more helpful if the agency had provided seeds for new crops or hand tools or even a basic irrigation system. These things cost a tiny fraction of the tractor, so many more villages would benefit and more people would see a change in their lives. Education on more efficient farming practices and how to build, use and maintain irrigation systems is also very effective and cheap. All too often the critical maintenance step is completely forgotten in the quest for a quick win.

More often than not isolated and remote people don't need a complicated water pump that requires electricity, maintenance and spare parts. A hand pump is a perfect simple solution that I saw and used in hundreds of small communities around Africa. It doesn't look as good on the cover of a brochure, but it genuinely helps people who need access to clean drinking water. Even better, it will work for decades because it's so simple.

In the case of the grain for Somalia, rather than simply flying in thousands of tons of foreign-grown food, the aid money could be used to help local farmers grow more for their own people. Grain could be purchased from the local market, providing jobs and incentive to grow more grain next season, which would alleviate the need for foreign-grown grain in the first place. Furthermore irrigation could be improved, farming techniques taught and locals could be paid to work on local farms. In this way foreign aid would meet the primary goal of providing food for the people who need it most and it would build the local economy and educate locals to be self-reliant in the future. In this scenario foreign aid could be slowly reduced and finally eliminated altogether.

Φ   Φ   Φ

Aid is such a tricky topic, and often people trying their best to make a difference get caught up in the doing without thinking enough about the why. Friends in Australia are involved with the Rotary organization which attempts to do good all over the world through fund raising and volunteer efforts. I heard many variations on the following story, and after my years in Africa I realized I saw it from an entirely different perspective than the thoughtful Australians doing their best to help.

An organization like Rotary sends a hard working crew of volunteers to install a solar water pump in an isolated and undeveloped village. Because the new water pump brings running water directly into the village, the ladies don't have to walk hours carrying heavy water jugs, and clearly their lives are better. The pump is installed and the volunteers fly home feeling great about the difference they've made.

A year later upon their return the volunteers are dismayed

to see the pump is not being used. A small part has broken, and nobody has been bothered to fix it. The volunteers can't help noticing the men of the village sitting around doing nothing, rather than repairing the pump. The volunteers are understandably frustrated and dismayed to see the pump they worked so hard to install being wasted. Eventually they conclude the locals are simply too lazy to do anything for themselves, and they'll just have to repair the pump themselves. This continues year after year until finally the volunteers give up, at their wits end as to why the locals can't get off their backsides to improve their own living conditions. Back in Australia they shrug their shoulders and conclude the locals don't deserve their help. If they're not willing to repair the pump then they simply won't have one.

While I understand the volunteer's frustration, after years in Africa I came to see this situation from the local point of view. I realized I'm more like them than I am the volunteers.

Before we go into any village and attempt to 'fix things' we must acknowledge the local peoples have been living the way they are for tens of thousands of years and their society and way of life is vastly older than ours, and has stood the test of time. They've never needed a water pump before, so it's odd to conclude they need one now. It's also good to remember that while their society has been successful for tens of thousands of years we're doing an expert job of destroying ourselves and the planet in just a few hundred.

It's also important to remember the water pump and associated plumbing is complicated machinery from the other side of the planet. It's made of plastic and precision machined parts that nobody near the village has any ability to make or repair. When viewed in that light, I completely understand why local peoples wouldn't trust their survival on a complicated device they have no ability to repair. If they relied on the pump as their sole source of water, they may very well die when it can't be fixed. If I were them I'd be wary of it too.

Finally, it's extremely difficult for people in the developed world to understand the significance of the two dollar part required to fix the pump. Two or even fifty dollars is insignificant for us to have running water, but to people living in undeveloped countries this is a significant amount of money. Furthermore, the majority of people have no access to paid employment. Trying to find a job and the perils associated with that only to fix a water pump isn't worthwhile when it's easy to walk and get free water anyway.

Also it's extremely difficult for us to understand how difficult sourcing a replacement part for that pump may actually be. The volunteers can't understand because they were driven to and from the village in an air conditioned 4x4 they hired at great expense. For the villagers to get into the city to find a part the story is much more difficult. What vehicle will they travel in, where will they get gas for the vehicle, and will the roads even be passable. Repairing a pump they didn't really need in the first place is turning into an expensive and time consuming ordeal.

After living this first hand, I completely understand why a person would take the 'lazy' approach and choose to carry water by hand. A hand pump may have been a good solution in this village, but I can think of an even better one.
The volunteers should have spent a few months with the local people before asking if there is anything they actually need. Chances are they have no problem carrying water, but something else cheap and easy would really make their lives better.

Ф   Ф   Ф

It's common for our Western culture to think we're the best, and that we must instill our culture and solutions around the world with the aim of 'helping' everyone be more like us. Unfortunately the way we think and solve problems is often not helpful for hundreds of millions of people living in remote villages across Africa. While I heard countless stories of aid doing more harm than good, I also saw with my own eyes how much it can improve the lives of millions of people when done well.

There is no doubt many parts of Africa could use help to improve livings conditions. Unfortunately, they very rarely need the help we think up while sitting at offices in the developed world.

Obviously it's better to teach people to fish than to simply give them fish, but it leaves out a very important step if you want to make an impact not just for a single season, but for years and even decades. We should always remember to teach people to repair their own fishing equipment so they can be truly self sufficient.

If you genuinely want to help, research organizations that have a track record of spending a large percentage of donations on real world solutions that make a difference. Look past the glossy brochures and websites, and find organizations that follow up on projects years later. Be suspicious of any organization promising quick results, and look for ones that have real people on the ground with years of experience.

Aid can and does make an enormous impact on the lives of millions around the world. When it's done well, it can even be a positive one.

Zambian Hospitality

Zambia
May 2018

CROSSING into Zambia at Victoria Falls I plan roughly a week for a quick look around this country I don't know much about. On my first night in a new country I like to stay in a campground if at all possible while I acclimatize, get some local currency and get a feel for the people. I find camping on the banks of the Zambezi close enough to hear the roar of the mighty waterfalls, and soon I bump into a friendly ex-pat happy to tell me about the Zambia. Michael has been working all over the country for five years and quickly gives me the important information I need. Gas is plentiful, Zambia is extremely safe everywhere and people are very friendly, if not a little shy. In a master stroke of luck Michael gives me his personal map of the country with red circles around the stunning places he has explored. I thank my lucky stars when I realize I've been given an epic Zambian itinerary, and suddenly my four week visa doesn't feel long enough.

My GPS shows a road splitting the two biggest and most famous National Parks in the country, cutting out hundreds of miles of back-tracking. I'm not certain if I can drive all the way through, and there's a question about a very large river crossing at the end that I'll just have to worry about later. I turn off the main road past a sign that says 'Strictly 4x4 only', and I know immediately I've made the right choice.

After sixty miles of good gravel I arrive at a small village with a checkpoint and boom gate blocking the road. The men manning the stop are friendly and offer input on the road ahead. They confirm there is a major river crossing towards the end, and they're not sure if I can make it through. In true Zambian style they say I can always turn around if I need to, and they look forward to seeing me then.

Over the next five miles the track drops steeply down to valley bottom, and the loose rock and severe washouts provide some of the steepest and trickiest low range 4x4 of the entire expedition. Dusk comes and goes and I simply move off the track at the only small clearing I can find to declare camp. A small fire drives away the surprisingly frigid night air and I sleep soundly in the utter silence.

I'm moving at dawn, and after just twenty minutes the Jeep is overwhelmed with huge tsetse flies. In the cool morning air I love driving with the window down, and dozens crowd inside before I realize. I learn soon enough the bite of these massive flies leaves a painful welt, and soon my arms and legs are covered. Tsetse flies carry sleeping sickness, a serious illness I would prefer to avoid. Driving with the windows closed I become virtually trapped inside and hundreds of the files swarm on and around the Jeep. Even bathroom breaks are virtually impossible, the flies are so think and ravenous.

The track conditions vary greatly throughout the day with a mixture of good dirt and gravel, dry river beds and sandy crossings. Thankfully there's no water to speak of and the Jeep moves forward in the usual slow and steady way. Throughout the day I see the tracks of elephant, lion, giraffe and more on the sandy road, though the animals never show themselves. Around midday I'm stopped at a checkpoint with armed and uniformed Military running an anti-poaching checkpoint. Then men explain the track with the massive river crossing has been closed for many months, so I'll have to take a different fork, which should be possible. I still have to cross a big river, but it sounds like the ferry should be running at this time of year. Of course, they don't know for certain.

Long after the heat of the day has passed I burst out on the shores of the mighty Luangwa River - wide, fast flowing and infested with crocodiles and hippos. I fumble along shore to the south until I locate what must be considered the ferry. On closer inspection I see plastic barrels have been lashed together to build a floating platform not much bigger than the Jeep itself. The men assure me it will hold the Jeep, though I'm worried they don't realize how heavy it is. As the weight of the front wheels transfer onto the ferry it pitches up, and I'm more than a little tense as I continue forward and ease the Jeep to a stop with the ferry more or less level.

This home made pontoon has no motor, so the two men simply pull it across the river using a steel cable strung for the purpose. The weight of us and the Jeep means the whole contraption sits very low in the fast flowing river, and watching hippos so close is not as enjoyable as I thought it might be. Going for a swim is not an option, the Jeep would surely be lost and the hippos and crocs would make quick work of us. Thankfully the men heave us across in less than ten minutes without incident. This is by far the smallest and sketchiest ferry I've dared to drive onto, and I'm relieved the whole exercise goes off without a hitch.

Late in the afternoon I'm still exploring dirt and sand tracks getting closer to civilization when I see vehicles for the first time in two days. In a sandy riverbed that must be seventy yards across I come across a mini bus helplessly stuck in the deep sand. The twenty passengers stand around looking glum while a solitary man shovels the deep and soft sand. The van is clearly beached, and with his tiny shovel it will take all night to dig out. I plow past in 4x4, having a hard time driving in a straight line in the very deep and soft sand. When I stop in front of the van everyone lights up as they realize what I'm planning. With the tow strap attached and in low range first gear the Jeep hauls the empty mini bus through the sand, dragging it's belly the entire way. Less than ten minutes of my time has saved these people from being stranded for many hours, and I love knowing how much of a difference I've made to their day. After a huge round of handshakes and smiles I pull onto a paved road packed with foot and bicycle traffic just as the sun hits the horizon.

A few days later I strike off into the wilderness aiming to find the Livingstone Monument. This remote marker was built on the exact spot where the famous explorer's heart was buried under a tree after he died of malaria and dysentery in 1873. I drive late into the afternoon on dusty and corrugated dirt tracks before I see the concrete and fenced monument is nothing to get excited about. The $10USD entry fee suddenly feels steep and I'm not so excited about seeing it up close.

I think for five minutes in the shade and realize if I just re-trace all those slow and bumpy miles I will have driven in here for nothing, which feels like a waste. I always prefer to go forward rather than back, so on a whim I turn deeper into the wilderness. I always roam with plenty of food and water, so I'm not concerned about those in the least. I don't usually have the auxiliary gas tank full to save weight, and I should be fine with just the main tank.

Over a couple of days I camp on a stunning wilderness lake, visit caves with ancient rock paintings and navigate a couple of small and muddy river crossings. By the time I reach a paved road the gas gauge is well below empty. The first small town I reach doesn't have a station, and twenty miles later neither does the next. With no choice I continue forward, using only my little toe on the gas pedal. I'm thoroughly distracted watching the dash and keeping the Jeep as close to 30 mpg as possible while rolling along in sixth gear.

I'm just four miles from a station when the engine abruptly dies. Without coughing or spluttering, it simply goes silent. I manhandle the dead weight to the side of the road without power steering which is much harder than I expected. Only after I roll to a silent stop do I see short concrete posts hidden in the long grass on the edge of the road. Hitting one of those would have made my day much, much worse.

I've coasted to a stop less than fifty yards from a Police road-block, and soon the friendly officers walk over to investigate. They laugh at my mistake, and immediately offer to help. The auxiliary tank is firmly bolted to the tire carrier, so I grab only my wallet and hope for the best. In less than two minutes the Police enlist the help of the next passing car, and the friendly family is happy to give me a ride. The Dad speaks good English and we chat about life in Zambia, and how much they love this wonderful country.

Ten minutes later in town I wave goodbye to my new friends and soon enlist the help of men sitting in the shade near the gas station. One man is happy to help, and together we walk five minutes to his house to collect a large plastic container I can borrow. Back at the station the attendant says it's illegal to fill plastic containers directly from a gas pump in Zambia, and she simply can't do it. Usually rules like this are negotiable in Africa, though try as I might I can't persuade her this time.

A nearby taxi driver sees my predicament and offers to help. We put the plastic container in his trunk before he convinces the attendant to fill it there. He reasons that nobody can see what we're doing, and it's basically the same as filling the tank of the vehicle anyway. He's very persuasive, and soon we're in business. The borrowed container was last used for diesel, so the taxi driver pumps in half a gallon and swishes the container around to clean it. I'm shocked when he pours that mixture into the tank of his own car, though he assures me it's run on much worse. For the first time I step back to have look at his mini van and get quite the shock. The interior has been almost completely stripped and it has no windows and barely any dash. The seats are a mishmash from various vehicles and there are no seat belts and a lot of exposed metal inside. I realize I've taken parts off vehicles in wrecking yards that are more complete.

With a few fresh gallons in the container the taxi driver chats happily on the way back to the waiting Jeep. He loves Zambia, especially how everyone is happy to help each other, even a complete stranger like me. He's clearly proud of his country and people, as he should be.

I'm happy when the Jeep fires right up without a single cough or splutter and I can only hope it didn't suck up the nasty gunk that must surely be lurking on the bottom of the tank. I follow my new friend back to town, thanking the Policemen profusely for their assistance as I pass. In town I buy lunch for the taxi driver and the man who lent me the container, and we sit to eat together in the shade of a large tree.

The main Jeep tank is officially 22.5 gallons, and back at the station I barely get 19 gallons in. Napkin math tells me there was somewhere around half a gallon in the tank when the engine stopped, so I gather the pickup can't suck up that last bit, which is probably a good thing.

Once again the fear of running out of gas was much worse than the reality. I was back on the move after just two hours, and I met friendly people all along the way.

Wildlife

W HILE dreaming of Africa I knew the wildlife would be stunning, though I had no idea just how close I would get, or how abundant the wildlife actually is. I regularly found myself utterly speechless, simply unable to believe the creatures directly in front of me. I had no idea it's common to look across a grassy plain and see zebra, giraffe, warthogs, antelope, gemsbok and many types of birds walking past nonchalantly while a pride of lions views the procession from a shady vantage point. Scenes like that had me rubbing my eyes and pinching myself to make sure I wasn't still just dreaming of African wildlife.

This is a collection of my favourite and closest encounters from around the continent.

Marienburg Chimpanzees

I follow the banks of the mighty Sanaga River on muddy tracks through dense jungle in southern Cameroon searching for the Marienburg Chimpanzee Sanctuary. Past a small village I park in a grassy clearing to ask directions, not certain if I'm in the right place. Before I realize what's happening a baby chimpanzee runs over and wraps himself around my leg. Totally stunned I look down as he stares up at me with enormous puppy dog eyes. For three minutes I'm unable to move, captivated by the tiny and expressive face staring inquisitively into mine.

As I've just experienced, this sanctuary is run very differently than most. All the chimps here have been rescued, and were previously kept illegally as pets, and they're confused about their place in the world. Often the chimps have been hand-raised like human children meaning they're incapable of living in the wild. Sadly, they would probably die if left alone so they need special care and attention.

The sanctuary encourages visitors and keepers to interact with the chimps until they can slowly be weaned off human contact. The youngest of the chimps are always outside, with a lot of human contact and care while the middle-age chimps that have been at the sanctuary longer spend many hours a day together away from people. When the chimps are confident in their group, they're moved to a nearby island in the river to live out their lives without human touch. Keepers do stop in occasionally to check on them, and the island is close enough I can hear the chimps screeching. While the chimps at this sanctuary will never live an entirely wild life, their future is bright given where they've come from.

Make no mistake about it - this setup is extremely controversial. Interacting with chimps like this is dangerous. Because we're genetically so similar, we could make each other very sick, and in fact entire chimp populations have been wiped out when they became infected with polio from humans. More than the danger of infection, there is also a physical danger. The bigger chimps could easily tear my arms off, or seriously injure me with a bite. These are extremely powerful animals, and chimp keepers around the world have been killed after their animals have broken loose and sought revenge for their captivity.

Because these chimps have been hand-raised the physical danger here is low, and during my visit not a single chimp shows any aggression. They're extremely gentle and constantly look at my face to make sure they are not hurting me. The young ones do play a little rough, but only because they don't understand how breakable I am.

In the late afternoon I setup camp on the banks of the massive river while listening to the endless screeching on the nearby island, happy to be surrounded by more chimps than people.

Φ   Φ   Φ

In the morning the youngest chimps are full of beans, and it takes an hour to make coffee and cook breakfast while they endlessly climb on me and the Jeep. They try to grab everything and from the second they see the open Jeep they desperately want to climb inside, an idea I don't love. Just like children, whenever I say they can't have or do something they want to do it twice as much. While repeatedly carrying them away I quickly learn the two little guys are as strong as me and have unlimited energy.

Sometimes they run into the trees to climb, though it's never long before they come running back and grab my leg, asking to be picked up. No sooner have I picked them up than they want to wrestle, play, or run away again. The games are endless, and it's hilarious watching their reactions when they fall or I hold them upside down and grin. It's clear they're having a lot of fun, and while they never actually roll around laughing, their toothy grins and cackling screeches are a close approximation.

I'm told we're going for walk in the jungle with the bigger chimps, and I'm not exactly sure what to expect. The keepers warn the chimps will grab anything people are interested in which puts cameras at the top of the list. I hide my GoPro in one pocket, and zip the Jeep keys into another.

When the enclosure is opened I freeze as six or eight large chimps excitedly rush directly at me. They look friendly enough, but they also look very big and powerful, and I have no idea how rough they are. A large female immediately climbs on my back, wrapping her arms and legs around me. She must weigh at least thirty-five pounds, and I struggle under her weight. Thankfully she's very content perched on my back and quickly settles down, clearly happy for the high vantage point.

With various chimps clamoring on various people we make a rag-tag bunch as we set off walking into the jungle.

Some chimps are happiest in the trees swinging on vines, some walk on the ground near my feet and others want to climb all over me or have me carry them. At times the young ones come running up and want me to pick them up, before scampering back down to the ground and running away. The large female sits peacefully on my back through all this, apparently happy to be out of the madness at ground level. She's extremely hot against my back, and combined with the intense humidity it's not long before I'm pouring sweat.

In the past I've merely been an observer to the wildlife, and now for the first time I'm right in the middle of everything. When two chimps have a disagreement it's often on my back or in my arms. When two chimps want to play tag they run between my legs and when one wants to walk on hind legs he uses my hands or legs for balance. It feels surreal to wander through the jungle with real-life chimpanzees who run, jump, climb, fall, smile, hoot, screech and whimper exactly like toddlers.

A few times I'm the cause of a disagreement when one chimp tries to climb onto me and another has already claimed that perch, though happily they never get genuinely angry or violent at me or each other. The two youngest thoroughly love when I spin or carry them upside-down and every which-way. Their front and back legs look similar, and sometimes I get confused which end of the bundle of fur is up. All I can do is lower them gently to the ground where they sort themselves out before coming right back for more.

A few times the young chimps test their teeth on my toes and fingers which never draws blood but does hurt. I sense the bigger chimps are very aware of how weak I am, so when they want me to move my arm they gently move it while watching my face to see if I'm happy with that. A smile and a pet has them at peace, and I can tell they're happy I'm happy.

The mellow chimps are also perfectly content to have me examine and play with them. I inspect their feet and hands and even tickle them on the belly which results in all kinds of laughter and attempts to escape my reach which lasts all of thirty seconds before they come right back. I'm intreiged to see they have fingerprints like mine and overall their hands are almost identical, just a lot more beat up and rugged. I'm filming with my GoPro when one of the boisterous chimps snatches it from my hand and races off into the jungle at full speed. Our guide tells us to stay put and charges away to give chase, so we sit quietly and play with the sole chimp that stayed behind, pushing him between us while he hangs from a vine, just like a child on a swing.

It takes almost ten minutes to retrieve the GoPro and the footage of the chimp carrying it while looking directly at the lens is hilarious. When the cartload of chimps return the lone one flips out, excitedly spinning around in circles and jumping up and down while grinning broadly. They're such social creatures it was clearly hard for him to be away from his friends.

The chimps continuously climb and swing on massive hanging vines just like I pictured. They're supremely confident in their skills and grip, even when thirty feet off the ground. On the rare occasion I see one fall or stumble I see a bashful, almost embarrassed response, as if saying "I hope nobody saw that."

For a rest we sit on the ground in a small clearing while the chimps play excitedly in the nearby trees and vines. The big female who climbed on me is extremely relaxed and soon sits on my lap to groom my beard. It's getting very wild and I realize my face looks more like a chimp than any of the other humans. With my face only six inches from hers it's captivating to watch her facial expressions and responses to mine. I pull faces which she mimics and she's always quick to laugh and smile with me. When I stare into the distance and point, she spins around to see what I'm looking at and using just the tone of my voice I can convey my meaning which she understands completely.

Sitting face to face with a chimpanzee and interacting with her like this I'm struck by the realization I am her and she is me. The similarities are so strong I can't possibly believe anything else.

When the time comes to say goodbye I feel a bit sad, though I'm happy to see the chimps bounce away, content to play with whoever else happens to be around.

Actually playing with chimpanzees is by far the most intense animal encounter of my life, something I'll never forget.

Mgahinga Mountain Gorillas

The decision to visit the mountain gorillas is not an easy one for me. Rwanda recently doubled the price to $1,600USD which is way outside my budget. In neighbouring Uganda a forty-five minute visit is $600, and after a lot of thinking I finally decide this will be my single most expensive activity in Africa. I notch it up as once in a lifetime.

On just my second day in Uganda I buy a permit at the National Park office in Kisoro, where two Uganda Wildlife Officers ask for a ride to the National Park. I'm always happy for friendly company, and their stories of working with the gorillas is a bonus. Both men carry AK47s like walking sticks, and I realize I've come to see them as a fashion accessory in this part of the world.

They explain the gorilla population has actually increased in recent years, due in large part to tourist visits. The National Park hires locals from the surrounding villages to work in the park, track the gorillas, keep them safe and guide tourists. This gives locals a big incentive to keep the gorillas safe, and the tourist money pays for the construction of new schools, hospitals and roads. It's a good news story, and the men explain they also work closely with wildlife officers from Rwanda and the DRC. Together they perform and annual survey of all the gorillas in the region, and work together to eliminate poaching, which does still happen but is much less common than years past.

Outside the park entrance is a beautiful little community campground with plenty of green grass where I'm able to spread out. I thoroughly enjoy soaking in the late afternoon sun and take the opportunity to repair multiple pieces of gear and clothing that are slowly falling apart. Overnight it's difficult to sleep because I'm way too excited about the day to come.

Early in the morning I'm given a quick overview of the area and the specific gorillas I'll be seeing. Here in Mgahinga there is only one gorilla troop consisting of eight gorillas and uniquely there are two massive silverbacks in this troop. One of the guides is proud to say the dominant male is the second-largest known in the world. After the brief twenty minute introduction I begin hiking up the lower slopes of Sabyinyo Volcano with four other visitors. We hike directly towards the three-way border of Uganda, Rwanda and the DRC.

After an easy forty-five minute hike through the light jungle we meet the trackers who explain the gorillas are very close. Peering eagerly through the foliage I catch a glimpse of the enormous animals just thirty yards further on and my heart leaps into my mouth. At this time of year the gorillas eat bamboo, which means they're mostly in the open and extremely easy to see and photograph up close. As we creep closer my brain stops, unable to comprehend the scene less than ten yards away.

The silverback is so enormous, and so close, I genuinely feel as if I'm watching a CGI movie. There's just no way this can be real. This gorilla weighs well over 500lbs of pure muscle, and his biceps, shoulders and chest are simply too big to comprehend. His head is three or four times bigger than mine, and he could easily crush my skull with one hand. Paradoxically, he's perched on his backside chewing bamboo with a quizzical look on his face, giving him a childlike innocence. His fluffy black fur looks extremely soft, and his enormous beer belly is perfectly smooth jet-black skin. I'm staring at a five hundred pound children's toy. He looks exactly like the huge plush toy prizes at carnivals, just way bigger and a lot more dangerous.

I'm sitting on the ground taking photos and video when the silverback slowly moves closer and closer. He walks forward with his knuckles on the ground and his head up, just like I imagined. Now he's in motion I see the true size of his shoulders and upper body with layers of rippling muscle. I want to retreat but a guide puts a hand on my shoulder and tells me to stay still, so I do. He assures me repeatedly I'll be fine, so with little choice I trust his judgement and enjoy the moment as the monster gorilla comes within five yards. A few minutes later I'm absolutely certain my eyes are lying.

After taking a stack of photos and videos I simply sit quietly on the ground and watch without distraction. It's clear they each have a distinct personality, with the younger ones clearly full of energy and the older ones happy to laze about while grazing in the bamboo. Occasionally they look directly at us, but for the most part they ignore us entirely.

The gorillas slowly move along a dry creek bed and we follow at a respectable distance, utterly captivated. It's clear the massive silverback is keeping an eye on the whole troop - it's his job to keep them safe after all. Once they find a new patch of bamboo to eat he lays on his stomach and rests his head in his hands, giving the appearance of being deep in thought. From time to time he glances around at his troop, making sure everyone is safe before staring off into space again. For five minutes I'm only fifteen feet from him before he suddenly stands and comes directly at me. I'm sitting down and decide there isn't anything I can do about it, so I just stay down and hope for the best. With a grunt he veers away at the last moment, easily passing close enough I could reach out and touch him. A guide explains that was a challenge of dominance and if I stood up or moved towards him the silverback would have attacked, and it would not have been pretty.

I struggle to believe this is actually real, and I try my best to soak it all in.

Twenty minutes later I move beside a tree to take photos before the other massive silverback comes over and starts eating the tree next to my face. He's less than a yard away on the other side of the tree and again the guides use hand signals to say I should remain in place. I cautiously lean forward to peer around the tree and I'm startled by him peering right back. He doesn't look angry or upset and I get the sense he might be a little curious about me. He's happy to keep munching and apparently doesn't mind me at all. Again I could easily reach out and touch him, though instead I lean back so the tree is once again between us.

Whenever the gorillas want a fresh bamboo stalk to chew they just reach up with one hand and snap one off with ease. After they move away I hang my entire weight on the same bamboo stalk and can't even bend it. They really are that powerful.

Just like chimps, the baby gorillas are full of beans and continuously wrestle, climb on and over anything in their path and chew everything they can. They take turns using the big silverback as a trampoline, and I'm impressed he never once does anything to stop them. Just like a human father he tolerates their play with endless patience, and it's clear the little ones thoroughly enjoy themselves while screeching, grinning and jumping up and down with excitement.

Too soon forty-five minutes has passed, and we tear ourselves away from the magical animals and hike down the volcano.

After all the stressing about the price, I seriously think about paying to go again. Once in a lifetime is not enough, it really was that breathtaking.

Mana Pools National Park

No less than thirty people have told me about Mana Pools National Park in the north of Zimbabwe, which places it squarely on my must-visit list. Camping is on the banks of the mighty Zambezi river, and as always I'm excited knowing the low mountains on the far shore are an entirely different country - Zambia. As I pull into camp on the first day a crocodile sits less than five yards away on the bank of the river, and just ten minutes later I watch an elephant wade through shallows to a small island. He really does hold up his trunk like a snorkel when the water covers his face, making the scene look more like a cartoon than real life.

Each morning I'm woken by hippos grunting loudly in the river only a handful of yards away before I freely roam the park in the Jeep searching for large African animals. During the intensely hot afternoons I rest at camp before setting out again before dusk to spot more animals.

One scorching afternoon I'm sitting next to the Jeep reading a book when I see an elephant a hundred yards away in the shallow reeds. Over the course of the next hour he slowly ambles closer until he's less than twenty yards away. He clearly knows I'm sitting calmly, and occasionally looks over to make sure I'm not doing anything crazy. He's perfectly content to wander from tree to tree searching out lunch and I'm perfectly happy to watch and photograph as he moves around. His movements are so slow and graceful it's hard to believe just how big he really is. When he's not stripping leaves off trees he's completely silent, and in fact I've been told repeatedly elephants are trouble makers because they move silently and often sneak up on people.

I book a walking tour in the hopes of getting close to the large predators and because we're going on foot the tour consists of a guide and a mandatory armed guard. The guard carries the now very familiar AK47, and I don't miss the fact he chambers a round as we leave the vehicles. As luck would have it a couple of researchers are tracking a pack of extremely elusive African painted dogs, and their radio-tracking equipment makes locating them almost a certainty.

I jump at the chance to tag along, and soon we're walking through tall dry grass and dense trees. Animal tracks are absolutely everywhere, and we spot a few elephants at a distance, but nothing super-close. I get the fright of my life when a lion lets out a mighty roar, and I'm seriously shaken when another returns with his own equally impressive roar.

My guide explains two different prides are talking back and forth, and we're right in the middle. Out of the Jeep I'm not feeling confident with lions so close, though the man holding the rifle doesn't seem worried at all. He explains lions almost never attack a group of more than three people, and he doesn't even take the rifle off his shoulder. I can't help thinking about how he said 'almost never' as we walk directly towards the very talkative cats who continue to roar. We close to within a hundred yards, though we never do catch a glimpse of either pride.

Months later on a similar walking safari in Zambia we come face to face with a lioness, less than thirty yards away. I get a huge fright when I first spot her couching behind a fallen tree watching us intently. She looks exactly like a predator stalking prey - us. Again the guides are relaxed, and don't bother to ready the .416 Rigby elephant rifle.
"If that was a hippo, I'd already have the rifle loaded and aimed," is all he says.

Back at Mana Pools we stop every five hundred yards while the trackers use the radio equipment to find a new direction of travel until we spot the pack of painted dogs sitting above the massive dry riverbed. We silently creep to within fifty yards before they start getting anxious. Through my zoom lens I have an excellent view, and the dogs look somewhere between a regular dog and fox, each with extremely unique and beautiful markings, giving rise to the name 'painted dogs'. One researcher mentions a female has been missing from the pack for a week, and he hopes she's found a den to give birth. This would be excellent news for the highly endangered dogs.

At camp that night I'm sitting around the fire with a group of South Africans when I hear a lion let loose with an almighty roar. Deep down my whole body instantly recognises the sound, and in the pitch black night it screams to run for my life. I have a hard time controlling my fear, but realize nobody else seems to care. The South Africans assure me it's perfectly fine, so we stay by the fire listening intently as the lion comes closer with each successive roar. Now on edge, I'm even more startled when I get up to fetch a drink and find a hyena less than ten yards behind me. Five have stalked up to our circle and now crouch just outside the light cast by the flickering fire watching us intently.

For the next hour we keep them back with our flashlights, and often we smell the stench of rotting meat before turning around to see the evil-looking creatures slink back a few steps. When it's time for bed I have to walk a hundred yards back to the Jeep, and I struggle not to run. While brushing my teeth a hyena walks a full circle around the Jeep to investigate. He slinks less than five yards from me, though he doesn't seem interested in a fight, and I easily scare him away with my headlamp. Not wanting to push my luck I quickly scamper upstairs, happy to be off the ground and out of his reach.

Wanting to soak in every possible minute I stay in the park until late the next afternoon and find a small clearing just outside the gate to camp. I'm exhausted after the long days and fall asleep soon after another stunning sunset. Normally I sleep soundly in my comfortable and elevated bed, and it's odd for me to wake. When I do, I immediately assume something is wrong and listen intently while looking around. Peering down to the ground through the fly screen I make eye contact with a large hyena standing at the rear tire of the Jeep, less than four feet from my face. He stares directly back, clearly aware I'm there. After sniffing around he finally moves away, and I struggle falling back to sleep. Later that night I'm woken by an extremely loud lion's roar and in the morning I find fresh elephant dung nearby. Apparently he snuck in and out without waking me. All of this, and I'm not even in the park anymore - this is just regular life in this part of Zimbabwe.

Φ Φ Φ

Early on the expedition in Mali I moved a rock to level the Jeep and got a huge fright to see a scorpion underneath. Lesson learned, I never again moved rocks or collected firewood without thick gloves. On many nights while getting ready for bed I was startled by scorpions in the sand around camp. Wearing flip flops with scorpions around might not be the best idea, though I never did have a problem with them.

I saw only a handful of snakes on the expedition, including a green mamba crossing the road in Mozambique. I never got particularly close or felt I was in any danger from them. I always gave snakes and spiders a wide berth, and they never gave me any trouble.

So abundant is the wildlife in Southern Africa I was often forced to stop on roads to allow herds of elephants to cross - that's not just inside National Parks, but simply driving on regular roads. I have no idea how much space elephants like, so I keep well back.

I was charged by elephants a couple of times while in the Jeep, most notably in South Africa. The biggest bull elephant I've seen before or since came directly at my driver's door with surprising speed, only veering away at the last moment. I fully expected him to graze the rear tire carrier, and he must have barely missed it. I later learned people were killed in that game park when elephants crushed them inside their car.

It was common throughout Southern Africa to pull off a small gravel track to wild camp and see a tower of giraffes lift their heads to investigate. Despite their immense size I always found them skittish, and unfortunately they would move away within a few minutes of my arrival. One magical morning I was about to climb down from bed at sunrise when a tower of giraffes walked past less than twenty yards away. Sitting upstairs meant we were able to see almost eye to eye, and for once the curious gentle giants weren't disturbed by me, even stopping to eat as they ambled past.

In the Central Kalahari I had to actually drive off dirt tracks to avoid lions lying in the shade, and I stopped so close I was afraid to lower the window. Sitting in the driver's seat the lionesses were less than six feet away and for the first time I realized the electric windows in the Jeep simply aren't fast enough. I have no idea how fast a lion can lunge six feet, and I have no intention of finding out.

At many wild camps I found lion prints on the sandy tracks, and it was an everyday occurrence to camp surrounded by elephant dung. Dirt roads are always littered with animal tracks, so even when I didn't directly see the elephants, lions, giraffe and warthogs I knew they were extremely close.

One evening while sitting outside at a wild camp after dark I heard rustling in the nearby trees. With no clue what animal might be sneaking up I prepared to scamper into bed. In the moonlight I was just able to make out a herd of elephants walking single file along the ridge holding tails with trunks. All I could do was sit in stunned silence, mouth agape. Later that night I was woken by extremely loud panting, which I assume was a lion very close by.

If you dream of visiting Africa and the stunning wildlife I urge you to go. It truly is a hundred times more breathtaking and abundant than I ever dreamed possible.

Treating People Like People

Burundi
September 2018

WHILE exploring the corners of Africa I've spent an immense amount of time pondering the major differences between 'our' world and the one I've been immersed in. There are a host of differences that scream for attention and are unmissable on the first days and months on the continent. Roads are very different, electricity and running water are spotty, armed Military personnel are an everyday sight and the weather can be counted on to be extremely hot and humid, except when torrential downpours last months and rainfall is measured in feet rather than inches. Of course there are also stunning landscapes and wildlife that literally makes my jaw drop.
These are the obvious differences.

But there is something more. Something deeper. Something intangible I haven't been able to pin down, hard as I might try. Something that has taken years to notice and feel, and I only became aware of once I was able to look past the obvious physical differences. Africa and Africans know something about life we don't. More accurately, they know something we've forgotten. Daily life here is different in a very good way because something is fundamentally different about the way people live and interact. *Something* about life in Africa is very different to our world and lately I've become determined to uncover this *something*, and I won't leave until I do.

Φ   Φ   Φ

At just under nine thousand square miles, Burundi is the fifth smallest country on continental Africa, and is seldom visited by foreigners. It lies in the very centre of the continent, and is torn between it's French-speaking West African neighbour DRC and it's more British-influenced neighbours Rwanda and Tanzania to the north and east respectively.

Full of curiosity, I apply for a visa at the embassy in Dar Es Salaam, Tanzania. A one month visa costs $90 USD, and must be applied for two weeks in advance. This is in stark contrast to the rest of Southern and Eastern Africa where visas are very cheap and are granted on arrival at land borders in less than five minutes.

The Ambassador welcomes me into his extremely clean and modern office, and I can't help but notice the classical music trying to drown out the low hum of the air conditioning fighting to keep the humidity in check. After flicking through my passport he asks about my home country of Australia, somewhere he has always wanted to visit. He asks about the people, and is curious to know about life Downunder.

I'm torn with which response to give, and feel compelled to tell the truth. I explain Australians are very friendly and easy going, but unfortunately they just don't have time. They're all so busy with work and responsibilities, Australians don't chat in the street like the Africans I've come to admire. Everyone is so busying earning a living they're always rushing to the next thing, always living by the clock.

The Ambassador listens attentively, and I see the disappointment in his eyes. In Burundi, he explains, everyone knows their neighbours, and everyone is part of a tight knit community. In times of need the entire community pulls together to help those who are struggling, and that's what makes Burundi so special. It doesn't have the best infrastructure or shiny shopping malls, but it does have very strong community, and people who have time and care deeply about each other. The pride on the Ambassador's face is impossible to miss as he says this.

He explains Burundi's troubled past, and it's continued struggles with poverty and lack of infrastructure. Even so, he's proud to add, Burundi has opened it's borders to those in need, and is currently home to tens of thousands of refugees from neighbouring DRC, fleeing violence and political unrest.

After thanking the Ambassador for his time, I leave with a sense of excitement for what lies ahead. The last few months in East Africa have not been as exciting as my run down the West Coast through Nigeria, Cameroon, Gabon, The Congos and Angola, and I miss that raw adventure dearly. Lately I've seen tens of thousands of tourists moving in air conditioned buses to crowded game parks. Speaking English every day has made me lazy, and supermarkets, campgrounds, wifi and even gas stations are similar to home. The whole expedition has become a bit too easy, and I've been a bit disappointed with that. I'm genuinely excited and a touch nervous to jump into a different world.

ɸ   ɸ   ɸ

After a month roaming Tanzania I climb into an unexpected mountain range before leaving the country through enormous steel gates. Immediately I feel that I've driven back into the thick of West Africa, and the déjà-vu comes in waves. Thousands of brightly dressed people mill about carrying everything imaginable, mostly on their heads. Hundreds of overloaded trucks wait in a long line and a stream of men soon run alongside the Jeep trying to sell me all manner of cheap Chinese plastic things. To top it off a man in Military uniform directs me to a small shack serving as an Ebola check station. I have my temperature taken and my Yellow Fever vaccination is confirmed before I can proceed. French is the go to language, and I find myself struggling to acclimatize back into a world that was so familiar not long ago. Taking stock of the basic infrastructure around me I feel as if I've driven backwards into West Africa not only in miles, but also through time.

Outside I haggle with men changing money, and a small crowd forms as we walk to my driver's door. I struggle with the big numbers in French, and I feel vulnerable holding a huge wad of cash and my irreplaceable documents. I've never once had the slightest problem exchanging money in Africa, though I always have my guard up and eyes open. I block the door with my body and put my documents on the seat before locking and slamming the door - and then immediately realize what I've done. Looking through the window I see the keys dangling from the glovebox lock. For the first time in over a decade I've just locked the keys inside. If I had a list of places I didn't ever want to do that, a bustling International border between two African countries would be number one.

A moment of stress passes before I put my contingency plan into action. Almost three years ago I secured a spare key to the underside of the Jeep, and I attract some funny looks as I crawl underneath and liberate it from the now permanent layer of rock-like mud. I'm relieved it's still there, and snapping the zip tie securing it to the frame is no problem. The key is not electronic, so the alarm sounds when I unlock and open the door, causing everyone to jump back in fright. After retrieving the electronic key I turn off the alarm and re-lock the doors before getting down to business exchanging one heaping stack of grubby bills for another.

Inside I hand my passport to a Tanzanian Immigration officer for an exit stamp who immediately passes it down the line to Burundi Immigration. The Burundians check my visa to make sure I'm permitted to enter before the Tanzanians stamp an exit in my passport. They do this to ensure I won't get stranded between the two countries. I'm taken by surprise and realize this is the most intelligent thing I've ever experienced at a border anywhere on the planet.

An hour later I move away from the border with a new stamp in my passport and new Customs paperwork for the Jeep. I'm impressed to see multiple signs encouraging me to drive on the right, the opposite side to Tanzania where I've just come from. This is only the second time I've switched sides on the continent, and the first time I'll drive on the right since Angola, nine countries and 24,000 miles ago.

I'm always a little unsure on my first night in a new country, so I get a cheap room in a guesthouse, only remembering the French word for room at the very last second. Within an hour a torrential downpour lets fly - the first of the season I'm told - which the locals are elated to see. This is not the first time I've brought the rains, and the hotel owner smiles broadly when he asks if I'm the rainmaker.

I order a beer and soon strike up a conversation with a uniformed Military man also enjoying the ice-cold local brew. He's excited to learn I'm a tourist interested in Burundi, a very rare thing. His words soon begin to slur and I can't help notice he finishes four large beers in the time I finish one, all while nursing a battered old AK47 across his knees.

Nearby James overhears our conversation and eagerly joins. He is from Kivu in the DRC, and is proud to say his impeccable English is self-taught. As we chat about the DRC and Burundi at length I realize James has seen and lived more in his thirty-five years than most will in their entire lives. Quickly I'm blown away by James' insight.

What James explains is so simple it's hard to believe I've missed it before now. People in Africa think about people. Their entire world consists of their family and friends, and those nearby in their immediate community. During good times or bad, people are there for each other, and they always treat each other with the utmost respect and courtesy.

The problem with our 'developed' world, says James, is that people have forgotten about those around them, and instead think about money and possessions. Because our world re-volves around material consumption, and the drive to acquire more wealth, we have abandoned the fundamentals of life and happiness. Too often we hear about a billionaire unwilling to provide sick pay for employees, or of people that have never met their neighbours. It's a sad reality that in the quest for more wealth and possessions, we've left out such a crucial piece of life.

Fundamentally, when people treat people like people, every-thing else falls into place, James says. The joy and sense of well-being this brings is on display around me each and every day.

Φ   Φ   Φ

In the morning after bumping along in first gear for the better part of an hour I finally give up. I'm technically driving on a paved road, though I wish it wasn't. It's so broken, and the potholes are so deep a gravel road would be much better. Even with the torrential rain mud would be better than the half-pavement potholes stretching endlessly in front of me. Reluctantly I pull over and get out to air down the tires. I have to remind myself that slowing down to the local pace is the best way to experience life around me, and while outside the Jeep no less than five people on bicycles stop to ask if I need any help.

I make a point to visit the few known tourist attractions in Burundi, and I venture off to find a few of my own. Famously Burundi claims to the southernmost source of the mighty Nile River, a hotly contested title among the countries in the area. From the top of a small hill water running off one side flows into the mighty Congo, while water bubbling from a small spring on the other side forms the Nile and will eventually flow into the Mediterranean at Alexandria in Egypt. There is a small pyramid and plaque, though it's clear the site sees few visitors, such is tourism in Burundi.

Nearby I find the extremely beautiful wilderness hot spring of Muhweza, easily the best hot spring I've visited in Africa. The crystal clear water is the perfect soaking temperature and I spend hours in the lush green valley washing away the miles. Later in the afternoon I wind down from the mountains and drop directly onto the shore of stunning Lake Tanganyika. This enormous body of water is the second deepest and the second largest on the planet by volume and is almost 5,000 feet deep. It's clearly central to life with fishermen heading out daily before sunrise and returning each night to a stunning sunset backdrop.

I camp on the sandy shore of a rundown resort and ask the caretaker if it's safe to swim. He assures me twice that it is, and I confirm explicitly there are no crocs or hippos. The words are not complicated in French - *crocodile* and *hippopotame* - and I'm confident I completely understand his reply - there are none. Feeling good about the situation I dive in alone for a refreshing swim just as the sun kisses the lake, streaking red over the DRC mountains on the far shore. I thoroughly enjoy the peace and quiet which can be hard to come by in Africa when I'm a huge source of curiosity for locals. I feel utterly alone with my thoughts for the first time in what feels like months.

In the morning I'm dismayed to see the sandy beach littered with the remains of what must have been a mighty hippo celebration. They came ashore to dine on the tasty green grass the caretaker is now watering. When I ask about the hippo tracks he grins widely.
"Sure," he says, "they only come on shore at night."
I was silly to think I had been alone for the swim after all.

Throughout Africa my Jeep has attracted a lot of attention, so I'm used to a crowd and a peppering of friendly questions everywhere I go. Here in Burundi the curiosity and awe have increased ten fold, and simply stopping for gas turns into half an hour of questions and answers. The people here are clearly not used to tourists, and they're eager to hear about the outside world and to inspect the Jeep.

The men always want to know the pertinent details - how big is the engine, how fast can it go and is it four wheel drive. I have to confirm multiple times the engine runs on gas, not diesel. The men here have never seen a 4x4 vehicle that is not diesel, and they're shocked to learn such a thing even exists. All agree that makes it better, because it means it has more power, and therefore has a higher top speed. I don't have the heart to correct them on these minor misconceptions.

The women are always extremely impressed by my kitchen ("He can cook!"), my sleeping setup and photos of my family on the roof. They're impressed I live in such a tiny space, and ask repeatedly why I don't have a wife and kids. They all agree a man of my age should have both and I get the feeling they would quickly sort it out if I stuck around.

Φ   Φ   Φ

Burundi's fledgling tourism industry bills itself as 'The Heart of Africa', and now I understand why. More than just being geographically at the centre of the continent, Burundi's people and their unmistakable sense of community really do bring to mind an emotional centre. Burundians have such warmth I struggle to see how an Africa without Burundi could survive anymore than a human without a heart.

When first dropped into Africa it's easy to feel overwhelmed like Dorothy when she first landed in unfamiliar Oz. We only need to open our eyes to realize we're a long way from Kansas. Less obvious, but equally important, are the emotional differences. Back in our world everyone is so focused on work, money and possessions, we've forgotten what we should really be focusing on - the people immediately surrounding us.

In South Africa the Zulu people have a saying - '*Umuntu*

ngumuntu ngabantu' which literally translates to 'A person is a person because of other people'. For hundreds of thousands of years the people of Africa have not forgotten this important lesson, and it's impact is as clear as the potholes in the road.

Africa has taught me more than I could ever write in entire volumes, and it has changed me in more ways than even I realize. More than any other, there is one lesson I'm determined to incorporate into my life as long as I live:
Once we treat people like people, everything else falls into place.

Disaster

B UTTING up against the mighty DRC in the remote south-west corner of Uganda lies the Ishasha Sector of Queen Elizabeth National Park, a seldom visited region that takes some getting to. I put in a massive day on nasty roads while watching enormous thunderstorms boil ominously on the horizon. Nearing the park entrance I know I'm on a good thing when I see multiple troops of monkeys and baboons playing near the road before listening to elephants trumpet while chatting to the guard at the entrance gate. I'm surrounded by the same familiar green rolling hills and grassland I came to love near the equator in West Africa and the humidity and imposing weather helps me feel like I'm right back in Gabon or the DRC, which is a feeling I love. The trumpeting elephants make me feel better about forking over the $90 entrance fee which grants me entry for today and tomorrow with camping for the night included.

This park is world famous for it's lions who climb and actually sit in trees. I'm told the lions climb on the hottest days of the year in search of a breeze. The torrential rains mean it's not overly hot during my visit and though I search high and low throughout the park I never do spot a single lion.

The massive thunderstorms build and swirl all afternoon and cast an eerie light on the grassland as I roam the park. The skies let loose at dusk just as I'm finishing dinner in the campsite. I'm the only person in the small clearing all evening, though I do share it with the hippos that infest the adjacent river.

In the morning I'm up and moving before sunrise, again exploring far and wide in search of wildlife. In multiple places I drive through deep mud and water, though as usual the Jeep doesn't have any problem in low range 4x4. I spot herds of elephants, buffalo and many different kinds of antelope grazing in the lush vegetation, including a lone male elephant that flaps his ears aggressively, a sure sign he wants to be left alone. Soon after lunch the skies open with an enormous torrential downpour, with the largest raindrops I've ever seen. The noise created by the rain pelting the roof is immense and I take it as a sign to leave the park and move north to new adventures.

Φ   Φ   Φ

Later that day I hear a disconcerting noise from under the Jeep, and wonder if I've damaged something in all the deep mud. During our two and a half years on the road I've become extremely attuned to her quirks and noises, and I know immediately this one is not normal. I continue a few miles and diagnose the ticking noise changes with road speed, and is not related to engine speed or the brakes. I finally pin it down to the front drive shaft, and that troublesome joint I had replaced in South Africa.

At first I just ignore it, but only a handful of miles later the slight ticking turns into a very loud clunking and I know action is required. For the first time in almost 100,000 combined miles during my two expeditions, I pull to the side of the road, get out my tools and lie in the dirt to work on my Jeep.

It takes me forty-five minutes to completely remove the front drive shaft so I can inspect it. The CV-style joint on the transfer case end clunks loudly when I twist it, and the end cap actually falls off. Inside the joint I see only a tiny amount of extremely dry and crusty grease, which is not good. Without adequate grease the joint never stood a chance. There is no way to repair it now, so it must be replaced again. I don't carry a spare, so I put the entire drive shaft inside the Jeep and I'll just have to continue without 4x4. I'll need to get a replacement joint, hopefully in the capital of Kampala, or maybe later in Nairobi, Kenya.

Back on the road the noise is gone which makes me confident I've correctly identified the cause. Later that night in camp I fix another minor issue, the heat shield above the rear muffler has come adrift, and has been rattling loudly against the exhaust. Lately the Jeep has sounded like a genuine African vehicle, rattling obnoxiously with every gear change. It's a quick fix to put a few large washers on the nuts that hold it on, and I get it bolted up solidly again. It's odd to have worked on two Jeep problems in the same day, though overall I feel good about it, even without four wheel drive.

In the morning I set out north, aiming to meet a friend at Murchison Falls National Park. The road deteriorates quickly, and soon I'm crawling forward exclusively in first gear bouncing over endless potholes. Chinese road crews are hard at work, and for a couple of hundred miles I drive through endless construction zones turning the muddy two lane track into a multi-lane freeway. On a couple of occasions I pull to the side to allow construction trucks to pass, and narrowly avoid getting the Jeep stuck in the slick clay without 4x4.

Φ Φ Φ

More than eight hours later on rough roads in the scorching heat I turn off onto a tiny track, searching for a small hot spring on the shores of mighty Lake Albert. The narrow track is dirt and rock, but doesn't present any kind of problem. Even without 4x4 it's easy for the Jeep, and we bounce along in our usual fashion. The sun is dipping low on the horizon, and I'm pushing my luck in terms of finding a place to wild camp. I haven't seen a good option for hours, so I decide to push on, hoping the hot spring will be the ideal spot. Searching for a wild camp near sunset is always stressful and I try to avoid it whenever possible. For whatever reason on long driving days I always convince myself to keep going rather than stop early as I should. It feels easier to just keep driving, so I do.

When the stunning lake comes into view I know I need a photo. I angle the Jeep across the track, pull the hand brake, turn off the engine and leave it in first gear. I've been lazy about adjusting the hand brake which I'm certain it's packed solid with stubborn Congo mud, but I just don't want to deal with it. I know it doesn't work all that well, so I've just been careful about where I park for the last six months. Once I have actually felt the weight of the Jeep overcome the engine, causing it to roll forward on a steep hill. On that occasion I was sitting in the driver's seat and it only moved about an inch every five seconds, which I assume is one cylinder rolling over at a time.

I stay in the seat for ten seconds while I drink water and grab my camera, and the Jeep doesn't budge, making me confident it's not going to move on the slope. As I walk away to take the photo I figure I'll just run back if it moves even an inch, which seems like a perfectly good plan.

I walk about twenty yards from the Jeep and climb the bank for a photo and as I look through the viewfinder the Jeep begins to move. Almost before I react it's traveled an entire Jeep length, and is picking up speed fast. I scramble to chase, but I already know I have no hope. I desperately run ten steps and barely close on the Jeep which is still picking up speed. I realize the situation is utterly hopeless.

After moving forward on it's own for six or eight lengths, the front driver's side tire slams into the rock embankment, flipping the Jeep over onto the passenger side. It violently slams onto the rocky gravel before skidding to a crunching halt. All of this happens in the span of five seconds, and I can't believe my eyes.

My heart pounds in my ears as the crash fades and the reality of the situation - and my stupidity - sinks in. Within seconds I feel more helpless and alone than ever before on expedition, maybe even than anytime in my life. Exhausted and terrified at the same time, I crumple to the ground, not wanting to look at my disabled and possibly destroyed home. I want to deny reality, and think if I stop looking it will stop being true.

I'm utterly shocked how quickly everything has gone wrong, and desperately want a do-over.

I'm so freaked out I feel close to tears, though even that's too much effort. When I first dreamed of this Africa expedition and posted details online I received an avalanche of hatred and negativity about how I was going to fail, and how I was a reckless idiot for even trying. Now feeling extremely vulnerable and alone, the comments about my certain failure come flooding back. I soon convince myself I really have failed, just like everyone said I would. All the years of saving, planning and dreaming have crashed to an end because of my own stupidity.

With every passing second I feel more stupid and terrified. Lying on it's side, the Jeep is utterly useless. I can't sleep, cook or shelter inside, and on my own I have no chance of getting it back on the wheels. I feel like my only course of action is to retrieve my passport and walk away.

Where I'll walk to, I have no idea.

Φ   Φ   Φ

I go through waves of despair, feeling horribly sorry for myself. I'm sitting in the dirt with my camera, so I snap a few photos. Even seeing the Jeep through the viewfinder makes me sick to the stomach, so I only manage to take three. A person is never truly alone in Africa, and soon locals materialize from the scrubby brush, attracted by the loud crash. Seeing the terror on my face they're immediately concerned someone has

been crushed, and they're relieved when I make it clear I'm the only person and I'm fine. While I reassure each person no people were injured, the locals ask what the big deal is.
It's just a car, they say. No big deal.
We can put it back right.

I stop shaking and start using my brain and I begin to see their point of view. It would be so much worse if someone was crushed by the Jeep, or if it veered to the right and gone off a cliff. Obviously the situation is bad, though it helps me get perspective realizing it could have been so much worse. It's not on fire, nobody was injured and it didn't go off a cliff. On a scale of bad to really bad, this is only bad. Seeing it this way helps me I see a glimmer of hope, and I see this isn't the end of the world after all.

Still in denial and not wanting to see the damage up close I walk a lap to assess the situation and formulate a plan. On the uphill side I see a few trees that are perfect for winching. If I can run a line to a tree and back to the frame with my snatch block, I may be able to right the Jeep without much hassle. I've seen this done as a demonstration, and I'm confident I can handle it. Always one to prefer action to inaction I get to work and immediately feel better. Even if the situation is hopeless, I feel better for doing something.

I need to retrieve the winch controller, so I start by climbing up the undercarriage, using the skid plates like ladder rungs. The view of the underside is disorienting, and it's strange to see the empty space the front drive shaft normally occupies. I can see the suspension better than ever before, and in my warped state of mind I briefly think this is a good time to grease the front U-Joints while they're so easy to reach.

Once I'm standing on the driver's side doors - now the top - I open the extremely heavy driver's door against gravity before lowering myself until I'm standing on the inside of the passenger door - now the bottom. The Jeep is still in first gear, and the hand brake is still all the way up, just how I left it. A quick glance reveals absolute chaos inside, including a pile of smashed glass bottles and eggs I just bought an hour ago. It's a problem for later, and for now I need to focus on the task at hand.

Holding the winch controller I climb back up and out the driver's door before climbing down the makeshift undercarriage ladder. I open the rear tailgate, needing to dig out recovery straps, shackles and a snatch block. With the spare tire, extra gas, hi-lift jack and maxtrax the tailgate is extremely heavy, and a few local men help me lower it to the ground without dropping it. Closing it against gravity takes the help of five men, and with a lot of struggling and grunting we barely manage.

I spool out the winch line as I walk to the nearest tree before discovering the winch line is not nearly long enough to reach the tree and return to the Jeep via the snatch block. Looking at the angles I'm fairly confident pulling directly off the tree will only drag the Jeep across the road, not actually lift it onto the wheels. One local man speaks reasonable English, and steps forward to help. Akram is tall and skinny, softly spoken and obviously wants to help in any way he can. He assures me the gathered crowd will be able to lift the hulking Jeep upright, as if it's something they do all the time. I'm skeptical they can lift the 6,000lbs of dead weight, though with no choice I realize there's no harm in trying.

Now my brain is actually working, I realize if we do manage to get the Jeep back on the wheels it will simply roll away again. After attaching the winch line directly to a tree I again climb up and lower myself into the driver's seat and stamp the brake pedal to the floor.

I take up the slack with the winch, and just as the Jeep starts to skid across the rocks I give the signal to start lifting the rear passenger corner. I'm shocked by how quickly the corner rises, and the winch holds the weight before my helpers reset and lift again. In this way the corner rises a foot at a time, and in less than thirty seconds the Jeep bounces back onto the wheels while I stamp on the brake pedal as hard as I physically can.

Pouring sweat and shaking like a leaf, for the first time I think I might just get out of this.

The Jeep is now partially in a ditch, though it's still on a dangerously steep hill. Now with zero confidence in the hand brake I have no intention of getting out until I'm certain it won't roll forward again. I manage to explain to Akram what I need, and he disconnects the winch line before I roll the Jeep forward a few feet to a better location. It takes five more minutes to explain to Akram I need him to chock all four wheels with large rocks. I'm still stamping on the brake pedal so hard my leg is shaking and I'm elated when he brings massive rocks which are clearly enough for the task.

Finally I feel confident the Jeep won't be having any more solo adventures, so I release the brake pedal and relax a tiny bit. I sit in the driver's seat for another few minutes, still reluctant to survey the damage. I still want to deny reality, and I'm terrified the passenger side has been badly damaged. It's entirely possible I've smashed multiple windows, torn both passenger side tires off the rims and bent suspension components. Worst of all I may have crushed the fiberglass pop-up roof, which will be utterly impossible to repair or replace.

When I finally pluck up the courage I'm amazed to see there are no broken windows, and the pop-up roof is virtually unscathed with only one tiny cosmetic chip in the fiberglass. Both plastic guard flares are torn almost entirely off the body, though I expected that and I don't care in the least. The mirror is dangling by the wires, and both door handles are broken and have buckled the doors which are also dented and scratched form the rocks and gravel. Apparently The snorkel took the brunt of the impact, and though it's badly scratched, there are no cracks and it looks perfectly functional. The severe impact pushed the snorkel into the A-pillar which has crushed right next to the windscreen, which is miraculously not cracked at all. Both wheels have scratches and scuffs, but all four tires are still perfectly round and ready to roll.

All things considered, I'm ecstatic the damage is not much worse. In fact, this is no problem at all.

I can't help thinking the Jeep would have been completely destroyed if it had veered in the other direction. I don't usually attribute my successes to luck, because that implies hard work was not involved. In this case I'm very willing to acknowledge I may be the luckiest person in the world.

Φ   Φ   Φ

With the outside cosmetic damage surveyed and more or less under control, I think about the engine and drive line. I left the Jeep in first gear and I know it didn't pop out. That means the engine was mechanically turning by the weight pushing it, which could easily be faster than the rev limiter would allow under normal circumstances. I don't know how fast it can go in first gear, and I can only hope it didn't go fast enough to cause damage. If it did, there's a good chance the engine has skipped a tooth on the timing chain, which would be a catastrophe. I don't have any way to check that, so I put it out of my mind.

I'm also worried oil may have leaked into the cylinders while it was on the side. If I start the engine with oil in the cylinders it will hydrolock and be destroyed. To clear any oil I must remove all the sparkplugs and turn the engine with the starter. The light is fading, the engine bay is scorching hot and I'm shaking from the exhaustion and adrenaline. After only five minutes of struggling to loosen the first sparkplug I realize there's little hope of me removing and reinstalling all six plugs without causing more damage.

After thinking for five minutes I rationalize the engine was not actually upside down, and it wasn't running when it went over. It also wasn't on the side for long, and so the chances of oil in the cylinders is very slim. I decide to let it sit for a few hours before I start it which will hopefully allow any oil to drain back where it's supposed to be.

Gorilla tape and zip ties do wonders to hold the fender flares on, and I cut the wires for the mirror before throwing it inside. I had visions of complete chaos under the hood, and I'm relieved to see everything appears sane, with just a hint of power steering fluid leaking from the reservoir, and a little engine oil leaking from the cap on the valve cover.

On the inside there's a pile of broken glass and smashed eggs squashed into the rear passenger door and under the fridge area. The storage cupboards burst open with the force, so my clothes, food and gear are soaking in the disgusting mess. Spice jars of curry powder have also broken open, and the inside already reeks like eggs, beer and curry powder all mixed together.

After topping up the engine oil and with a lot of trepidation I turn the key and immediately turn it off before the engine can fire and run. I repeat this a few times and everything sounds fine so I hold my breath while I start the engine. There is no smoke, no warning lights, and the engine purrs quietly as usual. Again, miraculously, everything appears to be fine and I have no reason to think I've caused permanent damage.

During all of this Akram has stayed to talk and reassure me, and he invites me to camp near his hut, less than fifty yards away. I'm relieved when the Jeep seems to drive fine as I reverse it up the hill to his hut. On relatively flat ground I'm happy the roof opens as normal, and I continue the massive clean up job long into the night.

In a strange twist of fate I then see one of the most beautiful sights of my entire life. Thousands of small fishing boats have rowed onto the lake and they each have a tiny kerosene lamp.

With so many twinkling lights the lake looks like an ocean of stars spread out beneath me. I'm awe struck by the sight, and feel reassured I'm not alone after all.

I'm still shaking when I finally climb up into bed near midnight, feeling like this has been a horrible nightmare.

I planned and dreamed of this expedition for so many years - but I never dreamed of this.

Φ   Φ   Φ

In the morning Akram jumps in the Jeep and takes me down to Kibiro Hot Spring on the shores of the lake, the reason I drove out here in the first place. It's a small spring in a beautiful valley, and has plenty of great soaking opportunities. While I usually love to explore hot springs, my heart simply isn't in it. I thank Akram profusely for his time, help and support which he says is no problem.

On the way out I park the Jeep near the scene of the accident to snap the photo I was originally trying to get. I park further up where the road isn't so steep and chock the wheels with large rocks. I'm not taking any more chances, and I think maybe I've learned my lesson.

I drive a hundred or so miles, and the Jeep seems fine. The roads are not paved, so I can't be sure it's driving completely straight or smooth, but nothing feels wrong, the engine is quiet and there are no warning lights on the dash. Driving on the wrong side of the road without a passenger side mirror is annoying and dangerous, so I'm determined to fix it one way or another.

A few days later I find a guy that assures me he can weld aluminum, not an easy thing to do without the right equipment. I'm soon impressed as I watch him work in the dirt on the side of the road. With an oxy torch he heats everything until the aluminum starts to melt before using a steel rod to push the liquid aluminum around until it bridges the gap and makes a strong enough weld. It's exactly like soldering electronics, and it seems to work well enough.

A day later I reassemble the mirror and continue cleaning out broken glass and eggs from inside. Tucked under a piece of carpet I discover a pile of squirming and stinking maggots, clearly loving the beer and egg mixture inside the hot Jeep. I disassemble the rear fender flare and reattach it with new plastic body clips, making it as good as new. The front fender has been held together with gorilla tape and zip ties since I clipped a tree stump in the DRC, so I just add a few new layers of each which is plenty good enough for an Africa fix.

A few days later I notice the front axle leaking oil from the end of the axle tube on the drivers side. The Jeep has never leaked a single drop and I wonder if hitting the bank so violently on that side has unseated an axle seal. I'll have to keep a close eye on it.

After all that it seems the Jeep and I can explore another day. Lucky does not even begin to cover it.

This lone male was not happy, and he's bigger than the Jeep

Taken from the driver's seat, watching me very closely

Camping in front of Mount Kilimanjaro, Tanzania

The silverback gorilla is mind-bendingly big

Crossing the Equator for the second time in Uganda

A lapse in concentration almost ended the expedition

I finally held an AK-47 in Ethiopia

The Jeep was issued Egyptian license plates - a first for me

With the completed map on the hood

Victory at the Giza pyramids in Cairo, Egypt

On Not Going Solo

DURING the Pan-American expedition when loneliness hit hard I promised myself I wouldn't go on another long expedition alone. The loneliness became front and center rather than the adventure, which meant I wasn't enjoying myself as much as I'd hoped. I very much wanted to improve on that the second time around.

In the years between the two expeditions those memories faded and looking back the loneliness didn't seem so bad, which made it easy to forget the promise I'd made. For the second time I decided it was better to go alone than not at all.

As fate would have it, I met a potential partner soon before leaving the Yukon. Like me, Em is a world traveler, adventurer and photographer and she had actually thought about driving to South America, so she was very interested in overlanding. Though we hit it off, I had already quit my job and left a few days later to build the Jeep while Em continued working.

A year later Em flew to southern Spain and we drove together through Northwest Africa. We were both new to the challenge and stresses of Africa, though we kept smiling and had a great time. Because she hadn't been saving for a huge expedition for years Em had to return to work, and I continued down the West Coast solo. A year later Em flew to Namibia, and we explored southern and eastern Africa together thoroughly enjoying the stunning wildlife and wilderness. Having a partner on the expedition was a huge change for me and I very much enjoyed the company and new dynamic Em brought.

I've become increasingly aware if I'm not careful I may spend the rest of my life alone on these crazy expeditions, which isn't ideal. With that in mind I became determined to round off my rough edges and grow as a person and partner. Of course it was amazing to have someone to share dreams and everyday life on the road. We roamed to our heart's content, living a life of adventure many people dream of.

Of course there were also downsides for two people living full-time in a small 4x4 in remote Africa. Obviously the living space was cramped, though the good weather meant we spent our time outside cooking, eating, reading and sitting around the campfire in the evenings. We were really only inside while driving or sleeping.

The lack of outside social life became an issue as time went on. We would often go weeks without talking to anyone else in depth, which put a huge strain on our relationship. It wasn't possible for me to have a boys night with friends, or for Em to catch up with her girlfriends. The time zone differences meant it was a continual struggle to call Canada or Australia and even when we did manage to speak to friends and family there was so much to say and hear about we never found time to talk about anything serious with them. With only the two of us we had to fill all the roles for each other we would normally get from friends and family, which got harder and harder the longer we were on the road.

I feel we also came into the expedition from different directions, and with slightly different expectations. I had been saving and working for years, filling both my bank account and my energy reserves. Working life had been a rest for me, so I went into the expedition fully charged. I dreamed of Africa for years, and I was determined to explore far and wide into the most remote corners I could push myself. I knew I may never get a chance like this again, so I wanted to see absolutely as much as possible. Before I even started I was well aware driving around Africa would be gruelling and easily the hardest thing I had attempted in my life. Overlanding is often romanticized as one long vacation, but I knew the reality, and I knew Africa would be much more exhausting than Latin America had been.

On the other hand Em had been working multiple jobs, literally running herself to exhaustion for years. She worked a full-time office job, ran her own business, worked freelance contracts and still picked up shifts as a waitress in the name of filling a savings account. Em arrived in Africa exhausted and rightfully in need of a vacation. The trip I planned did not provide that.

I was determined to make my quickly dwindling savings last, and simply spent continually less on non-essentials until it did. Completing the trip was always the goal, and I wasn't going to compromise on that, no matter what. Whatever it took, even if I had to eat nothing but rice and beans, I was going to complete the expedition. Because Em didn't plan and save for years like I did, she didn't have the same savings. Em wanted to enjoy the trip for as long as possible, and then would be forced to stop when her money ran out. Em wasn't possessed like me, and didn't want to reduce the trip down to the absolute bare bones just in the name of completing it.

Em's approach is clearly more sensible than my 'do or die' attitude, though I wasn't willing to compromise and my stubbornness caused a gap to grow between us.

While Em is extremely capable and confident, I also felt the burden of safety. If anything were to happen to her, I would feel one hundred percent responsible, and it was exhausting to try and look out for not only my own safety, but also that of someone who is extremely self-sufficient and determined.

As the months rolled on these tensions stretched our relationship to the limit, and we eventually went separate ways after eight months. I'm immensely happy I shared such a big part of my life - and the expedition - with Em. My memories of Southern and Eastern Africa are forever intertwined with Em and the good times we shared.

Φ   Φ   Φ

There were many other times I was not alone during the expedition, which also helped combat the loneliness. In West Africa a happy-go-lucky Danish backpacker named Ask jumped in the passenger seat for a few weeks. He aims to visit every country, and having seen almost a hundred he soon filled my head with dreams and ideas for my own future expeditions. Ask literally has no fear, and has been to some of the most wild countries on the planet. I was captivated by his story about riding the trans-Siberian train in the cheapest possible class with everyday Russians. During the day he would drink from a communal bottle of vodka passed around before meals were cooked in huge communal pots. At night everyone would just sleep on the floor of the train together. At stations he would dash off the train to buy another bottle of vodka before the train left, while his new friends cheered from inside the rail car. These are the kinds of raw adventures I've dreamed of my whole life and Ask and his stories are a true inspiration for me, and it was a pleasure having him ride along.

Sara the Doctor from Colombia jumped in the Jeep for a couple of weeks, and Sam the backpacker also jumped aboard for a couple of weeks. He was also exploring West Africa on foot, and couldn't find a good way forward without wheels. The timing was perfect and between us I don't think we stopped talking once, both clearly craving conversation.

I also convoyed with other overlanders on a few notable occasions. Sometimes we just camped together for a night or two, or if we were heading in the same direction we traveled for days, weeks or even months as with Dani and Didi. We became life-long friends as a result of the adventures we shared, and my memories from that part of the world are part and parcel with memories of them. Together we ventured to more wild and remote places than I dreamed possible, and I doubt I would have pushed my luck so far if I'd been alone. On more mornings than I can count we would linger in a stunning wild camp on the beach or in the jungle before one of us would ask "another coffee?", making all three of us grin with our shared desire for a rest day. More coffee was quickly brewed before we attended to our never ending job list in between resting in the shade.

When I was alone, loneliness did creep in just like before. Especially towards the end of the expedition I was exhausted and found it hard to keep going. I began to miss my family immensely, thinking of my baby Nephew and Mum's health. With no choice I knew I just had to get on with it, so I buried my head in work - logistics for the final leg of the trip, preparing my photography book, photographing and filming everything around me and writing articles for my website and magazines.

Like the first expedition, that was far from ideal. Unfortunately my tricks from last time didn't work too well because Africa has far less backpackers and travelers than Latin America, so it was very rare to bump into anyone else on the road, especially towards the end when I was intentionally exploring seldom visited places. Even with the hard times, I still think going alone is better than not going at all.

$$\Phi \quad \Phi \quad \Phi$$

On reflection I can't help thinking about everything I've sacrificed in life to undertake these expeditions. While working I become obsessed with saving money, walking a very fine line of not even enjoying life. I often turn down invites for dinner or adventures because of the cost, and I struggle to find a healthy balance. When on the road I become so stubborn and determined to reach my goal I won't let anything stand in my path, even when it costs a relationship. I've become so accustomed to forging ahead alone, it's the only way I know how to achieve my dreams.

Virtually all my friends from University and High School are married now. They have kids and houses and very full lives.

My brother Mike has a wife he adores, a son and a magical house they built with their own hands. Mike and I are so similar I often feel as if I'm looking in a mirror when we're together, though now his mirror is full while mine remains empty.

I don't know what the future holds, and I realize it's pointless to make promises to myself about any possible future trip. Clearly I'll just ignore that anyway. All I can do is continue to live the life that makes me happy, and keep an eye out for a partner who wants to share this wild ride.

It's a long shot, but I'm not giving up.

On Media Updates

Rwanda
November 2018

T HE more time I spent in Africa and the more I learned, I still couldn't come to terms with how the mainstream media portrays Africa. They pounce on any attention grabbing event and splash it across headlines for as long as they can milk it. Once the hype passes - or a more shocking event happens elsewhere in the world - the media move on and we never hear about that place or event again. In the minds of those following this news cycle that place is still in the state it was during the horrible incident. Without meaningful updates there is no way to know if or how the situation has improved. Because of this anyone who learns about the world from the media has a shockingly out of date understanding.

Never has this been more blatant than in Rwanda.

In 1994 Rwanda experienced one of the most horrific genocides in the history of the world. In the span of a few months an estimated half a million to one million people were brutally murdered by their countrymen, mostly by machete. Obviously this catastrophe drew enormous attention from the media at the time, with front page headlines continuing for months. So shocking was the genocide and so extraordinary was the media coverage that many people to this day still think Rwanda is a horrible and dangerous place.

What most people don't realize is the genocide was twenty-six years ago. Soon after, the media moved on. They had new disasters to report, and new shocking headlines to uncover. In the minds of many nothing has changed in Rwanda because they haven't heard anything about it since. Just the name of the country is synonymous with violence and death for many because they've never heard anything different.

The world has changed vastly since 1994. That was only three years after the collapse of the USSR and four years before the first section of the International Space Station was launched. Google didn't even exist, Facebook was ten years away and the iPhone wasn't invented for another thirteen years.

For almost three decades the media has neglected to update us about life in Rwanda for it's twelve million residents. The last most people heard the country was suffering the aftermath of a terrible tragedy. So strong is this lasting image that many people old enough to remember the genocide insist it's much too dangerous for me to even visit. Sadly, they're basing that on information that is twenty-six years old, and horribly out of date.

Rather than rely on such old information I would much rather find out today's truth with my own eyes.

Φ   Φ   Φ

When I roll up to the sleepy border everyone is friendly and polite, and after only thirty minutes I'm warmly welcomed into Rwanda. I drive forward with my usual excitement and curiosity, eyes wide open. Immediately I see a major difference from neighbouring Burundi. The road is extremely good pavement, and everything is spotlessly clean. This is such a shock it takes the next half an hour to believe it. Rwanda is much cleaner and better maintained than any country I've ever been in my life and I never see a single piece of trash in the entire country. .

Rwanda is nicknamed the land of a thousand hills, and I quickly see why. Virtually every square inch of the fertile land is dedicated to farming and small gravel roads twist and turn far into the distance through the picturesque mountains simply begging to be explored. I turn off the paved road and do just that, bouncing over cobblestones through tiny farming communities as I dive in.

Arriving at Chimerwa Hot Springs it's immediately clear I've found a very special place. This isn't just a hot spring as the name implies, this is actually an enormous hot lake. Boiling hot water bubbles to the surface of the massive lake, which is surrounded by spotlessly manicured gardens and grass. Most of the lake is much too hot to swim, and soon friendly locals invite me to join them and show me exactly where it's possible to soak, and even swim briefly. Later I wander the grounds and discover the lake flows into a river that stretches hundreds of yards through the lush valley, and I feel like a child when I discover hot waterfalls along it's winding route.

I soak late into the evening while watching an enormous thunderstorm roll through with an impressive thunder and lightning display. Feeling extremely safe and welcome I make camp in the dirt parking lot of the lake, and everyone assures me it's no problem. Soon after dark the Military come to check on me, and after explaining my story they assure me it's no problem to camp in the parking lot. After a very peaceful night I'm up at sunrise to soak and take in the stunning surrounds.

Φ   Φ   Φ

In the capital city of Kigali I'm impressed by the modern development I discover. Like all of Rwanda the capital is extremely clean and organized, and the skyline of towering glass skyscrapers is not at all what I expected. Quickly I learn Rwanda is much more developed than neighbouring countries, and after researching online I find my way to a bustling technology center in a high-rise building. Here hundreds of younger people with laptops are creating iPhone apps, writing software and designing hardware solutions for sale all over the world.

I use a locally-developed phone app to catch motorbike taxis all over town. It's ridesharing like Uber, though it's specifically designed to meet the unique needs of Rwandans. Riders mount their phone to the handle bars, and the app rates how safely they ride based on acceleration, braking and customer ratings. The app even has a feature where ladies can request female riders for safety, and of course it's all in multiple languages. This is just one example of an app designed and developed right here in Kigali, and it's being used be tens of thousands of people daily.

I thoroughly enjoying leaving the Jeep behind and ripping around town on the back these motorbike taxis, and one evening I attend a party at an art gallery where twenty and thirty somethings are eager to talk. They're all University students studying art, engineering, medicine and much more, and they want to hear what I think about modern Rwanda. Kigali is now the technology hub of East Africa, they explain, and it's booming.

Across town I visit the beautiful Genocide Memorial, an extremely moving place to spend time. Over a few hours I experience a huge range of emotions as I move through the displays that describe the conditions leading up to the genocide, what transpired, the aftermath, how the world responded and what we can do in the future to prevent this kind of thing from ever happening again.

I'm extremely moved to read panels about Canadian General Romèo Dallaire, the commander of the UN peacekeeping force in Rwanda during the genocide. In his book *Shake Hands with the Devil*[9] Dallaire documents the genocide as he experienced it over many months. Before any violence broke out he pleaded with the UN to intervene and prevent the slaughter he felt certain was coming. Shockingly, the UN did absolutely nothing, and Dallaire and his men were forced to stand by helplessly as the horrors unfolded around them because the strict UN

---

[9] *Shake Hands With The Devil* - Romèo Dallaire, 2004

rules of engagement prevented them from intervening. His book is one of the most unforgettable and most horrifying I've ever read, and seeing panels about him brought the memories flooding back.

Rwandans have made an obvious and conscious decision to never forget what happened and it's heartwarming to see how they've come together to grieve, forgive, and build their country into the success it now clearly is. They choose to keep the memories close to their hearts so they can remember loved ones and make sure it can never happen again.

The memorial explains how Rwandans are now united rather than divided, and that all Rwandans have a home here. To that end there is a monthly 'community clean up day', which explains the spotless streets and lack of trash. It's designed to get everyone in the country working together to achieve a shared goal, and is clearly working. Throughout the country it's forbidden to identify as one religious or ethnic group as opposed to another, now everyone is simply 'Rwandan' working together to build their beautiful country into the success it clearly is.

Φ   Φ   Φ

After almost a week in the capital I move north into the mountains, hoping to see mountain gorillas at the world class center. I decide not to fork over the steep fee, and instead take a much cheaper hike to visit the site where Dian Fossey lived among the gorillas for ninteen years. She documented her time in the jungle in the amazing book *Gorillas in the mist*[10], which was also turned into a movie. The entire site is stunning, and I throughly enjoy hiking into the jungle close to the DRC with friendly Military guys as escort.

It's clear to see Rwandans have united as one people and are quickly turning their country into the pride of East Africa.

---

[10] *Gorillas in the mist* - Dian Fossy, 1983

When the time comes to leave I find another sleepy border and the biggest delay is a very friendly lady from Rwanda Tourism who asks if I'd like to complete a survey about my time in the country. It's a shame the media failed to update us about this wonderful country, though the word is slowly getting out and it now hosts more than 1.2 million tourists every year. Now I know why.

$$\Phi \quad \Phi \quad \Phi$$

This lack of media updates and vastly different reality reared it's head time and again throughout Africa. The civil wars in Sierra Leone and Angola both ended almost twenty years ago, but without media updates we have no information about life in those countries now. Hollywood recreated the civil war in Sierra Leone in their blockbuster *Blood Diamond*, which depicted the horrors in stunning detail. Anyone watching that movie could be forgiven for thinking that's how things are now, though unfortunately it's terribly out of date.

The list of countries that have simply fallen off the radar is virtually endless, and we're left with a lasting impression of whatever bad situation we heard about last. Hollywood are all too happy to perpetuate these impressions of Africa that are twenty-plus years old because they're dramatic and gruesome which are very effective ways to hook us in.

$$\Phi \quad \Phi \quad \Phi$$

In his brilliant book *Factfullness*[11], Hans Rosling tackles this problem head on. He created a short multiple choice question-naire about the current state of the world. It's made of simple questions like the number of girls that go to school, what percentage of people have access to electricity and vaccination rates for babies around the globe. Each question has three possible answers, and it takes less than five minutes. Hans is

---

[11] *Factfullness* - Hans Rosling, 2018 (You really should read this book)

quick to point out that even a monkey guessing answers at random would score thirty percent correct, so surely we can do better. There are just thirteen questions, with nothing tricky or misleading. They are just simple questions about the state of the world today, all based on well researched factual UN data.

Hans has given this questionnaire many thousands of times to people from all walks of life all over the world. He has given it to world leaders, to high-level staff at the United Nations, to business leaders, teachers, engineers, medial students and scientists. Hans has also given the test to tens of thousands of everyday people from countries all across the developed world. Given how much we follow the news and most people consider themselves well informed, it would be reasonable to assume we can score better than the monkey who achieved thirty percent, and hopefully much better.

Sadly, that's not the case at all.

After giving the test to 12,000 people in fourteen different countries, only 10% scored better than the monkey who guessed randomly. A staggering 15% of people get every single question wrong, and only one person has ever scored all questions correctly. Even world leaders and high-ranking UN officials often perform worse than the monkey and it's their job to know about the world[12].

Not only do we all score terribly - clearly showing we don't understand the state of the world today - we all lean in the same direction. Universally, people from all around the globe from all walks of life think the world is more frightening, more violent and more hopeless than it really is. These results show just how terribly the media has kept us updated on the state of the world. Even worse, they've convinced us we're well informed when it's clear the opposite is true, and few of us have much of an understanding of the world today.

---

[12]I scored 15 percent, which is abysmal

Hans goes on to explain the facts show that in every measurable way, almost all countries in the world today are improving faster than his home country of Sweden did at any point in history. As one example just twenty years ago 29% of the world's population lived in extreme poverty, now it's down to just 9%, and still falling. Crime rates, deaths from natural disasters and preventable causes are falling while education, vaccinations and healthcare standards are rising across the globe.

Hans is by no means saying things are perfect everywhere. In stark contrast to the impression the mainstream media has given us, the facts very clearly show the global situation is much better now than at any other point in history and is improving much faster than it ever has.

Next time you hear about a country like Rwanda or Bosnia, take a moment to think about your impression of that country, and double-check how many decades out of date your information is.

Searching for Solitude

Lake Turkana, Kenya
December 2018

T HROUGHOUT my life I've always enjoyed solitude, and
in fact I've manipulated things so I get more. I'm not
sure what that says about me socially, though it's simply true
that I'm often content with my own company and a good
book or a walk in the forest. Across Africa I've sought out
the most remote places I could reach, which generally came
hand-in-hand with solitude and isolation.

It's common to hear people say 'You're never alone in Africa',
because no matter how remote you think you are, locals will
inevitably materialize from the forest or bush to say a friendly
hello. This frequently happens at the most inopportune moments - just as I'm about to eat dinner, or during a bathroom
break. East Africa is mostly densely populated, and lately I've
been longing for some real peace and quiet like I loved in the
remote deserts of Southern Angola and Namibia.

I should be careful what I wish for.

ϕ   ϕ   ϕ

For thousands of years Ethiopia has struggled with tribal
conflicts, and they've unfortunately escalated recently with
the new President attempting to re-claim territory previously
abandoned to the most violent tribes. While the interior of
the country is considered very safe, armed conflicts regularly
flare up near the borders and recently they have closed due to

gunfights between the Ethiopian army and local tribes.

The biggest crossing from Kenya to Ethiopia at Moyale has devolved into a war zone in recent weeks with gun fights, burning buildings and dead bodies left in roadside ditches. I spoke to one overlanding couple who were literally caught in the crossfire. While attempting to leave Ethiopia the officials said it was fine to proceed and then a few miles later they drove into an active gunfight. Rushing forward they found themselves trapped in the firefight after Kenyan officials abandoned their posts but left the gates locked. Tribal conflicts in Ethiopia are obviously very serious business.

It goes without saying I aim to avoid this at all costs, and in my research I learn of an extremely remote route along the shores of Lake Turkana, the world's largest permanent desert lake, and the world's largest alkaline lake. Stretching for more than 180 miles north to south, Turkana straddles the border of Kenya and Ethiopia and is the largest feature in the Great Rift Valley of Kenya. While researching the area and the lake I'm dismayed to read that it's also home to the densest population of crocodiles anywhere on the planet. I'll be sure to keep that in mind.

There are dirt tracks following both the east and west shoreline of the lake, and both are probably passable in the Jeep, as long as there's no rain. The western route is said to be the more barren, while the eastern is reportedly more beautiful, and utterly unpopulated after the only town to speak of. The more beautiful eastern route appeals to me, and further research indicates the border is so remote there is no legal border to cross. With no Immigration or Customs physically on site, I get myself and the Jeep stamped out of Kenya while in Nairobi. In a first for me, I'm legally stamped out a full week before I will physically leave the country.

While in the big city I perform a huge round of maintenance on the Jeep and gather visas for onward travel. I perform oil changes, a tire rotation and I finally replace the joint on the front drive shaft which makes me happy to have 4x4 again. I adjust the handbrake to prevent future solo Jeep adventures, though I think the Congo mud is so tightly packed in it doesn't make a huge difference. Likely I have to dismantle and clean each rear drum, and I just can't be bothered.

Northern Kenya doesn't have the best safety reputation, though as usual the reality is different than the media hype. Recently I spoke face to face with a German bicycle traveler who was held at gunpoint on the highway. Though he had all his worldly possessions with him, his assailant was satisfied with just one $10USD bill he peeled off a stack. The entire situation was so casual, he actually asked the armed bandit for a photo, though unfortunately the request was denied. After consulting multiple locals and people that have spent significant time on the shores of the lake, I feel confident the chances of me having problems of this kind are very slim.

I leave Nairobi on a good paved highway before filling every last drop of gas and water at the small town of Laisamis, my last dose of civilization for hopefully a week or more. In recent years a massive wind turbine project was built on the shores of the lake, and a new gravel road makes travel much faster than in years past. Never one to choose the easy route, I stay off this larger road and aim west on small dirt and gravel roads, passing through many tiny villages on route.

Over the day I pickup a couple of hitchhiking locals who are extremely thankful for the ride and happy to pose for photos. Most only speak a couple of words of English, and though I promised myself I would learn Swahili, I've done virtually nothing towards that goal, so communication is very basic. In the early afternoon I pull off the dirt road and make camp at the base of unexpected mountains. After just ten minutes I'm startled when a man wanders from the scrubby bush and says hello. He's been walking all day to visit relatives, and asks only for drinking water. We squat in the dirt and chat for twenty minutes before he disappears just as quickly as he arrived, eager to reach his destination before nightfall. Later when the stars blink into view I realize how invigorated I feel to be back in the wild after a couple of weeks running around the big city of Nairobi.

$$\Phi \quad \Phi \quad \Phi$$

In the morning the dusty and small road winds on, and eventually I find my way to the new wind turbine project built on the hills high above the lake. I'm told the station was built in less than a year, which is a huge achievement given how massive it is with hundreds of individual turbines slowly rotating in the wind. Cresting a rise I see the impressive lake for the first time, staggeringly big and dotted with dozens of rocky islands.

As I drop down to lake level and turn north on the mostly rocky track I'm staggered to see locals living in this extremely harsh environment. They live in round huts, and fishing appears to be their main food source. Remembering the crocodile population I'm bewildered to watch as fishermen wade up to their chests retrieving nets time and again. I can't help but wonder how many are killed each year, though I have no interest in getting close enough to the water to find out.

Arriving in the settlement of Loiyangalani I find a literal oasis in the desert. Home to around five thousand permanent residents it's built around a warm spring seeping from the rock which provides much needed water for the palm trees and lush green grass that fill the landscape. This is in stark contrast to the intensely hot and rocky landscape I traveled through today. A local explains the three main tribes living here had been in constant conflict for decades, though in recent years clean drinking water is in abundance thanks to an NGO tapping the source of the spring, leaving no reason to fight. I'm told gas is probably for sale here in drums, though after moving the thirteen gallons from my auxiliary tank into the main, I'm confident I have enough to reach the first town in Ethiopia.

Φ   Φ   Φ

I leave Loiyangalani early in the morning, again paralleling the lakeshore to the north and the difference in the road is immediately noticeable. It's now much smaller, and based on the few tire tracks I see it's obvious very few vehicles venture in this direction. As the hours roll by the road surface varies between rock, deep sand and occasional mud. The landscape is barren and harsh, and I'm not at all surprised when I see camels searching for what little food they can scratch up. How they find anything at all is a mystery to me.

In the scorching midday heat I stop for lunch under the shade of a rare and thorny acacia tree before pushing on to Sibiloi National Park, famously known as the Cradle of Mankind. It was here on the shores of Lake Turkana where the most complete early human remains ever discovered where unearthed, commonly known as 'Turkana Boy'. The rangers at the entrance are startled by my arrival, and they explain it's rare to see anyone. Often they wait a week without a single vehicle passing and they explain absolutely nobody lives inside the park, and it's unlikely I'll encounter a single soul before reaching Ethiopia, days to the north. They bid me farewell and good luck as I climb back into the Jeep, both excited and anxious for the road ahead.

For almost three years and 47,000 miles I've relied heavily on the Jeep to explore the most remote regions of the African continent. Not only is it my transport, but also literally my house, providing shelter, drinking water and food. Time and again it's proven capable and reliable, never leaking even a single drop of oil or giving the slightest indication of a problem. Unfortunately, that has recently changed.

Since the accident in Uganda I've been carefully checking the Jeep every couple of days, and I've found oil leaking from the front axle tube. On closer inspection I see the inside of the driver's side tire now rubs on the sway bar end link, which is impossible if everything is straight and true. After a lot of internal debate about the possible causes, I'm left with only one likely conclusion. I've bent the front Dana 44 axle tube, notorious as the Achilles Heel of this model Wrangler. It's a problem, but there's literally nothing I can do about it in remote Africa. Wrangler parts - especially replacement Rubicon front axles - are in short supply here. All I can do is keep an eye on it, occasionally top up the oil and hope for the best.

Now isolated from people and assistance, my mind runs wild thinking about the possibility of a major failure. I wonder if it would even be possible to walk out, and if there would be any chance of recovering the Jeep after the fact. With blistering daytime temperatures well over 110°F I begin to stress about the cooling fan that seems to be running almost non-stop. Minor noises and groans trouble me, and I become paranoid about dry grass collecting in the undercarriage and igniting on the scorching exhaust. More than once when I clear the grass from the skid plates I catch a faint whiff of the tell-tale odour of grass fire and I realize I'm not just being paranoid. I can't help thinking about how the passenger mirror is held on with gorilla tape and poor welding, and how the fender flares are also mostly held on with tape. To throw another item on the stack, the further I venture the more my gas reserves become a concern because the sandy conditions are causing much higher than normal consumption.

I'm not normally one to stress over things I can't control, though out here all alone the list is suddenly endless and my racing mind won't quit.

Adding to my woes, I'm not sure which faint track through the scrub I should follow. At first I decide to head directly west until I reach the lake, reasoning I can follow the shoreline north from there. After only thirty minutes I decide that route is so overgrown it can't possibly be the most used, so I backtrack and turn directly north. After another hour I'm again questioning my route choice when I see no tire tracks in the deep sand. All the rivers are dry, though the crossings are at least a hundred yards wide and cut deep into the rocky landscape. At one such crossing I completely lose the track, and after searching on foot for forty minutes the light is swallowed up by a monster thunderstorm closing in. Using my brain for possibly the first time all afternoon, I know I need to avoid any potential flash flood so I drive back out of the deep riverbed before making camp high on the bluff. While cooking dinner I'm treated to a stunning sunset mixed with boiling black clouds, crashing thunder and sheet lightning. Thankfully the rain stays on the horizon and the light breeze feels almost refreshing for the first time in days.

After climbing up into bed I begin to feel more isolated than I ever have in my life. I genuinely worry for the first time on the expedition, and my mind does not stop racing through thousands of possibilities - all of them bad. I sleep in fits and spurts, even dreaming about things going wrong.

Φ   Φ   Φ

I'm up and moving long before sunrise in an attempt to beat the scorching heat that is undoubtedly coming. Without a hint of breeze the temperature has not dropped below 75°F all night, and climbs relentlessly from the moment the sun crests the horizon. The prospect of trying to locate the non-existent track on the far side of the river bed is not appealing, and after debating my options all night I backtrack yet again. I will follow the faint trail west, and should at least be able to follow the lake shore north from there. I'm using up gas reserves I don't have, and I know this is the last time I can backtrack. From here on I must go forward.

I stop to explore a large petrified forest on foot, and I'm staggered to learn the perfectly preserved trees are a million years old. The significance of where I am fully hits me as I try to understand how these trees grew here a million years ago.

The more I think about it, the stronger the connection I feel to the ground I'm traveling across. For the first time on the continent, I feel very deeply this is where I come from, and that my distant ancestors are with me. Although I'm physically alone, the knowledge that people have been living here for over two million years is comforting, and in a spiritual sense I no longer feel alone. They managed to persevere through these harsh conditions, and so will I. I ponder these new feelings as I climb back into the Jeep and find a piece of mind that has escaped me for the last forty-eight hours.

The countries I'm exploring don't have the concept of search and rescue, and using a satellite phone to call friends or family on the other side of the world who can't help is only going to make them panic, so there's no reason to call them. Even if I called my embassy they won't be able to do anything because they don't have a vehicle and staff just sitting around waiting for a distress call. If I managed to get myself to the embassy they can help with paperwork problems, but they can't come and get me from the wilderness. All of that means a satellite phone is worthless. When I ran out of gas in remote Argentina, and again in Zambia or when I flopped the Jeep in Uganda, in fact whenever I've needed help, it was the people nearby that came to my rescue.

Now I know why I'm feeling so apprehensive about my current situation - there are literally no people for hundreds of miles in any direction. If I need help, there is simply nobody.

The faint track winds on and on, with sand and small salt pans becoming more common as I approach the lakeshore. Hours later I arrive on the windswept and barren lake before turning north into the nothing. The track degrades yet again into a continuous series of dry sandy riverbeds and steep washouts, forcing me to carefully pick entry and exit points to ensure I won't get stuck in the deep sand that has become extremely soft in the intense heat.

After camping another night in isolation I slowly climb up

and away from the lake on a rocky ridge with commanding views to the distant horizon. The first time I see children I'm a little disoriented, and then I see more and more people as I pass through the first of many mud-hut villages dotted on the northern extreme of the lake. These are the first people I've seen in two hundred and fifty miles and more than seventy-two hours, and I know everything will be OK.

Φ   Φ   Φ

Being alone is a truly powerful thing. With nobody to keep me grounded, and left unchecked, my thoughts and imagination ran away. I often say the thought of doing something difficult is worse than actually doing it, though for once maybe I had it backwards. Cut off from other people and feeling extremely isolated, my mind played tricks about the reliability of the Jeep and my chances of survival if I became stranded. For the first time in my life, I was genuinely concerned and began to stress about things outside my control. Everything turned out for the best, though I won't soon forget that sleepless night over a hundred miles from the nearest human.

This experience taught me a new perspective on solitude, and that I'm not as cool under pressure as I once thought. While time alone is still something I thoroughly enjoy, I suspect I'll be a little more cautious when venturing so far from other people in the future.

Ethiopia

Ethiopia
January 2019

CROSSING into The Federal Democratic Republic of Ethiopia is an extremely simple affair, and might be my easiest border crossing of all time. I'm so remote there are no Police, Military, Customs or Immigration to deal with, so there are no hold ups or any chances for bribery. In fact there are no buildings, no signs, and nothing at all to indicate I've driven into a different country. My GPS is the only indicator, and I celebrate for two minutes before I think about which side of the road I need to drive on now.

I'm fairly sure I have to swap sides for the fifth and final time, and I concentrate hard when the first vehicle in three days approaches. I notice the steering wheel is on the left, and there are characters on the license plate I've never seen before, confirming both that I need to swap to the right hand side of the road and I'm in Ethiopia, just as I thought.

Ten minutes later I see beautifully dressed men crouching on the side of the track, and I stop just for the pleasure of interacting with another human for the first time in a few days. They look friendly enough, though I can't help notice each cradles a battered AK47. While the infamous rifle has been a common sight across the continent, never before have I seen regular civilians carrying so much firepower. Throughout Africa I've occasionally seen men with battered old hunting rifles clearly looking to score dinner, however it's only ever been uniformed Police and Military who carry serious firearms.

As I soon learn, Ethiopia is *very* different in that regard, with virtually all farmers carrying an AK.

Even without sharing a language we manage to communicate with smiles and handshakes, feeling perfectly at ease. The men soon notice my interest in their rifles, which they affectionately refer to as 'Kalish'. I've asked repeatedly across Africa, though until now not a single officer has been willing to let me hold their AK - which I understand completely. I don't entirely understand my own interest in the rifle, I just want to size it up to better understand what it's all about. Without superiors and rules, it's clear these men have no such hang-ups about handing their rifle to a complete stranger and the rifle is quickly thrust into my hands. Gun safety is clearly not a high priority here. While I hold the rifle and look through the sights, the elder man repeatedly moves the selector between 'safe', 'semi-auto' and 'full-auto' while pantomiming the result of each.

Estimated to be responsible for over eight million deaths world-wide, the legend of the AK47 needs no explanation. With tens of millions of the rifle used in conflicts across the continent, they're a feature of everyday life in many countries. So common-place is the AK, in fact, it's on the official flag of Mozambique. Now holding one, I'm surprised by how compact and insignificant the rifle is in my hands. Both the stock and barrel are too short for my liking and hardly seem fitting for the infamous reputation the rifle carries. It's also very light, and doesn't feel very sturdy, almost like pieces are about to fall off. I continue to smile and nod at my new friends while being acutely aware of the horrifying power in my hands. Even while looking down the sights and sizing up the rifle I very carefully keep the barrel pointed down and my finger well away from the trigger.

I've always wondered if battered old rifles like this are even loaded, so using hand gestures I ask the elder man to remove the magazine for a closer look. After proudly showing the fully-loaded magazine he cycles the bolt to eject the round in the chamber, and his ear to ear grin tells me he's proud to have handed me the fully loaded automatic weapon without a care in the world. I'm shocked, but just go with it, continuing to smile and relax. The men are grateful when I give them drinking water, and after a farewell I continue on muddy tracks, now acutely aware I've left east Africa and am pushing into north Africa.

I knew I'd be cutting it close with regard to my maximum range, and after just over four hundred miles on horrendous sand, mud and rocky tracks from Kenya I roll into a small town and am relieved to see men siphoning gasoline from grubby containers. With less than twenty-five miles of range remaining, that puts a smile on my face.

Φ   Φ   Φ

A few days later I'm in the mountain town of Jinka, famous for it's proximity to the numerous ancient tribes that live in the area. These tribes hit international headlines in the '60s and '70s for their unique traditional customs, headgear and dress and have been visited and photographed by millions of tourists since. The Mursi tribe in particular are extremely famous for the enormous clay plates women insert into their bottom lips. These plates can be over five inches across and make for an extremely striking and unique appearance.

I arrange a mandatory guide who jumps in the Jeep, and together we descend a few thousand feet to the extremely hot and barren valley floor. Soon we begin seeing Mursi on the side of the road and my guide explains today is market day in town, and many people walk the thirty or so miles each way.

Before I can proceed we must collect and pay for an armed 'security escort', and a willing man hastily buttons his grubby shirt as he climbs into the back of the Jeep with the requisite AK47. We continue a handful of miles directly into a small mud hut village like others we've passed. My guide is friends with the chief so he's welcomed warmly, and the two men chat in the local language while I wait. From the minute I step from the Jeep I begin to interact with the Mursi people, some of the younger ones being as curious about me as I am them.

In the past it was customary to pay each person directly for any photos taken, roughly ten or twenty cents in the local currency per photo. The women especially are extremely striking, and obviously I want to take photos of them. I've come prepared with a wad of small Ethiopian bills, though the chief quickly explains things are done differently now. Instead of paying each individual who can spend the money how they please, I must pay the chief $10 which he will distribute among the people of his village. This will permit me to take unlimited photos, I'm told, and will make life easier for everyone. I see no way to object, and so I pay him the money and walk into the village.

Almost immediately I come to an extremely old and withered lady sitting on the ground and leaning on a hut. It's impossible to guess her age, though she looks to be in her late 70s or maybe even early 80s. At first she doesn't seem interested in me, but after my armed escort says a few words to her she poses for a photo, holding up her lip plate. I'm not even sure if she can speak, though she does manage to make a kind of moaning sound while holding out her hand to ask for money as payment for the photos I've taken.

Quickly my guide and the chief explain the new arrangement, and the look on her face tells me everything I need to know. She drops her arms in defeat, certain she won't get a cent from the chief.

It's late in the hot afternoon, and in the middle of the mud huts ladies grind corn for the evening meal while men watch or play with the many small children running around. My guide explains their lives have been extremely basic subsistence living for roughly 30,000 years. In true African style their lives are rich with celebrations and parties at every excuse, usually with nearby villages in an attempt to marry off those who've come of age.

On the far side of the village sits a striking young man and women, clearly a couple. From the look on their faces I can see they're extremely unhappy with my presence, and I think it best to leave them be. Having none of this my armed guard walks over and actually nudges them with the barrel of his rifle.

With a sickening realization, the situation becomes perfectly clear. The mandatory armed guard is not for my protection from these extremely gentle and friendly people, it's to force them to perform for the foreigner. I'm crushed to see how they're treated, and to realize that I'm the cause.

Now I just want to leave, and I hope these people can find peace away from horrible tourists like me. Unfortunately, that seems extremely unlikely.

Tourists have been visiting in droves for decades, paying for the mandatory guide, the armed guard and for photos of individual people. The Mursi tribes are such a popular destination and big business for the guides and tour companies each morning hundreds of tourists in separate 4x4 vehicles descend on these villages. My guide says the Mursi now rely on the tourist money simply to survive, and they would be much worse off without it. I can't help wondering what they did for the tens of thousands of years before tourists showed up.

On the drive back to town I see more and more Mursi walking back to their villages. I also see countless men passed out on the side of the road and my guide explains they're blind drunk, having spent all their money on alcohol in town. Somehow, I'm not sure tourists and their money are making a positive impact.

Φ   Φ   Φ

I've driven into Ethiopia in the midst of a huge gas shortage, which quickly becomes a problem. None of the stations in Jinka have any and I arrived planning to fill up here, so the Jeep is running on fumes. As much as I'd like to leave, I can't go anywhere until I find gas.

Early the next morning I'm directed to a station ten minutes out of town which supposedly has gas, or at least should be getting a delivery soon. When I arrive there are already at least fifty tuk-tuks and well over two hundred motorbikes clustering around the pumps. Everyone is shocked to see me line up in the Jeep, and each man wants to personally confirm the Jeep runs on gas and not diesel. Again they've never seen a big 4x4 that isn't diesel.

A few people speak a little English, and they're happy to translate while everyone comes to say hello and check out the Jeep and I. They want to know my story, and why I'm here waiting in line. Surely my driver should be doing that for me, they think. Everyone is on edge and the air is thick with tension. As much as I want to take photos I sense that's a very bad idea.

Over the next few hours more and more people arrive, and the tension only builds. Eventually the owner of the station stands up to make a speech, and I get snippets translated. He's trying to buy more gas from his supplier, but the entire country is experiencing shortages, so he simply can't get any. Today all motorbikes will be limited to two gallons each, while tuk-tuks will be allowed three and there will be no filling of jerrycans or containers. This way everyone waiting will get at least some gas, and we can all work together to get through this. He even mentions he will sell at the official price, rather than profiteering which he could easily do.

This all sounds very reasonable to me, and it's clear he's doing his best in a very difficult situation. Much to my surprise, I'm the only one who thinks this. Over the next hour I watch as almost every single man waiting goes over to verbally abuse the owner - screaming in his face, waving their arms and making it extremely clear what they think of his plan. Everyone is furious and bristling with anger and I think a riot might break out. The Jeep is trapped in the sea of tuk-tuks and motorbikes, and I realize I can't leave even if things get nasty. Mob mentality is very close to taking over, so I stay well back and leave my camera locked in the Jeep.

The anger and tension build further as more motorbikes and tuk-tuks cram into every possible space. After almost four hours of waiting I'm surprised when everyone starts revving their engines and screaming when the attendant begins to pump gas. I thought we were waiting for a delivery, but no, apparently it was in the underground tanks all along.

Now the madness kicks into high gear as the crowd of men yell, scream, and fill jerrycans and do whatever else they can to not cooperate with each other. Of course this only makes the entire process much slower and more painful for everyone, but somehow they can't see that, or simply don't care.

I continually maneuver the Jeep forward a couple of inches at a time to stop the swarm of tuk-tuks cutting me off, though they manage to sneak around anyway. When I accidentally give one a love tap with the front bumper I get yelled at with a stream of what I can only assume are profanities, and I try my best to apologize.

When my turn eventually comes I have to do a thirteen point turn so the hose will reach, and thankfully after I explain my situation the owner agrees I can buy a full tank. Feeling extremely conspicuous and with all eyes on me I thank him profusely before filling the main tank to the brim. I leave as quickly as possible before anyone can direct their anger towards me and before I'm forced to witness more abuse and stupidity.

Never before in Africa have I seen people treat each other so badly, and it's disconcerting to know Ethiopians have no problem yelling and screaming at each other. I can only wonder how I'll be treated.

$$\Phi \quad \Phi \quad \Phi$$

The extreme gas shortage forces me to abandon my plans of exploring the south, so I turn north to the capital of Addis Abba. On the way I'm forced to buy ten gallons of gas on the black market for double the official price, and later I fluke my arrival at a station at the same time as a filling truck. At stations with nothing the attendants quickly and quietly offer to sell me gas from the black market. It's obvious they fill containers when the station has gas, then sell it for twice the price when the station runs out. This is highly illegal, and at a few stations I see government people trying to keep the situation under control and stop this kind of profiteering.

Addis is a big city with a modern centre and I spend a few days ticking off jobs - getting visas for onward travel and planning my route. I try to complete as many jobs as possible on foot, and on countless occasions I'm invited to share delicious coffee with locals who are curious about me and my travels. The city has everything I could want, and I'm relieved when I secure the sometimes difficult visa for Sudan. With two others I'm turned away before I can even enter, and I'll just have to solve that problem later.

$$\Phi \quad \Phi \quad \Phi$$

In the mountains a few days later I encounter groups of children Ethiopia is infamous for. These children beg for money and candy on the side of the road, and after I don't give them anything they furiously hurl rocks. If I stop they scurry away, then quickly resume throwing rocks when I start to pull away. As much as I'd like to get out and teach them some manners, I know this is an exceptionally bad idea and it's very likely the adults won't take kindly to me yelling at their kids. I'm thankful none of the rocks hit windows, though one does take a large chip out of the rear tailgate.

In small towns young men rush the Jeep and grab door handles as I slow for traffic, trying to forcibly open the rear doors. They're all locked and I'm always able to drive away, but it unnerves me knowing they will do this so blatantly in the middle of the day. Never in all of my travels has anything like this happened before.

As I move across the country and further north I'm always lucky finding gas, and even fill up at stations that don't have a line - the only time I've seen this in Ethiopia

I hear from a Swiss overlanding couple I haven't seen since Cameroon who are heading into the Simien mountains, and I quickly decide I want to spend time with friends in the mountains. They've found a brilliant wild camp, and I'm more than a little skeptical that such a thing even exists in Ethiopia. The parts of the country I've seen so far are densely populated so whenever I stop the Jeep a crowd of children appears to beg and demand things from me. Because of this wild camping has so far been impossible. When I arrive at the co-ordinates my friends sent I'm not surprised to see them in the middle of an argument with a group of men carrying AK47s.

I'm so used to this it's just annoying and not the least bit scary and I walk over to greet my friends warmly, hugging and chatting while more-or-less ignoring the fifteen men with automatic rifles clustered around. The chief of the nearby National Park heard about my friends camping here last night, and has come to put a stop to it. After a lot of back and forward and anger on his part, he demands we pay for no less than eight armed guards and expensive park entry fees for today and tomorrow. All our maps show we're outside the National Park, but he doesn't care. He becomes extremely determined to get money from us, and is the opposite of friendly. It all feels downright hostile, and we soon tire of it. All of this anger and hostility is just not worth it, so we decide to give up and drive into the nearby town of Debark where we pay to camp in the crowded and noisy concrete parking lot of a hotel.

In the morning we stop at the ranger station to pay the mandatory National Park entrance fees, and I'm not surprised to see our friend from yesterday running the show. As soon as we set foot inside he starts right back with the anger and hostility, and I'm sick of it in five seconds. Clearly wanting to win today's argument, he insists we must pay for not one but two armed escorts while we're in the park, on top of all the permits, daily fees and camping fees.

The official park rules posted on the wall clearly state we only need one armed escort, though he doesn't care in the least. The argument becomes very heated and unfriendly, with lots of yelling from both sides. He digs in his heels and won't budge, instructing the staff not to sell us permits.
Not for the first time, I feel very unwelcome in Ethiopia.

I decide I'd rather be in the mountains than in this town, so I shell out a stack of bills and pay for entrance, camping and two armed scouts for three days and two nights. The scout I'm assigned is a gentle elderly man carrying just a bed roll and the requisite AK47. He doesn't speak a word of English and I've picked up only a couple of words of Amharic. Nevertheless, we get on well with smiles and hand signals.

Finally we're allowed to continue, and we drive directly into the National Park, high in the mountains. The scenery is stunning and the warm sun beams down as we climb higher and higher. I'd been expecting jagged peaks, though the mountains are much more friendly and accessible and a rambling rocky road winds into their heart. In the late afternoon we're short of breath when we arrive at our campsite for the night, Camp Chennek at 10,500 feet (3,200m).

From the moment I kill the engine the usual game starts, and I'm sick of it before it even begins. A man insists I can't park or camp where I am and insists I must park in the official lot. I carefully explain three times the official lot is completely full, but he doesn't care.

After a lot of loud arguing between him and I, and then him and my friends, I try a different angle and attempt to negotiate a peace deal.

"The parking lot is full," I say, "Please tell us where to go."

I'm not ready for his reply, though I probably should be after a couple of weeks in Ethiopia.

"I'm not here to find a solution," he says with contempt in his eyes.

We're at the official campground of a National Park, after we've paid a good deal of money for entrance, mandatory armed escorts and camping for two nights, and this is the reception we get. Again I get the distinct feeling Ethiopians don't want tourists, and that I'm very unwelcome.

After moving our vehicles four different times and being told to move again and again we find our own place to park on the grass just off the side of the road. When we stop talking the man gives up arguing and walks away, so we call it home.

Ф   Ф   Ф

The temperature plummets overnight, and I'm staggered by how chilled I get wearing all my Canadian cold weather gear. In reality it only drops to about 46°F, and I realize my blood is now much thinner after almost three years of scorching sun. Trying to warm up I walk just before sunrise, and stumble across a troop of Gelada Baboons as they seek out the warm morning sun. Typically Baboons are nasty creatures that I avoid, but I'm pleased to discover these unique baboons are placid and even friendly. With wild hairstyles blowing in the wind and clearly distinct personalities I'm reminded of all my chimp friends from across the continent as I watch them play and forage in the short grass.

We feed our escorts breakfast and coffee, and soon I'm asked to fix a broken AK47. A plastic piece underneath the battered wooden stock is cracked, so I cover it in a thick layer of black gorilla tape, witch matches perfectly. He's elated with this, giving a huge grin and thumbs up. It feels odd to repair such a weapon with just tape, but somehow it feels like a fitting Africa fix.

We spend the day hiking to the top of a nearby peak, happy to be out of the vehicles for a change. The surroundings are simply stunning, and the warm sun warms us to our bones as we take in the immense views. Coincidentally it's my birthday again, and I sit on the edge of a cliff remembering the three birthdays I've spent in Africa. It's hard to believe there won't be a fourth.

After another chilly night we drive further up the enormous mountains, and after an hour of steep switchbacks we reach a pass on the summit at 14,081 ft (4292m). This is the highest I've ever driven the Jeep, and also the highest it will ever reach on the African continent. The whipping wind is freezing, and I even spot a tiny patch of snow in the shade, the first and only I see in Africa.

After taking in the stunning views we slowly crawl all the way down the mountain back into the chaotic world.

Φ　　Φ　　Φ

I move an hour south and setup camp on the shores of stunning Lake Tana while my friends search for a replacement tire in the city of Gondar. Late in the afternoon my friends arrive with bad news. While driving through a small town their vehicle was surrounded by yelling and screaming men. Unable to move they became trapped in their vehicle while the men hit it with sticks and stones hard enough to dent the steel and break plastic covers. Extremely scared they buried the horn and crawled forward until the crowd parted enough for them to get away. They're understandably shaken, and we agree they were lucky to escape before a window was broken and the situation escalated.

In the coming days we learn of a foreign bicycle traveller nearby who is hit in the head with a rock badly enough to require stitches, and the very next day is violently attacked and almost has his bike and all possessions stolen. Soon the owner of the campground brings more bad news. Just last month a foreign traveler was beaten almost to death only twenty minutes away and other overlanders were recently attacked in their vehicle just outside Addis. Their windows were smashed and they barely managed to drive away before being dragged from their vehicle.

I had already been feeling uneasy in Ethiopia, and now I feel downright unsafe.

In all my travels around the world this is the only country I've ever felt unwelcome and also genuinely unsafe. In stark contrast to my experiences elsewhere, people in bigger cities are fine with my presence, while people in rural areas are angry and openly aggressive.

Our host at the campground is originally from Europe and has lived here for almost seven years, though she has just decided to give it all up and leave. She explains one reason why many rural Ethiopians are fed up with tourists. Through they bring a lot of money, it all winds up in the hands of educated city people running tour companies and employing city drivers and guides. Tourists are seen every day being driven through smaller towns and rural areas to see the stunning sights, but the people from these rural areas don't get any money, and they're angry about it. Ethiopia's new President is also much more tolerant and open, and so Ethiopians have much more freedom of expression than before. Evidently they've decided to use this new-found freedom to express their anger at tourists by attacking them.

Whatever the reason, I genuinely feel foreigners are not welcome in Ethiopia, and I'm sorry to say I can't recommend a visit to the country. I feel disappointed that an entire country has gone this way, but I feel helpless to change the situation. It seems young men especially are extremely confrontational, and quickly resort to violence.

The following day in the small town near the campsite I'm sitting in the driver's seat planning my route when a group of young men grab at everything on the Jeep and try to forcibly open the doors and gas cap. It's broad daylight and I'm clearly sitting in the driver's seat watching closely. Even when I honk the horn they just snicker and keep at it. They're obviously taunting me, and I realize they want me to get out. I'm furious they have no respect, and again, this is the only country where anything like this has ever happened.

Many people absolutely love Ethiopia and I had been looking forward to it immensely. Unfortunately, at the time of my visit, it's simply not a nice place to be.

Φ   Φ   Φ

Now absolutely certain it's time to move on, my Swiss friends and I formulate a plan. The sole road from Ethiopia to Sudan is notorious for armed conflicts, and in recent weeks it has been an actual war zone. We talked to a couple traveling on bicycles who were caught in a gunfight at the border just a week ago when the border town was full of burning houses and even dead bodies on the street. Eventually they were able to join a Military convoy, and were forced to stop repeatedly so the Military on their bus could get out and shoot at bad guys in the bushes. Once again these troubles have nothing to do with Sudan, and are conflicts entirely within Ethiopia.

Getting into Sudan is not a problem, and we're not worried about that in the least. It's getting out of Ethiopia we're concerned about. We've been keeping our ears to the ground for the last few weeks gathering all the information we can in an attempt to make our escape as safely as possible, and with our visas running out we simply have to go for it.

Now more wary we stick together on the drive back to Gondar, and I have no trouble buying gas from a regular station that has plenty. Diesel is harder to come by, and we spend an hour asking at every station only to come up dry. On the edge of town we talk strategy, and my friends decide to push on with what they currently have. By chance we've stopped at the entrance to a huge Military base or training ground and over ten minutes I see a handful of extremely well armed men in vehicles come and go and I can only assume they're patrolling the road ahead.

One vehicle in particular sticks in my memory. It's a beat up old Toyota pickup with two large and stern looking men in the front. In the back is a mounted gun manned by a muscle-bound soldier who clearly means business. He's wearing camo pants, no shirt and has massive strings of bullets crisscrossed over his chest. Sun glistens off the sweat on his jet-black skin, and I notice he never takes his hands off the massive gun, endlessly scanning the crowd and streets. The scene is directly from a B-grade 80s action movie, but it's clear he means business. As much as I want to take photos, I'm too on edge about safety to ask.

Our route takes us down out of the mountains, and as we drop three thousand feet the temperature soars to well over 110°F. I've only been in the mountains for a week and I have already forgotten about the intense African sun. On the route we're stopped at only one Military checkpoint where they ask to see our passports and paperwork.
"Is the road ahead safe?" I ask hesitantly.
"It is unknown," is the only cryptic reply I get.

We stick close together and keep moving on a decent paved road past Military posts with armed men guarding vehicles and buildings, the occasional burnt-out vehicle and two villages that are burnt to the ground. Fortunately we don't see or hear any problems or violence, and we don't stop once.

Arriving at the border itself we're happy to see it looks relatively normal for Africa, and after shaking off the men asking to change money we manage to locate Customs and Immigration and complete the required steps in the scorching afternoon heat. When the boom gate is raised I let out a huge sigh of relief as we drive out of Ethiopia, happy to see a country in my rear view for the first time in my life. I'm extremely happy I managed to get through without experiencing anything nasty directly myself and I know it could easily have gone the other way.

On the Sudanese side the paperwork begins, and friendly people pop-up to help us with each step. We have tourist visas in our passports and Sudan also requires tourists to 'register' their arrival. Thankfully we can do it all here at the border so we don't have to rush to the tourist office in the capital.

After a lot of waiting and friendly handshakes we complete all the required steps and leave the border just minutes before the sun hits the horizon. A handful of miles later we dive off the road into the scrubby brush, just enough to be out of sight. The temperature is still scorching when I climb into bed and I fall asleep regardless, utterly exhausted.

On Government Warnings

Sudan
February 2019

S UDAN is a country that makes headlines for all the wrong reasons. After the government was labeled a 'state sponsor of terrorism' in 1993, the Sudanese people have suffered for three decades under heavy International sanctions. Virtually all countries have severe travel warnings against visiting Sudan, and it's assumed to be extremely dangerous. As I've seen repeatedly throughout Africa, the reality is more complicated than it first appears.

Φ   Φ   Φ

Driving into Sudan I immediately feel welcome and safe after the tense situation in Ethiopia which is a relief. On my first day in the country I wander through a small town buying bread and vegetables and I'm repeatedly invited to share food with shopkeepers and their families. I've picked up only a few words of Arabic, and even with the language barrier it's easy to see Sudanese people are serious about welcoming strangers.

International sanctions mean Sudan is cut off from global financial markets, which for me means my bank cards are useless. For locals it means getting currency from the outside world is virtually impossible, which they need to do business outside the country. This means foreign cash is in high demand and there is a black market on the Sudanese Pound which is rapidly falling in value. I'm stopped repeatedly in the street by friendly people asking to change money at almost double the official rate.

Crude oil is Sudan's second largest export, though the country itself suffers from never ending shortages of both gas and diesel. Apparently the government are more interested in selling their resources internationally than providing for their own citizens. The vast majority of gas stations are simply abandoned, and hundreds of vehicles wait in long lines at the few stations that have a limited supply. These lines stretch far into the distance in the scorching heat, though I never once see a single person become angry or yell. Everyone simply waits their turn, chatting to their neighbour or squatting in the shade in an attempt to escape the relentless sun. I sense this situation is perfectly normal for the Sudanese people, and they just wait patiently without complaint.

I join the back of one rambling line and almost immediately people insist I must go to the front. A Policeman soon arrives and is determined to escort me around the line. I feel bad for cutting the massive line, though I'm assured repeatedly it's fine because I'm just a visitor in Sudan. After all, they explain, they would be treated the same way if they visited my country. With the black market exchange rate I pay just thirty-five cents per gallon, filling the main Jeep tank for only $7USD. It's hard to believe, but actually true.

After leaving town my Swiss friends and I find a quiet place to make camp not far from the road an hour before sunset. We're sitting in the shade of an enormous tree beside a small river when a few men approach on foot. They're all wearing white robes and sandals and with broken English and hand gestures they make it clear they're farming nearby, and they're happy for us to camp. I watch with interest as they gather the fruit from a nearby tree and after they show me how to peel it I discover the fruit is sweet and sticky on the inside. We share water with the friendly men who shake hands before wandering into the barren landscape. Mercifully the temperature drops in the hours after dark, and I wake before dawn with a chill on my bare arms and legs which feels fantastic.

On the roads Police checkpoints are few and far between, and after showing the tourist registration stamp in my passport they're always friendly and fast. Everyone seems genuinely pleased to see a foreigner visiting Sudan and again the language barrier doesn't stop us communicating with smiles and handshakes.

Φ   Φ   Φ

I soon learn The Sudanese people are utterly fed-up with dictator President Al-Bashir who has ruled since 1989. Hoping to finally remove him from power they're staging protests in major cities throughout the country and I've been warned to keep well clear because the government might respond with violence.

Even with heavy international sanctions I recognise many international brands as I drive into Khartoum, the capital city. It's much more modern and developed than I'd been expecting, and doesn't look too different from other capitals in Africa. Camping in Khartoum is at The Blue Nile Sailing Club directly on the mighty Nile where I sit and talk with the many locals who come and go throughout the day. I'm fascinated to learn how people are able to continue with daily life under such oppression, and I'm impressed to see they do so with a big smile. Delicious meals and fresh-squeezed juice from local restaurants is shockingly cheap, and soon store owners in a five block radius of the Sailing Club wave as I walk by each day, learning the city on foot.

I exchange more US dollars with these friendly shop keepers, and already the rate is better than yesterday. The Sudanese Pound is crashing so quickly the rate changes noticeably from day to day and again I marvel at how these people can live under such conditions. I struggle to find bread for sale, and eventually ask the shopkeepers where I can buy it. They explain it can be hard to find in the afternoons, so instead they will bring it here in the morning. At sunrise the friendly guys arrive with an enormous bag of freshly baked bread rolls, and they absolutely will not let me pay, try as I might. They explain it's their pleasure to extend this hospitality to a visitor, and they hope I enjoy the fresh bread. Despite their oppressive government and the currency crashing they insist on giving a complete stranger food. I'm almost overcome by their generosity and thank them profusely.

Φ Φ Φ

As the big city fades in the rear view mirror a few days later the landscape quickly changes to a barren and rocky desert only broken by the occasional small dune shifting in the wind. Close to the Nile are lush green fields under heavy irrigation, and it's extremely clear how much the locals depend on this ancient river to bring life. I order lunch at a small truck stop using only hand signals by pointing at the meal being eaten by a nearby driver. I hold out the equivalent of a dollar to pay for the meal and the proprietor takes less than fifty cents before inviting me to sit in the shade. The spicy chunks of meat are delicious, and I only briefly wonder if it's actually cow, goat or camel. It simply makes no difference. Many drivers are napping on rugs in the shade, and after my meal I think it best to adopt this local custom and nap away the hottest part of the immensely hot day.

I continue north through the featureless desert for hour after hour and get a sense of how enormous Sudan truly is. It was actually the largest country on the continent before South Sudan split off in 2011, now the world's youngest country. Before the split it was almost 50% bigger than Alaska, and now even without the South it's still 30% bigger. As I watch the heat haze rise from the blacktop in waves I start to feel the immense desert is equal parts impressive and intimidating.

Late in the afternoon I find another isolated and quiet place to camp alone in the desert. While taking photos at sunset I see the temperature is exactly 100°F.

Φ Φ Φ

The following day I drove through the city of Atbara asking at multiple stations for gas. All the stations I see are abandoned, and I have no idea where to look. A few young men stand in the shade at one station, and one who speaks a little English volunteers to show me across town to a station that likely has gas. Five minutes later I know he's right when I see what must be at least five hundred vehicles waiting in a huge snaking line paralleling the road. Again everyone insists I go to the front where the owner of the station is happy to shake hands before asking me to wait. An hour later the Jeep is full to the brim again and when I drop the young man back across town he asks for nothing. He simply shakes my hand and wishes me all the best for my time in Sudan before rejoining his friends.

Leaving Atbara I turn west, leaving the Nile on a paved road that slices through a desert of huge scraggly dunes. Almost immediately a brutal headwind springs up that becomes so strong the Jeep struggles to maintain sixty miles an hour. Sixth gear becomes useless, and the Jeep burns much more gas than usual working overtime against the wind. When I step out for a three minute leg stretch the wind whips sand into my face and eyes until I can't stand it. Late in the day I realize I've become a virtual prisoner inside the Jeep because it's the only place I can escape the tormenting wind.

I much prefer to keep the main tank above half full so I don't get caught by the shortages, so I join another line in a small farming town. This region apparently has many tractors and old 4x4s that all run on diesel, so that line stretches far into the distance while the line for gas is only a handful of vehicles. It's only men in line, and they happily joke and banter with me despite the language barrier, and many are curious to see inside the Jeep. They insist on inspecting the engine to make sure it does in fact run on gas, and are only satisfied after I point to the spark plug wires. I'm always happy to show curious and friendly locals around my house, and I sense I'm a welcome distraction from the day of waiting in the hot sun.

In the late afternoon I veer into the dunes, driving a few miles before stopping on the lee side of a monster collection of dunes. When darkness falls the wind drops to light a breeze, and I enjoy hours of silent stargazing while I struggle to comprehend the size of the desert surrounding me.

Φ   Φ   Φ

I cross the river to the western side and continue north in search of the Temple of Soleb ruins. In West Africa I often felt like Indiana Jones exploring the thick jungles, and now I have the same feeling wandering through the massive temple built from immense stone blocks and columns which are all covered in carvings. Soleb is more than 3,500 years old, something I can't begin to understand. I wander the site alone for an hour and thoroughly enjoy having it all to myself. Not for the first time in Sudan I feel as if I've driven into a world with endless breathtaking sights, but no visitors to see them.

Later in the day I wind through the maze-like streets of a tiny village before locating a small ferry to again cross the Nile. For just $1 the Jeep and I cross the mighty river which is so large and calm it looks more like a lake. Again everyone on the ferry is friendly and welcoming, and they're even happy to pose for photos after I ask permission.

Days later I pinch myself as I drive into the famous town of Wadi Halfa at the border of Egypt. Overlanders have used this crossing for decades, and the bureaucracy and time required to cross here have been the stuff of legend since before I was born. In town I wander through a bustling street market buying my usual food stocks and pickup enough vegetables, fruit, meat, eggs and bread to last a week for just a few dollars. A group of happy kids escort me around while helpful locals occasionally translate. Again when buying products I simply hold out my hand full of money, and shopkeepers take the right amount - always much less than I'm expecting - before giving change.

In the market an elderly man introduces himself before inviting me to sit for coffee in front of his nearby shop. Asim lives six months of the year in London and six months here, which explains his impeccable English. The Sudanese brew excellent coffee, and soon I'm buzzing from the delicious espresso packed with so much ginger it's both spicy and hot. When I comment on the scorching sun Asim says I'm lucky to be in Sudan in winter. During summer it's easily 135°F every day, unbearable even for him, he says.

Asim is comfortable talking openly about the ongoing protests, and how the Sudanese people deserve a better leader. He explains that just a few months ago he would have been afraid to speak so openly in public, but now the people have a lot more courage to demand change. Asim is clearly excited for the future, and he does believe change is finally coming. When I ask about taking photos in the vibrant market he explains I had better not. I'm perfectly safe, though it's not a great idea to walk around with my big camera on display. Understandably everyone is a little tense and they might mistake me for a government spy.

When it comes time to pay, Asim refuses my money. Again he insists it's the Sudanese way to host a stranger, and it has been his pleasure to host me. Asim invites me back the following day, and I'm happy when he accepts my gift of apples in exchange for coffee and conversation.

Two days later I bid farewell to Sudan and the extremely friendly and welcoming Sudanese and drive towards what is likely the most bureaucratic border on Earth.

Φ   Φ   Φ

As I learned, government travel warnings are a tricky thing. On one hand they seem really helpful and something I should watch closely. On the other hand I've come to learn they tell us almost nothing about everyday people. Sudan is colored red with warnings because the President and government are evil, not because regular people are. In my experience people I've met suffering under oppressive regimes have been some of the friendliest and kindest I've ever met. Despite these countries having dire travel warnings I've always felt extremely safe.

Governments warn us that a foreign government is doing something they don't agree with, or treating their citizens badly, but unfortunately that tells us extremely little about the regular people there, or how we will be treated.

There is really only one way to get up to date information about the real situation in a country you might be interested in visiting. If you want to get the facts, free from bias and political motivations, seek out ordinary people who have been there recently and listen to what they say.

Φ   Φ   Φ

Two months after my visit the Sudanese Armed Forces staged a *Coup d'état* and removed President Al-Bashir from power, placing him under house arrest. In late 2019 he was convicted of money laundering and corruption after $130 million was found in his home, and was sentenced to two years in prison. He will soon face multiple charges by the International Criminal Court.

Sudan is now transitioning to democracy, to be completed by October 2022.

The Pyramids of Giza

Egypt
February 2019

WILD camping in the dunes outside Wadi Halfa is supremely peaceful, and after a few nights soaking it all in and waiting for paperwork, I get moving early one morning. I've managed every border so far without a Carnet De Passage, despite the insistence of many it's utterly impossible to drive a foreign vehicle through Africa without one.

Unfortunately, Egypt is utterly impossible without one. After extensive research I conclude there is simply no way around it, so I resign myself to getting one for the final country. International Carnets are not cheap, and Egypt is famous for requiring a deposit eight times the value of the vehicle. This is way outside my budget, so I find another way. I contact a well-known fixer at the border who organizes a local Carnet issued by the Motoring Club of Egypt. It costs $500USD and is only valid in Egypt, though it's much cheaper than the alternative and good enough for my needs. Driving into Egypt will be by far the most expensive border of my life, though I decided long ago it was well worth it.

From the minute I arrive at the border itself I discover the Sudanese officials don't - or won't - speak a word of English, and flatly refuse to help. I've been told this border is utterly impossible without a fixer, and already I see why. Long ago I made a rule never to use fixers, though here I really don't have a choice. For the first time in my life I pay $5 to a very friendly man who quickly gets my documents stamped and completed at Immigration and Customs. While he runs around to the various offices I wait in a local coffee shop drinking extremely strong espresso and chatting to truck drivers.

After waiting two hours on the Sudanese side I'm free to drive forward to the enormous steel gates that fence the Egyptian border zone. Here I meet my fixer Kamal who hands the Carnet directly to an Egyptian Customs officer. Kamal is very well known among overlanders as *the* fixer for Egypt, and his warm smile and easy-going attitude make it easy to see why. As I pull forward into the border zone the real madness begins.

Over the next five hours Kamal works tirelessly, first securing a visa and entrance stamp for me, before moving on to Jeep paperwork. Kamal has been helping foreigners get vehicles in and out of Egypt for years, and has it down to a science. He knows every officer and even their assistants by name, and every time we visit a photocopier he knows exactly how many copies to get, even when it seems insane. I don't understand how this can possibly require twelve copies of my visa and passport, but it does.

For the first time in my life I'm issued a local driving license completely in Arabic and in another first the Jeep is issued temporary local license plates also in Arabic. I zip-tie the plates on the front and back which I'm assured is plenty good enough. I"m also forced to purchase local insurance, and again I can't read a single word on any of the paperwork because it's all in Arabic. In all my travles a mix of English, Spanish, French and Portuguese have gotten me through, but at this border I have absolutely zero language skills. I put my trust completely in Kamal who does a superb job of negotiating all the hurdles and mountains of paper.

This border is vastly more complicated and convoluted than anything I've experienced before, and the whole thing borders on insane. Kamal explains the authorities continually add steps and bureaucracy, and although locals are fed up with it, there's simply nothing they can do.

After almost seven hours Kamal claims victory, and we warmly shake hands before I depart the border zone. I could never have done it without him, and when I say as much he just replies, "I know."

As I drive forward into country number thirty-five I struggle to understand I've just completed the last border crossing of the expedition.

Φ   Φ   Φ

During my years driving through Latin America and around Africa I've seen more outrageous driving than I need in five lifetimes. I've witnessed countless displays of recklessness that border on suicidal, often so crazy they're hard to believe. In Peru it was so common for buses to round hairpin corners entirely in my lane I was forced to bury the horn all the way around blind corners. In Kenya I watched countless severely overloaded 18-wheel transport trucks overtake multiple vehicles directly towards oncoming traffic. In horror I watched as approaching vehicles were forced to dive off the road at high speed, and was dumbfounded when those approaching vehicles were sometimes also transport trucks apparently playing chicken. Even after hundreds of experiences like those, driving into Cairo three weeks later is utterly shocking.

I approach the city from the east on a huge two-lane freeway that could be in any major city in the world. As the sprawling city grows on the horizon the number of lanes and traffic steadily increase. Soon there are eight marked lanes, though everyone crams in wherever they can fit meaning ten or twelve lanes of vehicles actually surge forward. Evidently emergency stopping lanes and shoulders are just extra driving lanes and getting crushed in the center divide or pushed off the edge is a real possibility. We race along at fifty miles an hour with barely a foot between each vehicle side to side. Front to back the gap is a much more respectable two feet, and I watch the brake lights in front of me like a hawk.

Because everyone ignores lane markings the flow of traffic is entirely free-form. When someone swerves to miss a pothole, all lanes must swerve together to avoid side impacts. Vehicles wedged against barriers have to slam on the brakes and funnel behind into a different lane before an all out race to reclaim their previous position.

The snaking line of traffic appears to be alive, and actions ripple down the line like a snake slithering forward. To keep things really interesting there are steep speed bumps even on the freeway which force everyone to jump on their brakes before a twelve lane drag race. The Jeep doesn't win any drag races, but being so large and with steel front and rear bumpers I'm afforded a degree of respect by the much smaller vehicles around me. The European trend of tiny commuter vehicles has apparently caught on in Egypt, which makes pushing in much easier for me.

This madness continues for over two hours as I stream towards the city center, over the mighty Nile and south to a small campsite in the back paddock of a working farm. I arrive just as the sun hits the horizon, thankful to be off the road before dark.

Φ   Φ   Φ

In the morning I move through the familiar city traffic while holding my place in my imaginary lane. Driving through a maze of high-rise buildings I'm shocked when I catch a glimpse of an enormous stone structure between buildings. I knew the pyramids were close to the city, I had no idea they're actually *in* the city.

The Police in Egypt are very concerned about tourist safety, so security at the main gate is extremely tight. After multiple stops, searches of the Jeep and repeated questions about what I'm doing, the head of the Police wants to see for himself. After a long discussion he doesn't feel comfortable about the large cooking knives in the kitchen, and makes it clear they're absolutely not permitted. The Police remain very friendly and polite, though it's clear they are not OK with my knives. They don't want to allow the Jeep to enter at all, and I wonder if I've driven around Africa to be denied the last half mile.

Over twenty minutes I manage to convince them how important it is to me, so we strike a compromise. I will leave my knives at a metal detector and collect them on the way out. I'm extremely happy with this deal, and thank everyone repeatedly.

As I drive through the entrance gate the monster pyramids loom large in the windscreen, and I'm stunned into silence. I park less than thirty yards from one and walk over to touch the staggeringly large stone blocks.

During the last three years I've thought about this moment many times, in fact I've even dreamed about it. I built the pyramids up in my mind as a huge milestone on this enormous undertaking, and I thought about them many times over the years. When I was terribly sick and scared with malaria, when I was worried about Mum, when I was lonely and feeling down or wondering why I even set out in the first place, I thought about arriving here and completing my dream.

I spend hours wandering in the warm midday sun, exploring the various pyramids, the Sphinx and the surrounding area. The city really does begin within fifty yards of the Sphinx, and the entire area is packed with thousands of tourists from all over the world. I enjoy feeling separate from them, and I'm not interested in paying for a camel ride or buying trinkets from the hundreds of street vendors lining the walkways.

I can't stop grinning like a fool as I pose the Jeep for photos, constantly looking at the pyramids through the view-finder and then again in real life. I can't help pose for a victory photo with the Jeep, complete with an extra large fist-pump.

I've driven the Jeep around Africa, completing my dream. I faced all the challenges, and I overcame all the hurdles. There were countless unforgettable and breathtaking days and also more difficult days than I care to remember.

I feel equal parts elated about reaching my goal and sad the journey is coming to an end, making the moment bittersweet. Although I'm exhausted deep in my bones, I have one final challenge to face before I can call this complete.

End Of The Road

Alexandria, Egypt
March 2019

W HEN I first dreamed of exploring Africa, my ultimate route was to complete a loop, finishing where I started in Morocco. Prior to the Arab spring in late 2010, it was common for overlanders to explore Algeria, Tunisia and Libya, all of which are stunningly beautiful. By the time I hit the road in mid-2016 those countries were off-limits, and I hoped things would calm down by the time I drove around to Egypt.

Unfortunately that's not the case, and Libya is still in the midst of a horrible civil war. Obtaining a tourist visa is impossible, and the permits to drive across are even less likely. Furthermore the government of Egypt is extremely protective of tourists, and it's very unlikely they would allow me to drive anywhere close to the Libyan border, even if I had a valid visa. The border between Algeria and Morocco has also been closed for many years, and nobody knows what would happen if I managed to arrive there.

As a fall-back plan I've been investigating driving east across the Sinai Peninsula into Israel. Driving off Africa to finish my time feels like a fitting end to the expedition, though this region is also prone to the occasional terrorist attack, and the various routes open and close sporadically. In a strange twist of fate I would likely be permitted to cross, though the Jeep would not. The Egyptian Military are concerned about a strong 4x4 being captured by ISIS and used against them, so they won't allow a vehicle like mine across. There's a chance

I could talk my way across, though it's far from certain and sounds like a lot of aggravation I don't particularly want.

With all of that, Egypt will be the end of the road. Without any viable options to continue, I will ship the Jeep out of Egypt to finish my time in Africa and the expedition. That turns out to be a lot easier said than done.

Φ   Φ   Φ

I camp for two more nights in Cairo, cleaning the Jeep until it's spotless inside and out. I plan to ship the Jeep directly into Canada, and it must be exceptionally clean to avoid any extra Customs fees. Sand, mud, twigs and everything else imaginable has been accumulating inside for almost three years, and I spend hours using a vacuum cleaner for the first time in Africa. Outside I pressure wash repeatedly, slowly removing all the stubborn Congo mud from the undercarriage. After all my efforts it's mostly clean enough, though I still find hidden pockets of mud when I really search.

I move directly north on a new toll road to the city of Alexandria on the Mediterranean Sea. Just as I hit the city the skies let loose with an immense torrential downpour and I have to think hard about the last time I saw rain, months ago in Kenya.

Purely by chance I met a friendly Egyptian while applying for my Sudanese visa in Ethiopia who invited me to stay at his place. Omar has a permanent smile plastered on his face, and is extremely kind and generous. He has ridden the East Coast of Africa multiple times on his adventure bike, and like me, he's thoroughly addicted to overland travel. After navigating ten miles through the monster city I find his bustling neighbourhood which I call home. I feel like a fish out of water as I bring things out of the Jeep to sleep inside for the first time in months.

Φ   Φ   Φ

In the morning I'm on the move at 6am, battling rush hour traffic while still half asleep. It's so bad it takes me almost two hours to drive just ten miles into the heart of the city. There isn't nearly as much traffic as Cairo, though the drivers make up for it by stepping up the insanity. Five or six lanes of moving traffic cram into three and again the pace in frantic. There are also murky puddles covering huge sections of road where the rain has pooled. I quickly learn these puddles are shockingly deep because they hide all the potholes and train crossings where the pavement is cracked and broken. In less than ten minutes the Jeep is no longer clean.

In the city center I make my way to the shipping company where I meet my contact Aymen, who I like immediately. He must be in his mid-40s, has a huge grin and a very easy-going demeanor. Although he's the boss, he's also the only person in the office that speaks English, so he assigned himself to guide me through the shipping process. I've been warned repeatedly shipping in or out of Egypt is a bureaucratic nightmare unparalleled in any country on Earth, which makes me excited to see if I'm up to the challenge while simultaneously being so exhausted I don't want to find out.

Aiming to get the ball rolling we drive across town to the law courts to get a Power of Attorney endorsed. This mandatory document allows me to authorize Aymen and his company to act on my behalf for the purposes of exporting the Jeep from Egypt. I realize I already don't care about the 'why's' of what we're attempting to do, and I just keep my head down so we can get it done as quickly and painlessly as possible.

Inside the high-rise building we struggle past hundreds of people waiting in lines. Aymen explains every aspect of life in Egypt revolves around this building, so Egyptians from all walks of life must visit this building to lodge a huge stack of paperwork for all legal matters. After struggling to find the right line we're told an official translator is mandatory. Even though Aymen speaks perfect English, he doesn't have an official certification so he can't do it. Halfway up the stairs to the eleventh floor I ask Aymen about using the elevator and he just shakes his head. When we eventually locate the official office for translators, we're told there are no translators. This is a problem, and Aymen says we'll just have to deal with it later. How, exactly, he has no idea.

Putting that on the back-burner we drive to a shipping port so enormous it's the size of most large towns. Days from now I want to drive the Jeep into the shipping container myself to ensure it's safe and secure and I'll need a permit to enter the port, which has very strict security. Ayman takes the lead, and over the next four hours he collects five of the required seven signatures on the lengthy application form. The Police, Military, Traffic Police, Customs, Immigration, Port Officials and finally the head man all need to have their say before I will be granted permission. To complicate things our documents from the shipping line are in English, so only Aymen and I can read them.

Soon the confusion is very real, with Aymen doing his best to persuade every official it's fine and we can proceed. I quickly see Aymen is a master negotiator, and his warm and friendly demeanor is a huge asset. In every office, corridor, building and waiting area men chain-smoke cigarettes, even in the government buildings. Soon my eyes are burning and my throat is scratchy adding to my exhaustion and impatience for stupid bureaucracy. With nothing better to do while waiting I down multiple cups of extremely strong and delicious Egyptian coffee, and soon add severe jitters to my sore eyes and scratchy throat.

At 5pm the office closes, so we leave without completing our goal. Aymen assures me we should be happy with our progress, though I'm not so sure. I drive back through the same traffic, again spending almost two hours to cover just ten miles.

Shipping lines are understandably terrified about fires on their
enormous ships, so the Jeep must be virtually empty of gas
before shipping. I have no idea how many more times I'll need
to drive to and from the city before we load the Jeep into a
container, so I play the game of keeping the gauge at or below
empty by only paying for a couple of gallons at a time and
using the trip meter to make sure I won't run out.

I'm exhausted as I walk the streets to get a pizza for dinner
and fall into bed at 10pm, ready to start over the next day.

Φ   Φ   Φ

The following morning plays out in exactly the same way. I
battle traffic and meet Aymen before we go back to the law
courts and wait to get the Power of Attorney endorsed. At
9:20am we're given number 192 and I wonder how long this
could possibly take.

While waiting we drink coffee, talk strategy, and sit in a
room with many hundreds of other people stuck in the same
situation. I can't understand how Egyptians deal with this
every day, and Ayman explains they've just learned to live
with it. He quietly adds it wasn't nearly this bad in years past,
and the current authoritarian government is making life worse
for regular people.

Sitting in the waiting room is fantastic people watching, though
it gets a little scary when men completely loose their cool and
blow up at the employees. People yell, scream and even punch
the desk while everyone else just stares glassy-eyed, including
the employees.

By 2:50pm the count has reached 180 when Aymen is told I
need a special stamp in my passport that says I'm 'legal' in
the country before we can complete the Power of Attorney. I
gather there is no way around this because thirty seconds later
we're running across the city to another government building
in the hopes of getting the stamp. Arriving short of breath

I'm shocked when the guards won't even let us in. The boss went home at 3pm, fifteen minutes ago and without the boss, nobody can stamp my passport. Ayman pleads in Arabic, though it's hopeless.

With no choice we slump our shoulders and walk back to the law courts to resume waiting. When our number is called we're immediately told nothing can be done without the all-important stamp we didn't even know about an hour ago.

I try to remain positive, though the reality is clear - we've wasted the entire day on our feet waiting in a crowded and smokey building to achieve literally nothing. I try not to dwell on it while driving home and get a laugh when I stop to buy another two gallons of gas at the same station as yesterday and the guys can't understand what game I'm playing. It's obvious they think I'm crazy and with the language barrier I just let them think it.

ɸ ɸ ɸ

At 5:30am the next morning my alarm sounds, and groundhog day is real. I drive directly to the law courts, hoping to get a low number. I arrive before the office officially opens at 8am, and I'm called over to have my name written on an informal list. A friendly man explains this will be used to issue real waiting tickets, and I will be given number 79.

In the coming hour hundreds and hundreds of people arrive and push directly to the front of the small waiting area, yelling, shoving and chain smoking as they go. When the doors briefly open at 9am a few people are permitted to push through, while the rest of us wait. Eventually a man starts calling names from the list, though everyone is yelling so loudly it's impossible to hear. I'm thirty people from the front, and even on tiptoes I can't see or hear much. I think maybe some people from the list are going in, and then the man holding the door lets in a random wave of ten people. Everyone else waiting then pushes and yells even more, making it even harder to hear the names being called. I don't want to get caught up in any real anger or violence, so I hover near the back of the crowd with a few other men who also clearly think the situation is absurd.

After forty-five minutes of watching wave after wave of random people push to the front and get in, it becomes painfully obvious waiting is a waste of time.

The men I've been waiting with insist I should use my passport to push to the front and while I don't like playing the foreigner card, I rationalize I've tried my best to follow the rules and that I was supposed to be number 79 anyway. With effort I'm just able to push to the front without offending too many people or stepping on too many toes. At first the guard blocks my entry, though when I flash my passport he steps aside and waves me through. Without a word of Arabic I make it clear I need a number from the same department as yesterday, and I'm handed number 123, much to my relief.

The yelling, pushing and screaming I've seen until this point have been utterly stupid, and I can't fathom why people behave this way. I'm tired, over caffeinated and fed up with the clouds of cigarette smoke and I can't understand how anyone thinks this is an intelligent way to get things done. In the last month I hit my limit of exhaustion, and I don't have the same patience for bureaucracy I once did. I can tell I'm over it, but I have no choice. I'll just have to dig deep to get this done.

Nevertheless I have a number, and I'm happy for the fresh air as I walk to the other building for the all-important stamp in my passport. In that building I guess my way to a line, and commence waiting. There are about ten of us waiting in an orderly single-file line, and I watch as a man pushes directly to the front and shoves his documents through the window. Although it's all in Arabic it's easy to understand what happens next. Much to my satisfaction the young lady behind the counter lectures him about waiting his turn, and directs him to the back where he belongs. After trying repeatedly he gives up and does the walk of shame as the now smiling lady helps the rightful next person. After waiting an hour the stamp takes less than five minutes, and because it's in Arabic I can only hope it's the right one.

In the afternoon Aymen arrives at the law courts with a translator in tow just before my number is called. Hilariously the translator speaks very bad English, in fact much worse than Ayman. When my number is finally called copies are made, stamps are stamped and fees are paid before we move to another window to duplicate it all into a computer. At yet another window everything is duplicated for an unknown reason, then half is duplicated and filed away before we wait patiently in line at the window of the boss-lady.

Aymen explains she is the ultimate authority. Every document in the entire building must pass across her desk for approval, including ours. I stare blankly for thirty minutes as she hovers her big stamp above hundreds of documents, either giving it, or waiving disappointed people away to complete some unknown extra step. Amazingly Aymen has maintained a great sense of humor about all of this even though it's his life, and he and I chuckle back and forth trying to guess her decision based on how much she frowns at certain documents. We wonder out loud what happens when she's away sick. "Probably everything just stops," Aymen says while rolling his eyes.

By some miracle she smashes her mighty stamp onto our papers, and we have officially completed the Power of Attorney. Aymen pays the translator, and I realize all he did was show his official ID and didn't translate a single thing. Walking out Aymen and I feel like winners, and while I'm happy this is likely the last time I will ever set foot in this building after three painful days, I feel bad knowing this is Aymen's life.

I drive home on autopilot, buy delicious street food for dinner and even manage to print postcards of my victory photo at the pyramids before crashing at 9pm.

Φ   Φ   Φ

Again I'm moving before sunrise, and again I'm battling traffic for longer than makes sense. At first I was intimidated by the driving style here, often backing down when challenged for lane supremacy, and slowing to a crawl for potholes and puddles. After a few days of experience I've adjusted my style and now I take it in stride.

That, or I simply don't care anymore.

I use the Jeep to push in much more than I usually do, and I don't feel bad at all. Most cars are smaller than me anyway, and I feel justified knowing the usual law of the road applies here - the biggest vehicle has the right of way, no matter what. I'm bigger, therefore I go. I hit big potholes much faster than usual, and the Jeep takes the abuse without complaint. After everything we've been through, I know she can handle it. I'm aware this is a clear sign I'm exhausted, but I don't change my driving style.

Aymen thinks if we have a good day we *might* just get the Jeep loaded today, so right away I drive to a car wash he recommends. For the next three hours they meticulously clean the Jeep top to bottom, inside and out. I'm impressed when they even lift it to clean the undercarriage and use bright white rags to wipe every surface inside. I don't think it's ever been so clean, and finally I'm satisfied. Fingers crossed Canadian Customs will be satisfied too.

Together Aymen and I drive back to the port where we gather the remaining signatures needed for my entry permit. A few hours later I'm issued a security pass that looks like the kind of fake ID a high school student would make, and we laugh thinking we should have just made it ourselves.

At the main port entrance I'm finally permitted to drive the Jeep inside, which feels like another huge milestone. Even with my new security pass the guard wants some 'backsheesh' (a bribe) to let me in, and once again I know my patience for

Africa is wearing thin when I make it clear what I think of his request. The Traffic Police are first on the list, and they inspect the Jeep top to bottom before removing the Egyptian license plates and stamping a mountain of paperwork. I quietly ask, but there's simply no way they'll let me keep the Egyptian plates as a souvenir.

At Customs I drive into a dark and dusty warehouse full of vehicles in transit. There are Ferraris, Lamborghinis, luxury SUVs and now my shiny Jeep. I wait many hours while Aymen and his helper run back and forth completing paperwork and shaking hands in too many offices to count. Around lunchtime Aymen and I pay a visit to the men who will be securing the Jeep inside the container. Knowing it's going on a long journey across the Atlantic, Aymen explains he paid top dollar for the best company, and wants to confirm everything is ready. In the office they're quick to show us the large ratchet straps and wooden blocks they have purchased specifically to secure my Jeep, and Aymen assures me repeatedly they're the best. This is a very good thing, and I'm happy Aymen has gone to the extra trouble to make sure it's done properly.

Late in the afternoon we're told Customs are closing for the day, and they must keep the Jeep overnight in the warehouse. It's no longer legal in Egypt, so there is no way I can drive it home. I don't feel good about it and I really get upset when they say I must leave a key in case they need to move it. I'm one hundred percent dead-set against this and I've never given the keys to anyone before. I have no intention of doing so now in this dark and dingy warehouse deep in a shipping port in Egypt where anyone could take anything they want. Aymen assures me it will be fine, and we discuss this back and forth before we come up with a plan. I park the Jeep out of the way and lock everything in lock boxes before giving Customs a non-electronic key. I don't tell them, but this key will only open the doors. It won't start the engine, and it won't open any of the lock boxes. This is the best I can do, and I keep my fingers crossed it will be OK.

In front of the port Aymen helps me catch a public bus, and I ride home half asleep standing in the crowded aisle.

Φ Φ Φ

Now utterly stuck in groundhog day I'm back in the city at 8:30am, the frantic pace no different on the bus. I notice the driver pushes in a lot more than I did. At the port entrance the guard makes a very big deal of letting me in even though I have my permit. He wants backsheesh again, and I almost tell him to stick his backsheesh. Aymen just shrugs his shoulders and explains this is just normal life in Egypt.
What can you do?

We arrive at Customs at 9:10am and resume the familiar waiting game. After many hours the head man comes to see about this foreigner with a tricked-out Jeep. He's only in his 30s, though clearly commands respect from the men scurrying around him. He asks to see everything in the Jeep from my clothes and camping gear to cameras and hard drives. He meticulously documents everything, including details about the Jeep like ABS, traction control and other seemingly irrelevant details. Aymen explains later he's simply being thorough, trying to avoid vehicles being illegally transported through his port.

Just after 3pm we're given the all clear and Aymen and I drive the Jeep deeper into the port. Aymen spends a lot of time here, and clearly knows his way around the confusing maze of streets, buildings, containers and waiting vehicles. We drive into a virtual city of tightly stacked shipping containers where trucks frantically sling them to and fro and men on forklifts load and unload all manner of goods. Aymen dashes off to complete some final piece of approval, leaving me to my own devices. Sitting alone is a shiny new twenty foot container, which is all mine.

The Jeep has upgraded suspension, taller solar panels and

slightly larger tires than when I shipped into Belgium almost three years ago. I've been trying to determine if it will fit through the container door for the last couple of weeks, and now it's trivial to first measure the door height and then the Jeep. After checking twice I'm satisfied it will fit with about four inches to spare and I don't need to let air out of the tires. Taking a good look I see the front axle is still leaking a little oil, but that's not important now. We made it.

Again I wait, and the shadows grow long before Ayman returns with the final papers. I carefully reverse the Jeep into the container, fully aware this is the last time I'll drive it on African soil. Height is not a problem, and the side mirrors clear by about five inches each, leaving barely enough room to squeeze out the driver's door. While I disconnect the battery the port workers chock the wheels and lash the Jeep using the new ratchet straps I was shown yesterday.

The men are in such a hurry they have the door half closed before I squeeze out, leaving me barely a few seconds to snap a quick photo before the door is slammed shut and sealed.

Suddenly, the Jeep is gone. I've spent virtually every day on expedition within sight of it.
I've slept in it almost exclusively and I have cooked the vast majority of meals in it. Through all the good and bad she's kept me safe and we've had unbelievable adventures together. She has literally been the perfect adventure vehicle.

Now all I see is a huge steel box, indistinguishable from the thousands of others stacked around and I feel like a limb has been cut off.

Thirty minutes later we're issued an official Customs seal, and together Aymen and I add this to the massive latch on the door of the container, completing our work. I keep my fingers crossed the container won't get lost, or dropped, or fall off the ship as it crosses the Atlantic, but there's literally nothing I can do about it.

I bid a fond farewell to my new friend Ayman, thanking him profusely for all his help and encouragement. I honestly don't know if I could have survived that without his positive attitude and sense of humor. Although I'm exhuasted I can't help feeling triumphant on the bus ride home.

Φ   Φ   Φ

In the morning I sleep in before wandering the streets on foot. I sit to enjoy a coffee, and order another as the sun begins to warm me. I feel a calm wash over me, and for the first time in a very, very long time I'm able to take a step back and see the forest for the trees.

At 6pm I catch a taxi to the airport and watch my final African sunset, breathtaking as always.

Almost a decade since I first dreamed of exploring Africa, my dream is complete.

After 999 days and 53,426 miles through 35 countries, I step onto a plane and bid farewell to the continent that has forever changed me.

Thanks

ONCE again there were many hard working people behind the scenes who helped make the expedition a success. From care packages to wisdom and just talking when I felt stuck, these people were key. It's impossible to overstate how important it was to have a good team behind the scenes. More than just the physical support, their encouragement is what gave me the courage to keep forging ahead. Without the help of these people, I never would have made it to Africa, much less completed the expedition successfully.

There are also thousands of kind, generous and warm people from all across Africa who welcomed me into their communities and homes. They gave me family when I was so far from mine, and it meant the world to me. I never could have done it without their love, happiness and joy.

Massive thanks for the following people:

- Melissa & Reg once again for support from the beginning.
- Jamie & Ian for helping design & build my dream Jeep.
- Don for all the blood, sweat and tears.
- The team at Ralph's Coffee Shop for the support & caffeine.
- Liz and Simon for the support and temporary home.
- Mike and Ash for teaching me what family is all about.
- The Zampiello Family for being my second family again.
- Mum & Dad for encouraging me, even when it was scary.
- Bari for all her hard work and still putting up with me.
- Em for trusting me enough to jump aboard.

- The Sleeping Camel crew for a hilariously fun time.
- Dani & Didi for being the best travel buddies of all time.
- The team at Zone Offroad in Johannesburg.
- The entire 'Zim Network' for their generosity.
- The Shoesmith Family for treating me like family.
- Jess and Kobus for being awesome in so many ways.

Two need special thanks:

Eric Walton believed in me from the first minute I laid out my crazy plan. To say I couldn't have done the expedition without him is a huge understatement.

Ricard Doney gave me a home, encouragement and advice when I thought the whole thing was a failure. Richard also poured his own time into building the Jeep, prioritizing it over his own projects. Richard played a big role in making this dream come true, and I feel genuinely lucky to have met such a kind person when I needed it most.

Thanks to my corporate partners for the support, trust and belief and thanks to my team of editors for helping shape the book - Kylie, Stu, Jeff, Cody, Dani & Didi!

More photos from Africa are in my full-color photography book *999 Days Around Africa: The Road Chose Me*[13] on Amazon.

I also filmed video from all thirty-five countries on YouTube: *http://youtube.com/theroadchoseme*[14]

To research and plan your own global Overland Expedition, see *http://wikiOverland.org*[15] which contains everything from routes and budgets to paperwork and gas and diesel prices for every country in the world.

---

[13] *999 Days Around Africa: The Road Chose Me* - Dan Grec, 2019
[14] *The Road Chose Me - YouTube Channel*
[15] *WikiOverland - The Community Encyclopedia of Overland Travel*

Afterword

Australia
March 2019

I NTERNET access is severely restricted in Sudan and Egypt. Both governments keep tight control over what can and can't be done online, meaning social platforms like Facebook are blocked entirely and phone and video calling tools like Skype also don't work. This made it difficult to keep in touch with my family, though I did manage to bypass the blocks briefly using a VPN, and I was able to video chat Mum and Dad from central Egypt. Mum was doing well and just sleeping a lot in the afternoons which was becoming the new normal. The Doctors decided to stop chemotherapy because after more than two years it was doing more damage than the cancer.

While planning the dates for shipping and my own travel plans, I emailed my sister Liz in the UK to let her know I would probably be dropping through on my way to Canada after the Jeep had sailed. Crossing the Atlantic would take the Jeep three weeks, and I wanted to spend time with my sister and her fiancé Simon.

At first I was thoroughly confused by her email replies. She had taken unpaid leave from work to spend time in Australia with Mum and Dad. She felt like Mum wasn't doing well, and that Dad could really use the support. I was taken aback to hear this, and didn't understand the need to fly around the world. Given that Liz wouldn't be in the UK, it made sense for me to also fly to Australia to spend time with my family while waiting for the Jeep to ship.

During the whole shipping process I kept my family up to date on my progress. I was doing absolutely everything possible to make the process go faster, but of course there was delay after delay and there was really nothing I could do.

Φ   Φ   Φ

After sealing the Jeep in the container and returning to my temporary home in Alexandria I try to book a flight for that night, but nothing works. Instead I settle for the following evening, leaving just twenty-four hours in Africa.

I fly through Saudi Arabia, then somewhere in Asia I can't remember. After forty-three hours of travel I step off the plane in Melbourne with my eyes hanging from my head. An Immigration officer is shocked to see bearded and long-haired me with only a small carry-on bag, and wants to talk. Literally everything else I own is in the Jeep in the container, hopefully sailing across the Mediterranean to France by then. She grills me for five minutes, and I think my long and rambling tale about driving a Jeep around Africa and occasionally returning to Australia to visit family is so detailed and complex she can't imagine how I could make it up. Once I flick through almost sixty pages of colorful visas and stamps in my passport she's convinced and welcomes me 'home' to Australia.

My first indication something is wrong comes when only my sister-in-law Ashleigh and my now one year old nephew are at the airport to greet me. In my jet-lagged and sleep deprived state I can't understand why my brother and sister didn't come. Ash explains Mum is not doing well, and they don't want to leave her side.
Oh. I was not expecting that. Not at all.

On the two hour drive to Mum and Dad's house Ash explains Mum has gone downhill very, very quickly in just the last two days while I was flying around the world. My family knew I was doing everything humanly possible to get home quickly, so they decided not to keep me up to date because it would only have caused more stress, and there wasn't anything I could do about it anyway. Being left out of the loop feels strange, but I know it was the right decision.

When we arrive everyone greets me in the entrance and tries to prepare me. Mum is at home in her own bed, sitting up, and even manages a slight smile in my direction when I enter the room. She's struggling to breathe, and for all intents and purposes can no longer talk. I sit on the bed next to her with tears streaming down my face, trying to be strong and failing miserably.

I talk about everything and nothing for a couple of hours while holding her hand, trying to make the most of the time we have. I'm so unsure she understands I ask if she knows it's me, and if she knows I've completed my Africa dream she was so enthusiastic about and such a huge supporter of. Mum raises my hand in the air and looks directly at me.

Yes, she knows.

My family spends the afternoon and early evening together with Mum, before exhaustion overcomes me and I collapse into bed.

Φ   Φ   Φ

Liz wakes me at sunrise to say the end is very close and in a zombie-like state I follow into Mum and Dad's room where we all sit together with Mum for just a few moments before she takes her last breath and passes away peacefully.

Mum passed away less than fifteen hours after I arrived home from Africa and I have no doubt she held on until we could all be together.

Φ   Φ   Φ

The next week is a blur of emotions, jet lag and disbelief as preparations are made and friends and family fly in from all over the country.

We hold a small and beautiful funeral in the local church and together with my brother Mike and two uncles I carry my Mum's coffin to the hearse.

In the years since her diagnosis Mum made sure we had all the conversations we needed to have, and we were able to make our love for each other very clear, for which I am extremely grateful. Although the loss is heartbreaking, I'm so thankful we had plenty of time to say goodbye.

We receive many messages from people who Mum taught at Elementary school years ago who say how great of a teacher she was, and the lasting impact she's had on their lives. Of course, this makes the tears flow even more.

Φ   Φ   Φ

Mum was always extremely determined and proud, and she fought cancer on her own terms. She disliked hospitals, and from the very beginning was adamant she would not spend her last days in one. From the original diagnosis she was given six to twelve months to live, and she fought hard for nearly two and a half years, completely shocking all the Doctors. It was extremely rare to hear her complain about anything in life, and that didn't change with cancer. During my visits Mum would be out of bed at 7am to walk with her friends and she would literally drag me along, coffee in my hand. On many evenings Mum elbowed Dad and I out of the way in the kitchen to take over cooking dinner. She simply loved to cook for us. Cancer be damned, she was going to live her life, she said.

I'll be proud if I'm half as brave and strong when my time comes.

Φ   Φ   Φ

In the weeks and months that follow, through all the talks and tears, one thing repeatedly comes to the front of my mind. Mum was exactly thirty years older than I am. If I live as long as Mum, I only have thirty years left. That's only thirty more summers of hiking, camping and fishing. It also means only thirty more winters of wood fires, snowboarding, ice fishing and beautiful stars.

I have an enormous list of things I want to achieve, places I want to explore and adventures I want to have before then. Not to mention all the laughter, good food and family time I'm immensely looking forward to.
There is literally no time to waste.

I continue to dream and plan, bigger than ever. Volume 3 doesn't yet have a firm destination or timeline, but I'm more determined than ever to make my dreams come true.

In loving memory

Julie-Anne Grec
July 12 1951 - March 10 2019

All my tenacity, drive and perfectionism comes from you.
I'll look for you at sunrise.

Printed in Great Britain
by Amazon